POVERTY IN THE UK

Poverty is a root cause and effect of many social inequalities in the UK, due to the disproportionate impact on those living in poverty of their access to basic resources, services and opportunities. This important book covers a wide range of experiences relating to the everyday realities of living in poverty, providing timely and relevant insights for all areas of social work practice.

Written by those with lived experience of poverty, each chapter dives into a key topic related to poverty in the UK, including parenting, schooling, housing and homelessness, mental health, cancer, disability, trauma and addiction, as well as discussions related to being in prison, a refugee, a carer or care experienced. Taken together, these insights will help readers to develop and inform their appreciation of the challenges and potential solutions required to advocate for those in poverty.

Offering bitesize formal knowledge on UK legislation and policy, alongside reflective activities which foster criticality and transformative learning, this book will be of great interest to professionals, academics and students in the fields of social work, social care, health, education, police work and media, as well as students and academics of sociology and the social sciences more broadly.

Mel Hughes is Professor of Social Work at Bournemouth University, Academic Lead for the PIER Partnership and Deputy Director of the Research Centre for Seldom Heard Voices.

Debbie James, mother of two adults, is a writer and performer with The Outsiders Project, Community Commissioner with BCP Poverty Truth 1, and active member of Bournemouth University's PIER partnership.

Carrie-Anne Mizen is a parent and silent activist against poverty and trustee of the poverty truth network.

POVERTY IN THE UK

The Lived Experience

Edited by Mel Hughes, Debbie James and Carrie-Anne Mizen

Routledge
Taylor & Francis Group
LONDON AND NEW YORK

Designed cover image: Getty Images / stellalevi

First published 2026
by Routledge
4 Park Square, Milton Park, Abingdon, Oxon OX14 4RN

and by Routledge
605 Third Avenue, New York, NY 10158

Routledge is an imprint of the Taylor & Francis Group, an informa business

British Library Cataloguing-in-Publication Data
A catalogue record for this book is available from the British Library

Library of Congress Cataloging-in-Publication Data
Names: Hughes, Mel editor | James, Debbie (Workshop leader) editor | Mizen, Carrie-Anne editor
Title: Poverty in the UK : the lived experience / edited by Mel Hughes, Debbie James and Carrie-Anne Mizen.
Description: Abingdon, Oxon ; New York, NY : Routledge, 2026. | Includes bibliographical references and index.
Identifiers: LCCN 2026008720 (print) | LCCN 2026008721 (ebook) | ISBN 9781041070245 hardback | ISBN 9781041070238 paperback | ISBN 9781003638476 ebook
Subjects: LCSH: Poverty--Great Britain | Poor--Great Britain--Social conditions
Classification: LCC HC260.P6 P6885 2026 (print) | LCC HC260.P6 (ebook) | DDC 362.50941--dc23/eng/20260408
LC record available at https://lccn.loc.gov/2026008720
LC ebook record available at https://lccn.loc.gov/2026008721

ISBN: 978-1-041-07024-5 (hbk)
ISBN: 978-1-041-07023-8 (pbk)
ISBN: 978-1-003-63847-6 (ebk)

DOI: 10.4324/9781003638476

Typeset in Times New Roman
by SPi Technologies India Pvt Ltd (Straive)

CONTENTS

Lists of illustrations *vii*
List of contributors *viii*
Acknowledgements *xi*

Introduction 1
Mel Hughes, Debbie James and Carrie-Anne Mizen

1 What poverty means to me 10
Curated by Debbie James

2 Understanding poverty in the UK 19
Sam Crowe

3 Co-creating solutions to poverty in the UK 31
Martin Johnstone in conversation with Claire Brown, Tracy Goodwin, Tricia McConalogue, Dusty Thomas and Rachel Williams

4 Poverty and cancer 42
Carrie-Anne Mizen and Orlanda Harvey

5 Poverty and being a carer 53
Val McKie and Kate Jupp

6 Poverty and being care experienced 68
Caitlin Turner and Tilia Lenz

7 Poverty and disability 80
Steve Huxford and Sally Lee

8 Poverty and homelessness 92
Sam and Kate Parker

9 Poverty and housing 106
Dominic Watters and Julia Armstrong

10 Poverty and mental health 119
Sarah and Christopher Ademuwagun

11 Poverty and prison 133
Gary Lee and Mel Hughes

12 Poverty and raising a disabled child 147
Taliah Drayak and Stefan Kleipoedszus

13 Poverty and being a refugee 162
Alan Hamidi and Katharine Harrison

14 Poverty and school 177
Luke James, Debbie James and Richard Williams

15 Poverty, trauma, and addiction 185
Debbie James and Mel Hughes

16 Poverty and where you are from 198
Mary Brennan and Andrew Grinnell

Conclusion 209
Mel Hughes, Debbie James and Carrie-Anne Mizen

Index 213

ILLUSTRATIONS

Figure

8.1 What makes a house a home 102

Table

6.1 Placement types 72

CONTRIBUTORS

Christopher Ademuwagun is a senior social worker, AMHP (Approved Mental Health Professional) Lead and Senior lecturer at Bournemouth University with interests in Forensic Mental Health and deprived teenagers, especially of ethnic minorities.

Julia Armstrong is a social worker with adults, lecturer at Bournemouth University, therapeutic counsellor and eco therapist, as well as an activist against social injustice.

Mary Brennan has been involved as a commissioner with the Poverty Truth Commission in Leeds.

Claire Brown, Tracy Goodwin, Martin Johnstone, Tricia McConalogue, Dusty Thomas and Rachel Williams, authors of Chapter 3, have all been involved in Poverty Truth Commissions in various parts of the UK. That involvement has shaped and informed who they are today and the work that they do.

Sam Crowe has worked as a journalist and public health specialist in England and sub-Saharan Africa for 30 years.

Taliah Drayak is a parent carer, children and families advocate and visiting researcher at the University of Cambridge. She is also an appointed Poverty and Inequality Commissioner for the Scottish Government. She has volunteered for many years with ATD (All Together in Dignity), Fourth World and GRIPP (Growing Rights Instead of Partnership), both human rights and anti-poverty movements.

Andrew Grinnell is a facilitator of the Leeds Poverty Truth Network and Co-Director of the Poverty Truth Network.

Alan Hamidi is a civil and human rights activist, independent journalist and student of English.

Orlanda Harvey is a Senior lecturer at Bournemouth University with an interest in Intimate Partner Violence and Abuse and critical reflection on practice.

Katharine Harrison is a proud nana, mum of five adult children and a supported lodgings carer, with a passion for community development.

Mel Hughes is Professor of Social Work at Bournemouth University, Academic Lead for the PIER Partnership and Deputy Director of the Research Centre for Seldom Heard Voices.

Steve Huxford is a foodbank volunteer and has lived experience of disability and poverty. Like many others involved in this book, he is passionate about speaking up for those who feel they don't have a voice.

Debbie James, mother of two adults, is a writer and performer with The Outsiders Project, Community Commissioner with BCP Poverty Truth 1, and active member of Bournemouth University's PIER partnership.

Luke James is a 22-year-old security operative living in Bournemouth.

Kate Jupp is a PIER (Public Involvement in Education and Research) Officer at Bournemouth University, supporting and mentoring people and communities to inform and lead on the design and undertaking of research. Kate has a background of working both in hospitals and the community and is a qualified therapeutic counsellor.

Stefan Kleipoedszus is a qualified social worker/pedagogue specialising in Child and Family Social Work and works as the Associate Head of School for Health and Care at Bournemouth University, where he teaches Social Work Models and Methods and researches Secure Care for Children.

Gary Lee has an honours degree from the University of Life. He believes in changing one person's world at a time, rather than changing the whole world. He works with people in the care industry.

Sally Lee is a social work lecturer at Bournemouth University after many years of frontline practice. She is passionate about fairness and learning from the living experiences of other people.

Tilia Lenz is a Social Worker and academic at Bournemouth University with longstanding experience in front-line Children's Social Care as a practitioner and manager.

Val McKie, MA, is an executive coach and entrepreneur who turned the pain of her experiences of poverty into a passion to support others to thrive, creating a fairer and more equitable society.

Carrie-Anne Mizen is a parent and silent activist against poverty and trustee of the poverty truth network

Kate Parker is the Strategic Lead for Shelter Dorset and is driven by the belief that a safe home is a human right.

Sarah is an autistic, perimenopausal woman with chronic depression and complex post-traumatic stress disorder who just wants to feel understood.

Sam is a survivor advocate, live-in carer and systems reform contributor, working with Homewards, Groundswell and Shelter to strengthen housing, homelessness and domestic abuse responses through lived-experience leadership and compassionate community insight.

Caitlin Turner is a care-experienced changemaker, committed to challenging injustice, improving support for young people and ensuring that every child is seen, valued and safe.

Dominic Watters harnessed his council estate–lived experience to visually redefine the Four Pillars of Food Insecurity. Dominic is currently doing a PhD including research that collaborates with his neighbours, who all live in a food desert in the Garden of England.

Richard Williams is a Visiting Fellow at Bournemouth University. He retains a keen interest in how skilled educators can engage and inspire to make a significant difference in someone's life.

ACKNOWLEDGEMENTS

For all our children and their future selves, in the hope that poverty will be a thing of the past.

All royalties from this book will be donated to the National Poverty Truth Network, which is guided by the belief that better responses to poverty will be made if they include people who have experienced it. It is that simple and that challenging.

As co-editors, we are delighted to donate all royalties from the book to support this work.

Debbie, Carrie and Mel

INTRODUCTION

Mel Hughes, Debbie James and Carrie-Anne Mizen

Poverty in the UK: The Lived Experience is a textbook for students, practitioners, activists and policy makers, including those studying social work, health, social care and social sciences. Contrary to many textbooks, this book is written and edited by people with lived experience, giving you, as the reader, the opportunity to understand the causes of poverty, the experience of poverty and the solutions to tackling poverty, from the viewpoint of those directly affected.

Who we are

The textbook is edited by Mel, Carrie and Debbie, who met through the Bournemouth, Christchurch and Poole (BCP) Poverty Truth Commission, which brought together community commissioners with lived experience of poverty (including Carrie and Debbie), with Civic and Business commissioners who are local leaders and people in positions of power (including Mel). The aim of a poverty truth commission is to work together to be part of the solution. There are Poverty Truth Commissions across the UK that are working together to create a movement that is seeking to challenge poverty in a different way. We want to demonstrate the value of harnessing lived experience expertise in conceptualising and tackling poverty and show how building relationships can bring lasting change. This voice is often absent in literature on poverty.

Our own positionality (our social identity in relation to others) and that of our contributing authors are central to this textbook. Our experiences shape how we understand, view and interact with the world around us. Our views are formed from these experiences, and as such, we all have knowledge, expertise and insights to share.

DOI: 10.4324/9781003638476-1

Debbie is a powerful and passionate writer, sharing her experiences of poverty, homelessness, trauma and addiction through poetry and prose. Debbie is a member of the Outsiders Project, which gives voices to those on the fringes of society, and was a community commissioner (person with lived experience) in the first BCP Poverty Truth Commission. Debbie is a mum of two adult children and has written her own chapter (Chapter 15: Poverty, Trauma and Addiction) and contributed to her son's chapter on poverty and school (Chapter 14). As co-editor, Debbie has been instrumental in providing guidance, feedback and editorial comments to contributing authors on the content and presentation of their chapters.

Carrie describes life as a roller-coaster, having always lived in poverty. She was a community commissioner in the BCP Poverty Truth Commission and is a representative and now Trustee with the national Poverty Truth Network (PTN). Carrie is a lone parent, including of children with special education needs, and has lived experience of cancer, having lost her mum to the disease and having survived cancer herself. She shares these experiences within Chapter 4. As co-editor, Carrie has been a powerhouse in seeking and supporting contributors from across her national networks developed through her involvement with Poverty Truth and other anti-poverty campaigns.

Mel is Professor of Social Work at Bournemouth University (BU), and champions lived experience expertise through her roles as Academic Lead for the PIER (Public Involvement in Education and Research) partnership and Deputy Director of the Research Centre for Seldom Heard Voices. Mel was a business and civic commissioner in the first BCP Poverty Truth Commission. She has a track record for developing inclusive, arts-based, co-created and community-led research and co-designed education. Mel is a mum of two young adult children who, like Carrie, includes support for a neurodivergent teen. As co-editor, Mel has used her role and platform to bridge the gap between lived experience and academia, creating the opportunity for people with lived experience of poverty to write a textbook. She brings what Carrie and Debbie describe as her 'knowledgy, professorry, academiccy' experience.

Why this book and why now

'No Poverty' has been identified as number 1 of the 17 United Nations Sustainable Development Goals (SDGs). No. 1: to eradicate extreme poverty for all people everywhere by 2030. Poverty is a root cause and effect of many social inequalities in the UK due to the disproportionate impact on those living in poverty on their access to basic resources, services and opportunities. For readers from the social work profession, this is an urgent issue. Alongside reports in the UK that social workers are seeing an increase in poverty, there are reports of social workers feeling powerless in the face of poverty due to a lack of system responses for dealing with the root causes. Specific issues relating to poverty have been highlighted by the anti-austerity and anti-poverty work of the British Association of Social Work and Social Workers' Union. It is essential that students, social workers, other health, social care and community practitioners, activists, social scientists, civil servants and policy makers have opportunities to seek a deeper understanding of the causes, experiences and potential solutions to tackling poverty, so this can inform solutions. Focusing on the everyday realities of living in poverty, readers can develop a better understanding that informs their appreciation of the challenges and potential solutions to poverty so that they can advocate for and enact these in their practice and everyday lives.

How the book is co-produced – drawing on lived experience expertise

Poverty in the UK: The Lived Experience is written and edited by people with lived experience of poverty, giving readers the opportunity to consider the causes of poverty, experience of poverty and solutions to tackling poverty, from the viewpoint of those directly affected. The book is rooted in the work of the Research Centre for Seldom Heard Voices and the PIER (Public Involvement in Education and Research) Partnership, both based at Bournemouth University, with the support of the Bournemouth, Christchurch and Poole Poverty Truth Commission and the national PTN. It builds on the work of previous textbooks edited by Mel Hughes and the BU PIER partnership on *Statutory social work interventions: The lived experience* (2019) and *Social Exclusion in the UK: The lived experience* (2022) which collectively seek to amplify the voices and harness the expertise of marginalised people and communities to ensure they are central to understanding root causes of inequalities and in designing solutions.

For each lived experience chapter (Chapters 4–16), we reached out across our networks and invited people to share their experiences and expertise on poverty, in relation to a different aspect of their lives, e.g., as a parent, a carer or a cancer survivor. Each author was paired with a co-author to support them in writing their chapter in whichever way they chose. Some wrote their chapter independently with feedback from their co-author, others shared their story over many cups of coffee with their co-author writing up the content from the recordings so they could shape the chapter together. Our approach was to be inclusive and to tailor any support or mentoring to the individual needs or preferences of the first author. The results are very powerful. Whilst as editors we provided a guide regarding structure and feedback on drafts, authors were free to write their chapter in whichever style they chose, highlighting and focusing on what they wanted to share; what messages they wished to convey, and their own thoughts and insights into what needs to change to eradicate poverty. As such, each chapter takes on its own distinctive tone and character, reflecting the diversity of those involved throughout the book. The stories provide deep and rich insights into the realities of poverty. We make no apology for how some may be hard-hitting, don't pull any punches and may be triggering. The stories are real and reflect each author's reality. Their purpose isn't to shock or upset but to educate. We do, though, encourage you to recognise your own needs and triggers when reading each chapter and to access the support and care you need.

Definitions of poverty

Throughout the book, we seek to unpick and explore what poverty is and means from a lived experience perspective. There are varying definitions of poverty which inform government policy, underpin the welfare state and inform decisions about what is considered 'enough to live on'.

The most commonly used measures of poverty are based on disposable income:

- **Relative** low income refers to people living in households with income below 60% of the median in that year.
- **Absolute** low income refers to people living in households with income below 60% of the median income in a base year, usually 2010/2011. This measurement is adjusted for inflation. (UK Parliament 2025).

The government defines median income as 'the point at which half of households have lower income and half have higher income' (UK Parliament 2025). Critically, this can be measured before or after housing costs are deducted. Measures of absolute poverty are based on the idea that there is a poverty line, which people, families or households are referred to as above or below. This fails, though, to take into account individual circumstances or the marginal differences above or below this supposed line.

Poverty is about far more than income. It is also about someone's personal circumstances and needs and what this income needs to cover. Relative poverty seeks to address this by taking into account other considerations, such as the availability and access to basics, which affect quality of life, such as healthcare, nutritious food, transport and suitable housing. The current UK government has committed to drawing on other measures of poverty which account for differences amongst households, e.g., costs of childcare or disability, savings and access to assets.

It remains a financial measure, however, on what is deemed 'enough to live on' with very little consideration of the impact of poverty on a person's life; how it feels to live in poverty; how you are viewed by others; and how the system both creates poverty and sustains it.

More recently, there has been work in the UK to develop a consensual approach to measuring poverty, which seeks to go beyond basic needs and 'keeping your head above water' by achieving a consensus on what it actually means and the costs to have a good quality of life (Lansley and Mack 2015). We will explore this further in our conclusion chapter.

What we do know is that the experience of poverty is subjective. The book aims to explore what poverty means to people through the lens of different individual circumstances to enable us to understand the impact of system-level decisions on individuals and to draw on lived experience expertise, to identify what this means and solutions to eradicating poverty. We start as editors by reflecting on what poverty means to us.

What poverty mean to us?

For Carrie, I am a lone parent to neurodivergent children, a cancer survivor, a champion of sleeping through alarms and a silent activist on poverty alongside my work with the national PTN. Every time people think of poverty, they often associate it with money. For me, money has been a problem at many times in my life, but the biggest problem for me is how this restricts access to services, help and support. As a person who doesn't 'fit' in the normal boxes of society, it can be a real struggle.

I am currently struggling with the 'new me' after my cancer treatment. I suffer from fatigue so much. I literally could sleep for hours and still be tired. I am a lone parent, and I don't have any real family support, especially those who could help me day to day. Most of my friends are lone parents as well, who have children in different schools or other commitments.

Poverty is definitely relative to the things you and your direct family require. This is not fixed to one thing and could cover multiple areas. Life isn't easy, and I wish people in 'power' would learn more from people with lived experience about how their decisions affect our lives.

For Debbie, in my experience, poverty has been entwined in a life that goes against everything society disapproves of; it's a vicious circle of hardship, stigma and blame, lack of identity and self-worth, which leads to distrust of authority and rejection of support. Then the cycle begins again and again.

When I became a parent, the stigma and judgement were much more obvious and damaging to me and my family unit. Social Services and the schools were the worst. They sat in judgement, in the classic position of power versus powerlessness. It's a dangerous dynamic. And it drove me to my knees. I had a string of people barge into my life, who thought they could lecture me about budgeting, cooking and providing for my kids. My response was usually 'Who the fuck are you to tell me how to spend my money'.

My life has been a series of trauma responses, and that detail was never recognised or addressed by anyone in authority. For me, poverty was an injustice which has been an integral part of my experience. Although my life satisfaction has improved, I still live in poverty today. One of the things I still struggle with the most is trying to understand how so many people in positions of power can get away with looking down their noses at someone who is simply trying their best to survive.

For Mel, it is a humbling experience to reflect on the same question: what poverty means for me. The reality is, I have the privilege of not having given it as much thought as Carrie or Debbie, other than in my role as a social worker and academic. I have spent far more time in my career exploring and seeking to understand what poverty means for others. The reality, though, is that I am from a comparatively privileged background. The times when money has been short, and I have gone without, have always come with the safety net of being temporary, short-lived due to the coming of a monthly paycheque, access to a credit card with available credit or the 'bank of mum and dad'. This safety net goes far beyond the availability of money. It provides a foundation from which to make choices and take risks. It brings security that creates space and mental bandwidth for dealing with other pressures of life. I do not, though, take this privilege for granted. Allyship is about recognising our privilege, seeking to understand the experiences of others and taking positive actions to eradicate poverty. Amplifying lived experience expertise is one way to achieve this.

How to use this book?

Throughout the book, the authors challenge taken-for-granted assumptions and norms around poverty by sharing first-hand accounts and the expertise and insights they have gained through lived experiences. The book includes chapters focusing on poverty and parenting, homelessness, disability, mental health, school and housing, amongst others. The main voice is that of those with lived experience, underpinned by text boxes sharing formal knowledge, such as links to legislation, policy, research, wider literature and evidence to show the extent to which each contributor's lived experience is illustrative of the wider UK context.

There are reflective activities throughout encouraging you as the reader to put yourself in the shoes of each author and to consider poverty from different perspectives. You are encouraged to consider your own experiences and how you can use your learning from the book to inform your own practice in ways that recognise and address the causes and impacts of poverty at a personal, cultural and structural level. Authors of each chapter have suggested further reading, listening and/or viewing for you to continue this exploration beyond each chapter.

Overview of chapters

Whilst Chapters 4–16 focus on a range of lived experiences, Chapters 1, 2 and 3 set the scene regarding poverty in the UK.

Chapter 1: Throughout the writing of this book, our goal has been to be inclusive and to capture a wide range of views and experiences of poverty. In addition to the lived experience chapters, we created space for shorter contributions. An additional 12 contributors share their thoughts and definitions of poverty under the title of 'what poverty means to me…'. Contributors were invited to submit poems, quotes and thoughts, and we invite you to consider these alongside the definitions of poverty outlined in this introduction.

Chapters 2 and 3 provide a policy and practice framework for the book. Key policies, theories and concepts are explained and explored in relation to poverty and the UK context. This includes views on the political landscape and ideology. Themes emerging from these chapters are applied and considered throughout the book in relation to different lived experiences.

Chapter 2: Understanding poverty in the UK

We invited a fellow civic and business commissioner and Director of Public Health in our region, Sam Crowe, to collaborate with us on a scene-setting chapter around the policy framework for addressing the root causes and impacts of poverty in the UK and the extent to which these have failed or been successful. The chapter explores some of the historical context of poverty in the UK and the impact of poverty on wider health, economic and social inequalities. A personal and professional perspective is given as to possible reasons why public sector institutions have found it difficult to make significant progress on reducing poverty, and how we need to address power imbalances and other structural factors if we are to make genuine progress.

Chapter 3: Co-creating solutions to poverty in the UK

We invited Martin Johnstone, one of the Co-Directors of the national PTN, along with Poverty Truth Commissioners: Claire Brown, Tracy Goodwin, Tricia McConalogue, Dusty Thomas and Rachel Williams, with direct experience of the struggle against poverty, to collaborate with us on a scene-setting chapter which explores the evidence of how poverty is something that can be eradicated. Building on the themes identified in the introduction and Chapters 1 and 2, it provides evidence that, as a society, from social workers to policy makers, we have the power to enact change by working in collaboration with people with lived experience to address the root causes of poverty. The chapter includes reflections and learning from the national network of poverty truth commissions and includes specific examples of where the act of people with lived experience and those in positions of power coming together has led to change.

Chapters 4–16:
The main content of the book is authored by people with lived experience in collaboration with co-authors who are academics or those working in social work, social care or community settings. Chapters 4–16 are written from the perspective of people who have experienced poverty. Each chapter provides a personal account and reflective narrative of the first author's experiences in relation to an identified topic, such as poverty and parenting or poverty and mental health. Authors were asked to consider:

- Based on my experience, I would describe poverty as…
- How I think others view poverty (covering commonly held views, pre-conceptions and stereotypes and any examples of this)
- My story (my life and experiences, the causes of poverty for me, the impact of poverty on me and those around me)
- The impact of poverty on the topic I have offered to explore, e.g., parenting, homelessness, health or disability
- What needs to change – My message to others

Text boxes are incorporated throughout each chapter to provide formal knowledge (legislation, policy, research, wider literature and evidence) in the form of bitesize quotes, statistics or short explanations, to underpin the author's experience. For example, if a contributor discusses their experience of using a food bank, a text box has been used to identify statistics which demonstrate the prevalence of this in the UK. This is to enable you, as the reader, to consider the person's lived experience in the wider UK context. Reflective activities have also been incorporated into each chapter by the authors, enabling you to reflect on your own views and perceptions.

The conclusion has been written by the three editors and draws the book to a close with an overview of what the book has sought to achieve and what the learning from it might be. We draw out some key themes from the different chapters and consider the impact (positive and negative) of different experiences as we see them. Throughout the book, each experience is unique to the person who shared it, and so we encourage readers to consider the wide range of experiences and expertise that you could draw on so as not to assume that this applies to everyone. In this section, we provide suggestions for further work in the future to tackle poverty and signpost readers to anti-poverty and anti-austerity campaigns for examples of how to take action to end poverty in the UK and beyond.

References

Hughes, M. (2019). *A Guide to Statutory Social Work Interventions: The Lived Experience*. Palgrave.

Hughes, M. (2022). *Social Exclusion in the UK: The Lived Experience*. Critical Publishing.

Lansley, M and Mack, J (2015). *Breadline Britain – The Rise of Mass Poverty*. Oneworld Poverty Truth Network The Social Workers Union (SWU).

UK Parliament Research Briefing Number 7096 Poverty in the UK: statistics, published Wednesday 10 December 2025. Available at Poverty in the UK: statistics - House of Commons Library

1

WHAT POVERTY MEANS TO ME

Curated by Debbie James

It was important to us as editors to capture a wide range of views and experiences of poverty in this book. We wanted to give people with lived experience, who did not have the opportunity to write a full chapter, a space to contribute, and have their voices heard. We asked a range of people from around the UK to write a paragraph, a poem or a quote of 100 words or less on "What Poverty means to you". When I say "we", I mean mostly Carrie, who has a wide range of contacts across the Poverty Truth Network and beyond. She was the champion of tapping on metaphorical shoulders and sending countless emails back and forth. As contributions came in, we realised that some people had gone above the word limit, but their pieces were so valid, informative and generously shared that we couldn't leave them out without compromising our own commitment to our purpose. We made an executive decision to break our own rule and include them. This chapter is the result of diversity sourced across our networks, the wisdom of unheard voices and the power of lived experience … with a bit of rule-breaking to spice it up.

Do consider these "meanings" in relation to the formal definitions of poverty shared in the introduction chapter. Whilst the formal definitions focus on "measures" of poverty, our contributors focus on the experience.

KATHERINE HOLNESS

Poverty:

It's like learning to swim when you're drowning

DOI: 10.4324/9781003638476-2

NEIL, SOUTH DURHAM

Poverty:

It tastes like failure, it smells like fear
The mountain of debt will it ever clear

The kids go hungry and cry at the cold
with coats for blankets to keep the chill from their bones

They wear wellies in the summer, can't afford shoes
only to be met with ridicule as they go into school

It's a dark place I go to, each day full of fear, I
sometimes wish I was no longer here.

Everyday living hand to mouth, sometimes the
amount I eat could barely feed a mouse.

Every day is a constant slog trying to keep my mind
clear of this consuming fog.

Trying to find ways of robbing Peter to pay Paul, only
to find it doesn't work out at all.

I gaze at my children and I'm wracked with guilt,
knowing that today it will be heat or eat.

I gaze at my children and I'm riddled with shame
knowing that tomorrow they will have to endure
some more of the same.

Ladies and Gentlemen, as a wealthy nation in the
table we lie third. But the way our pensioners are
treated, don't you think that's absurd.

We send aid all around the world and of that I'll
make no bones, but don't you think it's time we
looked after those of our own.

I'll get down off my soap box now as I have nothing
left to say except I hope you will carry our message
with you as you go on your way.

Please remember Tomorrow begins with today.

GEORGE FROM POOLE

Poverty and being a carer

You are pulled from pillar to post trying to give your best to most
You had a car with mobility too but that was cut as reliance on benefits grew
Money was tight and put pressure on you, school trips, Christmas and birthdays too
Appointments, visits and so much work to do, how do you manage to find time for you?

TRACY PORTER

Stoke on trent

Voided legacy

There are cracks in the ceiling,
Cracks in the walls,
Cracks in society,
More visible than before!

Gaps in wages,
Gaps in spending,
Gaps between the balance,
& The balance pending.

There are rifts between families,
Rifts between cultures
Rifts between governments & political parties.

We need to join the endeavour,
To make amends & heal together,
Or one day we will find,
A void is the legacy we will leave behind.

ISHIE (MICHELLE), SWANSEA PTC/POVERTY INSIGHT LAB

I have walked through hunger's night,
where silence pressed against my chest,
and hope felt like a stranger.
The edge was near,
a cliff of despair,
yet I still breathed.
Then truth was spoken,
not about me, but with me.
In the circle of voices,
I found my own.
Pain became testimony,
poverty became power.
Now I rise,
not unscarred, but unbroken.
Hope is no longer distant—
it lives in my hands,
in the change we make together,
in the light of justice,
in the Poverty Truth Commissions.

ANDREW SHAW, DORSET

'Ten things poverty taught me'

It taught me silence, and the ache of being unseen.
It taught me hunger, and the weight of broken dreams.
It taught me how a door can close without a sound.
It taught me how to vanish in a crowd.
But it also taught me how to listen, how to notice, how to care.
And that—is something I still share.

KAS B

Looking back to the 1960/70s and knowing now it was poverty

Free school meals, bread and butter for tea, cake if lucky.
Bailiffs at the door "don't let them in and if they do come in say it's mums".
Free school uniforms "plenty of room to grow into" also became Sunday best.
Jumble sale and hand me down clothes and shoes.
Police at the door "say you have not seen him for weeks".
No power, the electric meter has run out.
Getting dressed in bed, ice on the inside of the windows.
Working from the age of 11.

KAREN, HAMWORTHY

Poverty isn't one thing, we've all got the same problems, but
we've also got loads of individual problems as well.
It's not just one thing, we don't just fit in a box,
we've got so many different boxes, and they are not the same as the next person.
We are all so individual but treated the same.

REBECCA SAMUELS, LANCASHIRE

Addressing poverty

The disconnection between services helping to combat poverty can be likened to rescuing babies floating down a river—pulling the children from the water is a noble thing to do, but at the moment, they're just crying and shivering on the bank. We have to link up the rescuers with other people or groups who can provide towels, bassinettes and formula. Working together is vital to create a true safety net rather than a landing net, or worse, a cycle of catch and release.

RONA

Wouldn't it be lovely

All I want is a nice home somewhere
With lots of comforts that we can share
Nice bath and somewhere to wash my hair
Oh, wouldn't it be lovely.

To go round the shops without a care
and to buy lots of clothes I need to wear,
to keep me warm when it is cold out there
Oh, wouldn't it be lovely.

Cuddle up in a nice soft bed
warm and cosy like I just said
No cares no money worries any more
Oh, wouldn't it be lovely

TRACY

Poverty for me, means hardship

Waking in the morning,
To see vapor in the air,
Walking into the kitchen,
To see the cupboard almost bare.
The carpet that needs replacing,
Will have to remain threadbare.
The many times we've had to say no,
When the kids want to go here or there.
No, we can't afford that,
You'll just have to make do,
I know the other kids show off their shiny new toys,
But lots of expensive gifts,
Just won't happen for you!
No holiday, again, this year,
The closest you will get to that,
Is the garden with a pool.

Walks to the park, or to the lake,
Maybe a carnival,
But only if we pay the bills late!
Of course they don't know,
You're just being mean,
When you say no.
I tell them they're lucky,
There are those that have less,
We gave them the best we could,
But that put us into debt.
Hardship feels like playing catch-up,
Always a few steps behind,
Never having quite enough,
And always having to find,
Ways to cut corners,
A cheaper option.

DEBBIE FROM BOSCOMBE

Poverty is living in an unfurnished house; that's not a home on a social housing estate.

My kids sleep on mattresses because the cheap second-hand bed they were given broke on the first night it was slept in.

The carpet's infested with fleas, and the bathroom floor is so rotten that my foot went right through it.

It's skipping meals so my kids can eat, choosing between milk or bread with the last pound in my pocket, and dragging heavy food bank parcels home because there is no other choice.

It's social services telling me I'm "neglecting" my children.
It's living in fear of losing them.
It's buying things on HP, even though I know the interest is sky high.
It's missing appointments because I cannot afford the bus fare and lying out of shame.
It's living unseen and misunderstood.
It's indignity after indignity
It's a daily relentless cycle of injustice.
It's exhausting.
Poverty is second-hand clothes, second-hand furniture, second-hand lives,
until you believe you are only worth that much.

GENIE JAIMA

I can't afford blaming my parents for my damaged childhood. Culture, religion, immaturity, and other factors made them be, **BUT I was** given the gift of being a parent myself now, and I am doing my best to be and do it better.

I can't afford grieving, not growing up in my homeland, the corrupt government and the war made us run away to Europe, **BUT I was** so lucky to grow up here and have all the freedom and possibilities there are to make it my chosen home.

I can't afford justifying myself in cases of racism and sexism, some of my own countrymen done really bad things to people, family members ignored the truth about all sorts of abuse, **BUT I can** and will stand up to racism and any kind of abuse there is, especially against women and children.

I can't afford working full-time and providing for us fully as a single mum, **BUT I am** studying for a higher degree in order to be more financially independent one day.

I can't afford staying away from my abusive ex-husband because he is the father of my children, **BUT I managed** to leave him, take my children away, start a new life, and be fully back in control of my own life, body, and soul.

I can't afford to do without all the financial support there is for my family, **But I can** appeal and re-appeal and not give up on my family's right to have a stable, normal income.

I can't afford to wish to be pain free for a day in my life, chronic illnesses won't go anywhere, **BUT I can** learn to live with it, not let it overtake my life and mind, make it my strength and not my weakness anymore.

I can't afford to do it all alone, **But I am** so blessed to have my family, friends, and all of you here to count on.

I can't afford to scream, be mad at the broken system, complain, and be frustrated **BUT I can** raise my voice, look for the right people to connect with, and help the next person, if not myself.

SAFIEH ESKANDARI FROM SALFORD

Poverty cannot be defined by a single standard; it encompasses a range of experiences shaped by various factors, such as education, financial wellbeing, health, and access to basic needs. What constitutes poverty for one family may not for another. For instance, the absence of a mattress may signal poverty for some, whilst others may not be affected by the wear of an old one. Poverty is not just about lacking food, shelter, or healthcare, but also the quality, security, and access to these essentials, along with the opportunities to learn, study, and enjoy the pleasures of life, love, and personal growth. It is also about social awareness and the right to live with dignity, free from judgement, and empowered to challenge systemic inequalities.

And finally, a note to end on…

ISHIE (M. HOPKINS)

Swansea

A wonderful society happens when the state ... sees people not as problems to manage, but as lives to uplift. When it replaces punishment with care, and silence with listening. When it breaks the cycle of poverty not with pity, but with justice—and never lets shame be policy. A society flourishes when people in our community ... refuse to look away. When we greet each other without assumption. When we remember that dignity can't be means-tested. When we build a culture where no one has to hide their struggle to be treated with respect. My contribution to a wonderful society is ... To speak up when silence is easier. To make sure stories of poverty are not told about people, but by them. To keep holding hope—and to never accept shame as the cost of survival.

2

UNDERSTANDING POVERTY IN THE UK

Sam Crowe

When I was asked to write this introductory chapter for this important book on poverty, I must admit to feeling a little conflicted. My professional background for the past 30 years or so has been public health, and before that, global health journalism. My interest in public health was sparked by working as a journalist in sub-Saharan and South Africa in the 1990s, alongside health organisations tackling malaria, HIV/AIDS and tuberculosis. These were the headline diseases that were attracting large-scale funding from Western donors. Yet what was obvious when working on the ground in countries like Kenya, Tanzania and Uganda was the realisation that poverty and malnutrition accounted for as many, if not more, poor health outcomes for people.

Poverty and malnutrition created the conditions that allowed these diseases to have such an impact on the people at that time. But it somehow felt 'easier' to focus our professional efforts on tackling the diseases. It was much harder to address the enormous structural and human challenges of simply not having enough of the basic necessities for a healthy life.

This experience grew into frustration at times during my public health training. During a lecture on global disease eradication programmes (smallpox vaccination – very important), I remember questioning why so much funding was going into trying to eradicate the very small number of cases remaining. It seemed to me, perhaps in my naivety, that the final rounds of funding from donor countries would have been better spent addressing sanitation issues, given the statistics on childhood deaths due to diarrhoeal disease in the same population.

What has this got to do with poverty in the United Kingdom today? Through my experience in Tanzania and Kenya, I learned that a narrow focus on

DOI: 10.4324/9781003638476-3

improving health through tackling disease will not be enough. You cannot understand how to tackle inequality in health without also understanding poverty. And yet, as professionals, we may find the subject of poverty and how to respond to its challenges overwhelming. It feels too big, and we may feel too powerless to do something about it. It is not a subject that easily lends itself to our comfortable professional disciplines of using evidence to take action … It feels as if it will take a lot of resources to solve.

When I was approached to join the first Poverty Truth Commission in the BCP Council, I had an inkling that this might offer a different way forward. I had spent the past 20 years or so working in public health in England. We focused on 'tackling health inequalities' and improving people's health and wellbeing. With relatively tiny budgets that were pretty much fixed in terms of what they could be spent on. We carried out needs assessments and became adept at using data and insights to describe our local populations, including areas with a higher proportion of people on low incomes, with poorer outcomes. And yet I think that this still skirts around the real issue. Inequality in our society.

In England, Sir Michael Marmot has been studying the importance of wider factors like income, education level and housing on health and inequality for more than 40 years. In a landmark study involving British civil servants, he showed a clear association between job grade and risk of death (Marmot, 1984). The study was powerful because it was designed to overcome some of the problems created by the use of general social class groupings. For example, trying to classify people in a study into higher or lower social classes may reflect subjective interpretations of 'status', but ignores income. In this study, administrative grade in one type of industry (the civil service) was used because it provided very clear ways of classifying job grades. And because grade determines income, it is a more precise way of capturing both social status (e.g. education level) and material factors like income. And between these grades were obvious social divisions. Men working in the lowest grades tended to be messengers or doorkeepers, compared with men working in the highest grades who were administrators.

What the study found was that men who were working in the lowest grades in the civil service were three times more likely to die from all-cause mortality compared with men working in the highest grades. The study tried to find out whether this difference could be explained by risk factors like smoking, blood pressure, obesity and physical activity levels. Even after controlling for differences in these risk factors, men working in the lowest grades were at twice the risk of death from heart disease compared with those working in the highest grades.

Sir Michael and his research teams have continued to study these relationships between social status and various health outcomes in a number of different studies, including Whitehall II – a study of male and female civil servants.

These social determinants of health have been shown in carefully designed studies to be closely associated with health outcomes. Ultimately, what Sir Michael has shown is that what we might call 'class' in this country is strongly associated with better health and a higher life expectancy.

These findings have been influential in UK government policy and led to the Marmot Review in 2010. *Fair Society Healthy Lives* proposed six policy objectives to reduce inequalities in health, ranging from ensuring the best start in life, through to fair employment and good work for all.

As a public health professional, I am trained to be guided by evidence. Sir Michael's work is highly influential in public health circles. Working at a local level, public health teams often produce health assessments using a variety of publicly available data. This tends to show associations at the level of a local council between measures of deprivation (e.g. the Index of Multiple Deprivation), say, and common measures of health in the local population. Sir Michael's report contained a landmark graphic that illustrated this starkly for England. It showed life expectancy in each neighbourhood in England, plotted against income deprivation for that neighbourhood (Marmot, 2010). This showed a clear trend – life expectancy increased as average income deprivation score decreased across all neighbourhoods in England.

It is tempting to make assumptions about the link between income deprivation, or poverty, and ill-health, because most, if not all of the areas experiencing the worst health outcomes are in the north of England, when viewed at upper-tier Council level. However, associations between poorer health and income inequality – sometimes called the 'fine grain of inequality' – can be found in almost every area when you look at smaller geographical units, such as electoral wards, or super output areas.

For example, in BCP Council, we have shown a consistent link between deprivation score in each electoral ward, and life expectancy for men and women (Iggulden, 2021) Looking in more detail, we have also shown consistent links between deprivation scores at ward level, and child obesity rates, educational attainment at key stage 4 and early deaths (before 75 years) from all causes.

So even at a local level, in a population within one unitary council in England of around 400,000 people, you can see patterns that link how deprived a small area like an electoral ward is, and the health status of people living in that area. Yet many people would not class Bournemouth, Christchurch or Poole as 'deprived' because the overall income deprivation score masks inequalities within the area. Similarly, assumptions are often made that poverty and inequality are an urban issue. In fact, rural poverty and income inequality can be just as deep but harder to recognise. The 2025 Index of Multiple Deprivation highlighted several rural areas to which this applies, including north Norfolk, East Lincolnshire, Cornwall and the Isles of Scilly, as well as rural towns in Herefordshire, Shropshire and Somerset (McLennan, 2025)

The challenge for a local public health team is that describing these patterns can lead to a sense of helplessness and anger at social injustice. It just feels too big, often ignored in public debate and risks stigmatisation and blame through oversimplified use of stereotypes and tropes. How often have we seen headlines that blame the poor for ill health (they smoke too much, eat and drink too much, watch too much TV …)? We lack the resources or influence locally to affect or impact structural policies that drive inequality.

As relative funding and resources for the public sector have declined over the past two decades in real terms (English councils' core spending has fallen by 18% during this period, Ogden, 2024), it has felt difficult to know what approaches locally might make an impact in what appear to be huge structural challenges. One response has been for public services to consider asset-based approaches – recognising that some solutions may be found by working with and alongside communities.

Asset-based community development was conceived as a method of sustainable development of communities, based on their strengths and potential. Developed in the 1990s, the idea was to empower communities by encouraging them to use resources that they already possess. Recently, Cormac Russell has argued that the focus on efficiency drives in public services, switching spending plus lots of organisational restructuring, may not be the answer to rising demand and pressure. He believes that sustainable services are more about re-orienting how services work in communities, alongside people. He has provided a compelling set of principles for how institutions should work with communities. This includes sharing space, sharing skills and economic power, but also offering support, solidarity and advocacy for communities in a way that builds mutual trust and alliance (Russell, 2025).

And yet the international evidence also shows how important it is to create fairer, more equal societies. It is not just about the levels of poverty, but the gaps between rich and poor. And these gaps can have impacts in surprising ways, beyond the obvious unequal income distribution.

I remember working in a rural village in northern Tanzania in summer 1997 – visiting and writing about how tuberculosis is treated in a remote rural community. When asking about where a good place might be to eat in the village (I had protein in mind – chicken, especially), it became apparent that no chickens were available for use in any of the dishes being served in the local café. This was because almost all were being sold to the encampment nearby, where several international NGOs resided. In short, locals could obtain a far higher price selling their chickens to foreigners, thus removing them from the local food economy entirely.

In *The Spirit Level*, Richard Wilkinson and Kate Pickett argued that more equal societies with smaller income gaps between the rich and poor perform better across a wide range of social and health outcomes. The authors present data showing that more equal societies tend to have lower levels of health and social problems compared with more unequal countries. They showed a clear relationship between the level of income inequality within each country and the extent of health and social problems (Wilkinson, 2009). They assessed health and social problems using an index that included life expectancy, maths and literacy levels, infant mortality, homicide rates, imprisonment, teenage births, levels of trust, obesity, mental illness, including substance misuse and social mobility.

Although the main argument has been criticised by some economists, who say that correlations at the country level between income equality and outcomes do not necessarily mean causation, the authors say that the consistent relationships between these correlations are meaningful, i.e., there is a link.

The implications of *The Spirit Level* are profound and indicate the importance of policy as a response to improving outcomes in health, education and crime rates. They studied data from Japan, Scandinavia, the US and US states and showed that the greater the level of income inequality, the greater the rates of worse health and social outcomes. The authors argue that policies which reduce income inequality (the gap between rich and poor) are, therefore, the most effective way of tackling poor health and social outcomes. This includes progressive taxation, having a strong welfare system, representation for workers and protection of rights, as well as limits on excessive executive pay.

It is impossible to understand poverty in the UK without also understanding income inequality. When I look back over the past 50 years from my personal and professional perspective, the change in society that has probably had the most impact on rates of poverty that we see today in the UK is the growth in income inequality.

I can vividly remember Margaret Thatcher's election as Conservative Prime Minister in 1979. I was eight years old, and in the playground at primary school in Manchester, Margaret Thatcher's election as PM was being hotly debated. A divisive figure, even for eight-year-olds at the time. Before the Thatcher Conservative Government (1979–1990), poverty rates were around 14% and had remained at this level for some time. But in the 1980s, wages and income rose significantly in the UK. And while income grew for many, the unequal distribution of wealth contributed to a 50% rise in the proportions of people experiencing poverty (Cebula, 2024).

By 1990, the proportion of the population living in poverty had risen to 23%, rising further to 25% by the end of John Major's government in 1997. Since the 1990s, the proportion of people living in the deepest poverty has increased. In 2022, this group made up the largest proportion of people living in poverty in the UK – about 40% of those in poverty overall, or 6 million people (Cebula, 2024).

Recent economic and global shocks, including austerity, the pandemic and the cost-of-living crisis due to inflation, have not helped people living in the deepest poverty. More recently, 'destitution' has been the focus of poverty campaigners.

Destitution refers to being unable to meet your basic physical needs – to stay warm, dry, clean and fed. About 3.8 million people in the UK experienced destitution in 2022 – roughly doubling in number since 2017 (Fitzpatrick, 2023).

From the evidence of these headline statistics, it seems as if government and public sector institutions have struggled to make progress in reducing poverty over the past 50 years.

During the 1970s, policies focused on building up public welfare provision and redistribution of wealth through progressive taxation. A range of benefits was expanded, including pensions, unemployment support and allowances for children. Social housing provision was helped through the supply of council houses. There was even a Royal Commission on the Distribution of Income and Wealth, introduced under the Labour Government in what year? as a standing body to analyse past and present trends in economic inequality.

Analysis by the academic Danny Dorling and colleagues showed that during this decade (1970s), the percentage of people living in poverty fell significantly (core poor, or income poor in absolute terms, and breadline poor, or living in relative poverty). Poverty fell among pensioners and families with children due to improvements in the welfare state (Dorling, 2007).

In the 1980s, a series of policy reforms driven by a market ideology led to cuts to welfare spending, with tighter eligibility criteria and more targeting to people's absolute needs. The sale of council housing under schemes like the Right to Buy, which enabled council housing tenants to purchase their property and become homeowners, reduced the availability of social housing stock. This led to long-term housing instability and rising housing costs. The Conservative Government at this time emphasised absolute poverty rather than relative poverty and shifted the narrative away from concepts like income inequality. Absolute poverty tends to be defined as when a household or person lacks the minimum income needed to meet basic needs, like food, shelter and clothing. Relative poverty is defined in relation to the economic status of other people in that society. In the UK, it is often defined as living in a household with income below 60% of the median household income after housing costs.

Prime Minister Margaret Thatcher argued during this period that even the poor experienced a rise in living standards, due to the so-called 'trickle down' effect. This economic theory suggests that benefits provided to the wealthy or businesses through tax cuts will eventually trickle down to everyone else, including the poor.

However, Thatcher's assertion of a 'massive rise in living standards' has been questioned due to the poor understanding of statistics on poverty and inequality during the 1980s. In a comprehensive review of some of the claims in support of the trickle-down effect, Felix Romer has shown that far from experiencing an 8.3% growth in income in this decade, the poorest 10% in fact experienced losses in income of 14% (Romer, 2022).

This analysis has also shown that under the government at the time, previous sources of official statistics on income and inequality (such as those produced by the Central Statistical Office, CSO) were suppressed. The first authoritative figures on poverty and inequality were not available until 1983/4, after a public campaign backed by the Trades Union Congress to 'save our statistics'. Partly, the lack of official statistics on income and inequality was due to cost-cutting in the civil service. But it was also potentially due to the view that the Government Statistical Service should fulfil the needs of the government. Romer writes that the provision of information to society 'was to be left to political parties, pressure groups and the media'.

Nonetheless, Romer points out that public discourse on poverty, inequality and social class had shifted by 1996. He quotes Steven Webb, an analyst for the Institute of Fiscal Studies, speaking in a BBC4 programme on poverty in 1996.

> The agenda has shifted by the Conservatives over 15 years or so, and they have got across the idea that there is no such thing as poverty, that it's all just relative poverty, that people are just further behind, they they've still got video players and cars and go on foreign holidays. And because that has become widely accepted the political pressure to do something about poverty has diminished enormously.
>
> *(Romer, 2022)*

This quote aptly sets the stage for a significant change in Government policy, with the election of the Blair Labour Government in 1997. During the 1990s, the Child Poverty Action Group had been campaigning for policies to reduce child poverty. Their campaigns were supported by legal test cases to challenge unfair welfare rules. This public and political pressure paid off, and many of CPAG's proposals were reflected in Labour's 1997 manifesto, especially the drive to increase child benefit and targeted support to low-income families.

Between 1997 and 2007, the Government developed one of the most comprehensive strategies to reduce poverty with the launch of New Deal programmes for young people, the unemployed and single parents, quickly followed by a National Minimum Wage, Sure Start centres and a series of tax and pension credit reforms.

By 2007, when Tony Blair stepped down as Prime Minister, there was clear evidence that an estimated 2 million children had been lifted out of absolute poverty (Joyce, 2013). A comprehensive analysis of the policy changes shows that overall, Labour's commitment to its objectives to end child poverty and end pensioner poverty was largely achieved. However, tackling income inequality was more complex – and statistics over this time show that incomes at the top of the distribution showed the strongest growth of all during Labour's period in office. In terms of income, the richest benefitted the most.

Within 15 years, the approach to tackling poverty had changed again, with the election of the Coalition Government (between the Conservative Party and the Liberal Democrats) from 2010 to 2015. The main policy reforms were aimed at simplifying the benefits system through the introduction of Universal Credit and requiring benefit claimants to agree personalised job search plans, with sanctions for non-compliance. This shift towards personal responsibility, with commitment expected from claimants (through Jobseeker's Allowance (JSA)), has been criticised as not addressing the underlying structural causes of poverty. In addition, JSA payments were seen as insufficient to cover basic living costs.

But perhaps the biggest impact on efforts to reduce poverty and inequality came through the commitment to address the budget deficit. This saw public spending fall by 2.6% overall, but the impact on non-protected areas like local government, housing and social care was far bigger, with estimated cuts of up to one-third (Lupton et al., 2015). Although the Government was committed to the importance of 'the foundation years' spending on early education, childcare and Sure Start centres fell by an estimated 25% between 2009–10 and 2012–13.

Sure Start was launched in 1999, initially targeting the most disadvantaged areas in England. It provided a range of services to families with children under the age of 5 – usually from a one-stop centre located at the heart of the community. Services included health services like health visiting and speech and language, parenting support, early learning and childcare and wider services such as employment support or benefits advice for parents.

A recent review of its impact by the Institute for Fiscal Studies found that having access to a Sure Start centre between the ages of 0 and 4 improved educational achievement significantly (Carneiro, 2025). And these benefits lasted until at least age 16, when GCSE exams are taken. The impact was measured by comparing educational attainment at various ages among the cohort of children living within 2.5 km of a Sure Start centre, with those who did not live within 2.5 km of a centre. The study also looked at the possible impact of Sure Start on hospitalisations in childhood, and the impact on social, emotional and behavioural outcomes. The results of these studies were more mixed. However, there are methodological challenges in this type of complex evaluation. These includes the difficulty of controlling for differences in a number of variables, using proximity as a proxy for attendance, and being able to isolate the effect of this policy intervention from several others that were also introduced at the time. The authors used a number of methods to mitigate against these biases. One of the strengths of the study was its ability to track outcomes over a long time period for millions of children to ensure consistency and comparability across large geographical areas and cohorts of children.

The Conservative Governments of 2015–24 continued to roll out universal credit and the move to incentivise work. By 2024, an estimated 6.8 million people were claiming universal credit (Full Fact, 2024). While the system aimed to simplify benefits, it has been criticised for delays in payment, gaps and extreme hardship during transition periods. The two-child benefit cap was also introduced in 2017 – aimed at being fairer to working families but linked with rising child poverty rates in larger families (Full Fact, 2024).

This period of Government also saw some global economic shocks, not least the COVID-19 pandemic, war in Ukraine and subsequent impact on energy costs, and the cost-of-living support introduced as a result of spiking inflation. There was a nod to regional inequalities through the Levelling Up Strategy, described as a long-term poverty reduction strategy (Hayes, 2024). This is a significant shift in policy, because it sets out to describe how living standards, pay, jobs and productivity can be boosted in parts of the UK where they are lagging by boosting the private sector. It also started to talk about the importance of 'place' and restoring a sense of community, local pride and belonging. The strategy also set targets to improve primary school level education and increase the number of people completing high-quality skills training. The overall aim of this approach was to reduce regional differences in income, health outcomes, education and infrastructure through 12 'missions' – especially between south-east England and the remaining regions. There was a focus on improving productivity, and using private sector investment to encourage innovation with a view to creating jobs and improving living standards in areas that 'had been left behind'.

However, the strategy has been criticised for a lack of objective metrics against which progress can be measured. The Institute for Fiscal Studies said progress had been 'glacial' with some indicators worsening, including primary school attainment falling, and further education course completions dropping, especially in low-skilled areas (Farquharson, 2024). Gaps in employment rates between regions also widened in this period. So, where does this leave us now?

At the time of writing, one year into a Labour government, elected in May 2024, we are on the cusp of more policy promises. A new Child Poverty Strategy is promised in the autumn of 2025 (Cabinet Office, 2024). However, the planned changes to welfare and the introduction of disability and employment reform have become difficult tests for the government, with widespread opposition to the changes, including from Labour's own backbench MPs. It remains to be seen whether the previous Labour government's success at lifting children out of poverty can be repeated. But it also feels as if the world has turned in that time, with continued financial and global pressures making it harder to deliver the growth to the economy that would help fund direct policy interventions similar to the tax credit reforms of the Blair government.

So, on reflection, looking at the past half-century of policies to tackle poverty and income inequality, it can be shown that focused and aligned policies to directly intervene to improve the incomes of the poorest did lift children out of poverty and improve the lives of the poorest families. Investing in the welfare state and introducing progressive taxation policies also improved poverty rates in the 1970s.

At the time of writing, it feels as if the headwinds for government intervention are far stronger, and there are different challenges. The growth in the number of people out of work due to ill-health – mental and physical – has shifted the focus to working-age adults. Unemployment has steadily crept up to nearly 5%, with job vacancies also falling, and fewer people on the payroll. As a reader, you can search online for up-to-date statistics to see what has changed.

What might the next few years look like, from this perspective? For me, it very much feels as if there is a need for multi-level approaches to tackling poverty and inequality. At the national level, policy must support a reversal of the growth in income inequality, as far as possible. It is welcome that the Government is keen on a return to Sure Start with its Best Start in Life policy, announced in 2025. There is also a drive to devolve power from the central government to local areas, through devolution deals. While these are encouraging councils to work together on a bigger footprint, there is also a growing sense that investment in neighbourhoods, with further devolved powers, is key to making a difference in many social and health outcomes as part of a new place-making agenda.

This is where, for me, the importance of asset-based community development, working with people's strengths, and Poverty Truth Commissions is important. The PTC motto 'Nothing about us without us is for us' shows that if local public service is to play its part in restoring trust and addressing power imbalances that have led to the UK being one of the most unequal of developed countries (Wilkinson, 2009). Empathy, listening with humanity to people's real experiences of what it is like to struggle for want of the basics, can be a powerful way of showing how we must all change if we are to challenge the patterns of the past 50 years.

What I learned from joining the commission as a public health professional was that change starts when we sit as equals. By listening to community commissioners, we can work together to change the seemingly small barriers that are perfectly within our gift: rewriting impersonal and impregnable housing letters. Training frontline professionals to listen properly without judgement and see the whole person, and ensure our processes are 'humanised'. Joining up information systems so that people don't have to repeatedly tell their story, adding to endless frustrations and feeling as if 'the system doesn't care'.

In 2025, the Government stated a commitment to 'neighbourhood health' as part of its ten-year plan for Health (Department of Health, 2025). And local government is being encouraged to develop new forms of community participation as part of the English Devolution and Community Empowerment Bill. If local public sector organisations adopt these approaches and genuinely involve people with experience of poverty and its challenges in the design, as equals, right from the start, we have a chance to re-wire public services differently and recover some of the lost ground from the political and policy failure of the past half-century.

For me, writing as a public health professional and drawing on my experience abroad and working in this country on inequality and health, I think we must keep poverty reduction firmly in our sights, whether our profession is health, social care or education. Poverty and inequality continue to lie at the heart of unjust differences in our society. Unless we address this directly, any policy or professional service improvements are likely to have transitory impacts at best. However, I do remain hopeful that the recent focus by the Government on neighbourhoods is important – but only if we see this as an opportunity to share power, resources and time with communities. This requires working in a different way, with different leadership skills and ways of working. Technical expertise and understanding the evidence of what makes a difference will always be important. But we must remember that for this to work well, it has to be led with local communities, not imposed. And on that note, the Poverty Truth Commission motto, 'nothing about us without us is for us', seems to me the most wise way of summarising this introduction. I hope you enjoy the rest of the book and are excited about the potential that working differently holds.

References

Cabinet Office (2024). 'Tackling Child Poverty: Developing Our Strategy'. *Policy Paper*, published 23 October 2024, last updated 18 June 2025. Available at: https://www.gov.uk/government/publications/tackling-child-poverty-developing-our-strategy/tackling-child-poverty-developing-our-strategy-html (Accessed: 30 November 2025)

Carneiro, P., Cattan, S., Conti, G., et al. (2025). *The Short- and Medium-term Effects of Sure Start on Children's Outcomes*. Institute for Fiscal Studies. Available at: https://ifs.org.uk/publications/short-and-medium-term-effects-sure-start-childrens-outcomes (Accessed: 3 November 2025).

Cebula, C., Earwaker, R., Elliott, J., Johnson-Hunter, M., Matejic, P., Milne, B., Taylor, I., Thompson, S., Wenham, A. & Joseph Rowntree Foundation (2024). *Understanding Poverty in the UK in 2024*. Joseph Rowntree Foundation. Available at: https://www.jrf.org.uk/pdf/15211 (Accessed: 30 November 2025).

Department of Health and Social Care (2025). *Fit for the Future: 10 Year Health Plan for England*. London: GOV.UK. Available at: https://www.gov.uk/government/publications/10-year-health-plan-for-england-fit-for-the-future (Accessed: 2 November 2025)

Dorling, D., Rigby, J., Wheeler, B., Ballas, D., Thomas, B., Fahmy, E., Gordon, D. & Lupton, R. (2007). *Poverty, Wealth and Place in Britain, 1968 to 2005*. Bristol: Policy Press.

Farquharson, C., Heath, L., Milsom, I., Tahir, I., Upton, B. & Vyas, G. (2024). 'How Do the Last Five Years Measure Up on Levelling Up?' *IFS Report R323*. London: Institute for Fiscal Studies. Available at: https://ifs.org.uk/publications/how-do-last-five-years-measure-levelling (Accessed: 30 November 2025)

Fitzpatrick, S., Bramley, G., Treanor, M., Blenkinsopp, J., McIntyre, J., Johnsen, S. & McMordie, L. (2023). *Destitution in the UK 2023*. York: Joseph Rowntree Foundation. Available at: https://www.jrf.org.uk/report/destitution-uk-2023 (Accessed: 30 November 2025).

Full Fact (2024). 'Welfare Reform: Explained', 1 July. Available at: https://fullfact.org/economy/welfare-reform-election-briefing/ (Accessed: 30 November 2025)

Hayes, E. (2024). 'Poverty in the UK: Government Policy'. *House of Lords Library*, 12 February. Available at: https://lordslibrary.parliament.uk/poverty-in-the-uk-government-policy/ (Accessed: 30 November 2025).

Iggulden, P, & Ireland, S. (2021). An Overview of Health Inequalities in BCP Council. Available at: https://www.bcpcouncil.gov.uk/documents/about-the-council/Health-inequalities-in-BCP-Nov-2021.pdf (accessed 31 October 2025).

Joyce, R. & Sibieta, L. (2013). 'An Assessment of Labour's Record on Income Inequality and Poverty', *Oxford Review of Economic Policy*, 29(1), pp. 178–202. Available at: https://doi.org/10.1093/oxrep/grt008 (Accessed: 30 November 2025).

Lupton, R., Burchardt, T., Fitzgerald, A., Hills, J., McKnight, A., Oboloenskaya, P., Stewart, K., Thomson, S., Tunstall, R. & Vizard, P. (2015). Social Policy in a Cold Climate, Summary Research Report 4 January 2015.

Marmot, M. (2010). *Fair Society, Healthy Lives: The Marmot Review*. Strategic Review of Health Inequalities in England post-2010. London: The Marmot Review. Available at: https://www.parliament.uk/globalassets/documents/fair-society-healthy-lives-full-report.pdf (Accessed: 31 October 2025).

Marmot, M. G., Shipley, M. J., & Rose, G. (1984). 'Inequalities in Death—Specific Explanations of a General Pattern?', *The Lancet*, 323(8384), 1003–1006.

McLennan, D., Noble, S., Penney, B. et al. (2025). *The English Indices of Deprivation 2025. Deprivation in Rural Areas: Supplementary Report*. Available from English Indices of Deprivation 2025: Rural Report (accessed 31 October 2025).

Ogden, K., & Phillips, D. (2024). 'How Have English Councils' Funding and Spending Changed? 2010 to 2024', *IFS Report, No. R318*. Institute for Fiscal Studies (IFS), London. Available from How have English councils' funding and spending changed? 2010 to 2024 (accessed 31 October 2025).

Romer, F. (2022). 'Poverty, Inequality Statistics and Knowledge Politics Under Thatcher', *The English Historical Review*, 137(585), pp. 513–551. Available at: https://doi.org/10.1093/ehr/ceac059 (Accessed: 30 November 2025).

Russell, C. (2025). 'Exploring the Potential of Community-centred Public Services', *New Local*, May. Available at: https://www.newlocal.org.uk/publications/community-centred-public-services-cormac-russell-stronger-things-2025 (accessed 31 October 2025).

Wilkinson, R. & Pickett, K. (2009). *The Spirit Level: Why More Equal Societies Almost Always Do Better*. London: Allen Lane.

3

CO-CREATING SOLUTIONS TO POVERTY IN THE UK

Martin Johnstone in conversation with Claire Brown, Tracy Goodwin, Tricia McConalogue, Dusty Thomas and Rachel Williams

It's About Relationships: The Story of the Poverty Truth Network

We have invited Martin Johnstone, one of the Co-Directors of the Poverty Truth Network, along with Poverty Truth Commissioners with direct experience of the struggle against poverty, to collaborate with us on a scene-setting chapter which explores the evidence of how poverty is something that can be eradicated. Building on the themes identified in the Introduction and Chapter 1, it will provide evidence that social workers have the power to enact change by working in collaboration with people with lived experience to address the root causes of poverty. The chapter will include reflections and learning from the national network of poverty truth commissions and include specific examples of where the act of people with lived experience and those in positions of power coming together has led to change.

The task of writing this chapter, like so much that is part of the work of the Poverty Truth Network, has been a joint effort. In the first instance, Martin spent some time with Tricia McConalogue. Both were involved in the first Poverty Truth Commission. Subsequently, he hosted a second conversation with Claire Brown, Tracy Goodwin, Dusty Thomas and Rachel Williams. They have been involved in a Poverty Truth Commission in either Gateshead, Morecambe Bay or West Cheshire. This chapter brings together some of what they shared together.

DOI: 10.4324/9781003638476-4

By Way of Introduction...

The first Poverty Truth Commission was launched in Glasgow in April 2009. Since then, the model has spread to over thirty different locations across the UK.

At its core, its practice of change is very simple. It brings together two different groups of people: those who experience poverty in their daily struggle for survival and those in leadership positions who are committed to tackling its causes and symptoms. It does that over a sustained period of two to three years, always beginning with those who experience poverty firsthand.

In 2019, the Poverty Truth Network was formally established. The Network supports local commissions and commissioners, as well as working nationally to enable change.

At the heart of that change is an understanding of the importance of building positive relationships, alongside the recognition that most people want to make things better. It strives to get beyond the divisions of "them" and "us," towards a "bigger us."

The Network is clear that real and lasting change is most likely to happen when people struggling against poverty are at the heart of generating and delivering that change. It takes as its motto a phrase developed through a range of social justice organisations, including the anti-apartheid and disability movements: "Nothing About Us Without Us Is For Us."

Every Story Starts Somewhere: Where This One Started

If you were to ask the almost thirty people who were part of the first Poverty Truth Commission how it started, you would probably receive at least that many answers. Martin has been involved in the Network from very near the beginning. Although it is the fruit of many different conversations and moments, including insights from many others in the UK and overseas, for Martin, it probably began around a table in John and Molly's living room. He remembers:

> This idea of bringing people together was beginning to niggle away for several of us. But we knew that we had to test it out rather than just jump straight in. So, John and Molly agreed to host a meal to which we invited a few people who knew about poverty in their guts. To ask them if this idea had any mileage.

Tricia was one of those who came along that evening. She went on to become co-chair of the first Poverty Truth Commission. Whilst she had experienced poverty in her own life and had been involved in anti-poverty organisations for many years, the Poverty Truth Commission felt different. "It was probably the most powerful thing that I have ever been involved in," she says, remembering in particular the opening event in front of an audience of about 400 people in Glasgow City Chambers.

> I thought, it will never work. For almost two hours people shared their reality of poverty through dance, rap, animation and testimony. And then, whilst we all enjoyed some food, fifteen key civic leaders were asked to leave the room and to think about what they were going to do about what they had heard. When they came back, they were clear. They wanted us to all work together, to form a single commission. We were all commissioners now.

The first meetings of the Poverty Truth Commission weren't straightforward. It met at first in the Council Chambers in Glasgow, with commissioners having to press microphones if you wanted to speak. It was familiar territory for some. And completely alien to others. "We don't want the mics. We don't need the mics," said Jessie.

So, the Commission moved to a dusty and somewhat damp community hall. We sat in a circle on rickety chairs with mugs of coffee and tea. And cake. Always cake.

We built relationships. And friendships. And understanding. We found common issues and tried to understand them better. And then we got our sleeves rolled up to do something about them. Martin remembers that there was a lot of anger, frustration and tears. But also, a lot of laughter, a huge amount of laughter. "Labels and lanyards were left at the door," he recalls. "And we met as human beings."

Two years later, the Poverty Truth Commission reported back to a packed hall in the City Chambers. But this time it was different. This time, it was not just those who knew about poverty firsthand who spoke. It was all the commissioners, sharing both what they had achieved and about the many problems that remained unresolved. However, people also spoke about how being involved had changed them. Often, it was the civic leaders who were most nervous. They were less used to talking about their feelings in public. It was emotional stuff.

Reflecting on the whole experience, Tricia notes:

> When you are in poverty you don't know where you fit in, where you can take the mask off and just be yourself. In the Poverty Truth Commission, we were all able to be ourselves. As well as making change happen, we were also becoming friends. Many of those friendships have lasted.

It was perhaps the experience of "doing things together" that was the most striking element of that first commission. This involved real, tangible change – for example, change to Kinship Care legislation in Scotland. But it also involved a change in the way of doing things. According to Jim, one of the civic leaders, adoption of the model would be nothing short of revolutionary.

Going Deeper: Four Stories

When the first Poverty Truth Commission concluded, few if any people expected there to be a second one. However, within a relatively short period of time, there was not only an appetite for a second commission in Scotland but also a growing interest in the approach from elsewhere. Further growth was, in part, because of the involvement of key members of staff from the Joseph Rowntree Foundation in some of the early Poverty Truth Commissions, specifically in Scotland and Leeds.

Commissions began to pop up in different parts of the UK, each trying to follow a similar process. Beginning with those who experienced poverty. Inviting civic leaders to join. Identifying key areas where they could make a difference. Sharing what they had done and what they had learnt, as well as how being involved had changed them.

It would be easy to tell the story of how the movement has spread. From Scotland to the North of England, to the Midlands, to the South, to Wales and to Northern Ireland. But it is how this way of working has enabled change that is perhaps even more striking. In preparing to write this chapter, a few commissioners got together to reflect and share their experiences.

Tracy, from West Cheshire, tells how she learnt about the Poverty Truth Commission whilst on the bus. She had recently been evicted along with her six children and was trying to get by in a single room on the outskirts of Chester.

> When the two housing officers evicted me and the kids, they fist bumped. Job well done! I'll never forget that. As a working mum with six kids, when they introduced the two-child limit, I couldn't afford to pay the rent. They went to court to throw us out. And they celebrated that they had succeeded.

Through the West Cheshire Poverty Truth Commission, Tracy met the housing association director whose company had been responsible for her eviction. Her name had been on some of the letters. In true Poverty Truth Commission style, they met first over a cup of tea. They discovered how important being a mum was to both of them. "I didn't want to," remembers Tracy, "but I discovered that I really liked her."

It wasn't instantaneous, but over a period of time, by working together as part of the Poverty Truth Commission in West Cheshire, they reduced the level of evictions by over 75%. There was a fresh understanding that forcing someone to leave their home represented failure, not success.

Dusty, from Morecambe Bay, by comparison, was involved much earlier in the process of establishing a commission in his area. By virtue of his many years as a community activist, he was there from the earliest conversations of the start-up group.

Dusty is someone who it is very hard to put a label on. He is an important reminder to avoid labels and stereotypes if at all possible. He is a community leader, a facilitator within the Morecambe Bay Poverty Truth Commission, and someone who has lived in generational poverty. Part of Dusty's advice would be:

> Trust the process. Take your time. Don't try fixing things from day one. Instead, listen and learn. Always remember that we have a great deal in common.

Perhaps because there have already been two Poverty Truth Commissions in Morecambe Bay, and a third one is underway, Dusty can point to lots of changes that have happened in the area over the years. These include: changes within the ways that a major energy provider deals with household debt (and the setting up of a department focused on preventing debt in the first place); the major refurbishment of a traveller caravan site giving its residents long-term security; and changes in the way that council departments engage with residents. Council and NHS staff have received training through the Poverty Truth Commission. They are actively encouraged to "be more humane."

Perhaps one of the most striking things that happened in Morecambe Bay – and it also happened through several other Poverty Truth Commissions – was during COVID. Several commissioners struggling against poverty, many of whom were particularly vulnerable, took to keeping in regular contact with senior leaders who were under huge pressure, checking in on their welfare and mental health.

Claire, from Gateshead, is currently chair of the Poverty Truth Network. But that is not a role she ever expected to assume. Like many other commissioners, she became involved because someone she knew, and liked, invited her. She says:

> We were struggling and Tracy was there to help. I didn't think that we were living in poverty, but we were really struggling. We have two boys with disabilities and my husband ended up losing his job because of all the pressure. I knew others who had always been in poverty and didn't feel like them. But I also recognised how disabilities pulled other people into poverty. People need to know about the struggles of being a fulltime carer.

In Gateshead, the Poverty Truth Commission helped housing providers to think about keeping carpets in homes at the end of tenancies. It seems like such a small thing, but having carpets instead of floorboards helps to make a house a home. These are the things that often get missed but can make such a big difference.

Launching and operating largely during COVID restrictions, the commissioners learned to keep in touch during lockdowns. It was a process that helped to inform some of the wider changes that were so essential at that point. It highlighted in real time the harsh realities caused by digital exclusion. It also ensured that people who were really struggling were heard by senior leaders in the area.

Although she has seen lots of good things happen, Claire remains involved because "there is still so much work to be done." She reflects on how, twenty years ago, she visited a friend whose son's bed was in their living room because he couldn't get up the stairs; and how, until recently, that was their own family predicament.

Claire is also passionate about the need for people to be treated with the dignity that they deserve and require if they are to survive, let alone flourish:

> Over the years we've had fifteen social workers. Fifteen. One of them used to come in, go into the boys' rooms and check the bedding. And go into the fridge and check what food we had. Of course, the place was going to be untidy. I had two disabled kids, was getting by on four hours sleep a night. You're there to help me, not judge me. You are not there to make me feel like the scum of the earth.

Rachel, from West Cheshire, could relate to Claire's pain. We all can. She remembered a time when, during a mental health crisis, she had been berated rather than supported. "They were awful," she recalls, thinking also of a friend who "they broke before they then offered to help."

Rachel, like Claire and many others, didn't immediately associate with the notion of being poor. It was a term that she more naturally associated with those in extreme poverty in the Global South. There was a sense of shame associated with it. Perhaps that's one of the reasons why in the Poverty Truth Network, we consistently talk about people struggling against poverty. Poverty should never define us.

However, where people started talking about failing services and food insecurity, Rachel felt that she could very much associate with these experiences and that she had something to contribute.

She has chosen to stick around because she has seen the changes which have happened. For example, how their food poverty group developed a resource that has been taken up nationally. Or the training that they now provide for Council employees, from frontline staff to directors. Or the way that they are helping to influence and inform academic research into poverty, so as it more faithfully reflects the process and values of Poverty Truth's ways of working.

One of the major achievements of the West Cheshire Poverty Truth Commission has been the decision of the Council in 2020 to establish a Poverty Truth Advisory Board with public, private, civic and community sector representatives to mainstream the approach across the Council. The Advisory Board operates in a pattern like that of a Poverty Truth Commission. It is co-chaired by someone with ongoing experience of the struggle against poverty.

All these changes have mattered for Rachel. But there is also something else that Rachel would wish to highlight:

> I stay because of the changes we have made together but also because of what I get out of it. It gives me a boost and confidence. I did something here. I helped to make that difference. I wouldn't have stayed had I not seen change. But it's also about relationships. It's about building a community.

Tracey, Dusty, Claire and Rachel are just four out of over eight hundred Poverty Truth Commissioners, drawn from three out of over thirty locations. Every commissioner would have their own story to tell. It is about being given the place to share your reality safely and honestly, and to listen to others share theirs. And it is about everyone working together to effect the necessary changes.

Going Wider: Helping Change to Happen

Across the Poverty Truth Network, we try increasingly to talk of the ripples of change which occur because of the activities of Poverty Truth Commissions and the wider Network. These changes happen at different levels: for individuals who are involved as well as for the organisations and communities in which they are rooted or influenced. But ripples of change also happen elsewhere; in broader changes in practice and policy, as well as shifts in cultural perceptions.

Poverty Truth Commissions tend to be rightly reticent in claiming too many of these changes for themselves. We are, at best, one factor amongst many. Nonetheless, some of the changes which have occurred can trace their roots back to conversations that began, rose to the surface or were energised in Poverty Truth Commissions.

Several commissioners with direct experience of poverty have begun to share their realities in other settings, including the training of social work students. The writing of this book is a collaboration that has grown out of the Poverty Truth Commission in Bournemouth, Christchurch and Poole.

In Lancaster, Joanna has taken some of what she has learnt through the Poverty Truth Network to change recruitment practice within her local Citizens Advice, and to use that experience to influence national change.

In Salford, the City Council reviewed their debt recovery and income collection systems to minimise hardship, distress or difficulty for vulnerable people. They also stopped using external enforcement agents when recovering debts from their more vulnerable residents. And everyone saved money.

In Leeds, five community commissioners worked with an independent film company to produce "Fighting Shame." Sponsored by The Guardian, this documentary has been viewed over 850,000 times on YouTube.

Good Company, the host organisation for the East Surrey Poverty Truth Commission, ran a laptop recycling project after hearing that children were having to do their homework over lunchtime because they had no access to computers at home. The scheme was replicated by several other commissions, and elsewhere, particularly during COVID.

Many other examples of change could be given. Indeed, it is one of the very precious things about the approach; it changes the way that people (and organisations) do things. And that change continues long after any Poverty Truth Commission has concluded.

Building Solidarity: Reconnecting with Purpose

Perhaps the real genius of the Poverty Truth Network is that it has found a way of working – albeit that it can be a slow and sometimes painful way – that humanises people and builds community in an age where many are quick to polarise and promote division. Increasingly, we have learnt to talk about this process as slow activism, or relationally based activism.

Poverty Truth Commissions bring together very different people with very different experiences. In an environment where people often seek simple analysis and straightforward solutions, there is an inherent risk of missing some of that complexity.

Society often pits one group of people struggling against poverty against another group of people in the same predicament. It is that temptation to kick those just above, or more often below, you, on the social ladder. Tricia, involved in the first Poverty Truth Commission in Scotland, describes it in these terms:

> At one point it was single parents. And then addicts. And then asylum seekers. It feels like there is always "an 'other' to blame." I remember walking through Glasgow with someone who had addiction issues. We came across an asylum seeker who was begging. And he turned to me, and he said: "They're taking our jobs."

Poverty Truth Commissions bring people together with very different experiences of poverty and help us to listen to one another – to discover what we have in common – and to get beyond the false, populist narratives. Martin recalls one commission that he was involved in where, over time, people struggling against poverty began to understand the struggles of others in similar predicaments. The tropes around immigrants, young people, benefit scroungers and addicts, as well as the false dichotomy of deserving and undeserving poor, gradually fell away as people got to know one another. It's an experience that is regularly repeated. It is much harder to hold myths about people as you get to know them.

Early on, there was a presumption that all the civic leaders would know one another. Certainly, in many cases (although not all), they are often in some of the same meetings. But there they meet for business, and to promote the purposes of the organisations that they help lead. Poverty Truth Commissions have offered a very different meeting space. Particularly in the early meetings of a commission, when people are asked to suspend the temptation to rush to solutions and to turn up as human beings, people have got to know one another in ways that have influenced their work in other settings.

Andrew, who has been involved in four cycles of Poverty Truth Commissions in Leeds, talks about how, when you are working in the city, leaders themselves often recognise others who have been involved in a Poverty Truth Commission by the posture that they adopt, and the ways that they strive to address issues.

If a deeper understanding of the plight of other people experiencing poverty and more impactful relationships amongst civic leaders are two of the not entirely expected outcomes of this relational way of working, a third, more planned impact, has been a deepening of the relationships between the two groups. Or, indeed, a blurring of the boundaries between them.

Commissions take time to listen to people's lives in detail. In some cases, that has involved writing up a person's life story and then, as a full commission, reading it paragraph by paragraph around the circle. This can take thirty to forty minutes. And at the end of it, there is rarely a dry eye in the room.

On one occasion, when this had happened, members noticed that the Director of Social Work was in tears. She told the group that whilst this was the account of someone whose life remained blighted by poverty, it could have been her story had someone not been there to put an arm around her at a very vulnerable moment in her childhood. It was out of gratitude for that person's actions that she had chosen to become a social worker. It was a poignant reminder, and there are many such reminders, that the vast majority of people are in public service to do the public good.

On many occasions, it is the utter brilliance of people who are struggling against poverty who shine when given their rightful place and the opportunity to fulfil their potential that takes your breath away. Of course, that is not true for everyone, but that isn't true in any walk of life.

Being the Change: Practices and Values

As the Poverty Truth Network has expanded over recent years, it has proven useful to seek to articulate more clearly the practices and values which underpin and inform its work.

The Network prefers to talk of a practice rather than a theory of change, emphasising the dialectic which exists between theory and practice. For us, our practices inform our theory, whilst inevitably our theories also inform our practices.

Our values and practices are:

- ***living wisdom***: we create environments where everyone participates so that a deeper wisdom may emerge.
- ***humanising everyone***: we encourage and support one another, recognising that our conversations often require bravery and courage and include laughter and tears, hope and despair.
- ***deepening relationships***: we encourage supportive relationships that focus on hearing rather than addressing each other's circumstances.
- ***paying attention***: we encourage a slow and deliberative approach so that we may listen with our hearts as well as our heads before we set our hands to action.
- ***seeing more clearly***: we are open to being changed by this work; our perceptions of people in power and people in poverty will not be the same again.
- ***enabling lasting change***: we want to change how society understands poverty and those who experience it.

We expect that these practices and values will continue to evolve as we get better at what we are trying to do and understand what we are doing more clearly. They not only inform how Poverty Truth Commissions function effectively, but they can also inform many other conversations and interactions, especially where there may be an inherent power imbalance within the relationship.

Some Final Words

Recognising that this chapter, and the wider book, will be read by, amongst others, those committed to a career in social work, we wanted our final words to be encouraging.

Tracy speaks about a social worker who supported her family at a particularly vulnerable time.

> We would not have got by without Michelle. I never felt judged by her. She would come in, flick on the kettle and make a brew for us. I knew that she wanted the best for the children.

Claire's advice was characteristically poetic and challenging: "Come into our lives with open ears and an empty opinion." Rachel would want social workers, and others in positions of authority, "to remember what motivated you – to help and not hinder." And Dusty would encourage us all to recognise: "We have a great deal in common. It's about relationships. It's always about relationships."

It is the resilience of people struggling against poverty that is often remarked upon by civic leaders once they get to know their whole story. As one civic leader put it: "We need to remember that the great majority of parents love their kids more than we can possibly care for them."

4

POVERTY AND CANCER

Carrie-Anne Mizen and Orlanda Harvey

Resilience and Courage: 'from thriving to surviving' – the Reality of a Cancer Diagnosis

My name is Carrie-Anne, and I am proud to be a member of the Poverty Truth Commission (local and national) and a member of Bournemouth University's Public Involvement in Education and Research crew. I am a lone parent of two children who have educational needs, and I am a cancer survivor. I wanted to share my story in the hope that through being open about the impact that poverty has had on my life, I might help someone else to know that they are not alone.

It is impossible to capture my whole life story in a short chapter, so my focus is on how poverty impacted my cancer diagnosis. First, I want to share one fundamental concept. When working with people, you shouldn't assume that they know things because you have met someone with this diagnosis previously, nor assume their outcome.

As co-authors, we cannot emphasise enough the importance of taking a relational and person-centred approach when working with someone. Feeding this understanding of the individual through into policy so it can be applied flexibly, and understanding that every one of us is shaped by our life history, and although there may be commonalities, we are each uniquely different. Consequently, the impact of something as devastating as a cancer diagnosis on each of us needs to be understood with compassion, empathy and tailored support.

DOI: 10.4324/9781003638476-5

My Childhood

My parents were poor. We had hand-me-downs and didn't have the gifts and presents that all the other kids had. I got a lot of second-hand stuff. Growing up, our living conditions weren't great. We didn't have central heating, just one heater. It was a leasehold house. My parents were hoarders; there was lots of stuff everywhere. I remember times when you couldn't even open the front door. My mum had chronic kidney failure when I was 12, and my dad was diabetic. We mainly lived off my dad's income. My mum had a small part-time job, and then she got poorly, and she could no longer work. She still tried to do the part-time job, but she would come home and go to bed all afternoon. Looking back now, it is possible mum also had a mental health condition, but she would never have said anything; she bottled everything up. It might be a generational thing, even with the cancer diagnosis, my mum was very much a closed book. I had my first daughter when I was 18. Then I gave up college and started working. Sharing a little of my background is important as it shows how I was brought up and how influential my parents were in my later life.

My Diagnosis

It was a week before my 35th birthday, I found a lump in my right breast and went to the doctors and was given an urgent referral to the hospital. I went for some scans and biopsies. I was told I had breast cancer and was going to have my first ever operation – a mastectomy. It was daunting. They found six tumours in total. I'm lucky that they removed the whole thing, because it was so full of it – 21 centimetres of cancerous cells. That's why I'm quite pleased that, although it's been traumatic having to have the operations, they saved my life.

UK STATISTICS: CANCER

- On average, someone is diagnosed with cancer at least every 90 seconds in the UK. (Cancer Macmillan Support, 2025).
- There are an estimated 3.5 million people living with cancer in the UK (Cancer Macmillan Support, 2025).
- Cancer incidence varies with age and sex: The overall incidence of cancer in England was 21% higher in men than in women in 2020. Over half of the people newly diagnosed with cancer are aged over 70. Amongst people aged 25–59, incidence rates are higher in women than in men. Amongst people aged over 65, incidence rates are around 50% higher in men than in women (UK Government, 2025).

- According to Breast Cancer UK, breast cancer is the *most common cancer in the UK*, and every year, around 56,000 people are diagnosed with it. That's around 150 women a day.
- Cancer is the cause of just over a quarter of all deaths in England in a typical year. In 2022 in England, 138,579 people died from cancer (UK Government, 2024).
- According to Macmillan UK, cancer survival rates are up to 25 years behind other European countries, and they estimate that around one in four (25%) people with cancer are living with the long-term consequences of cancer or its treatment (Cancer Macmillan Support, 2025).

Across the Globe countries with persistent poverty have higher cancer mortality rates than other countries (Moss et al., 2020). In the UK, a study by Cancer Research UK (2025) found that people living in the most deprived areas of the UK are much more likely to die from cancer, with death rates almost 60% higher than in the wealthiest areas, with around 28,400 extra deaths from cancer a year linked to socioeconomic inequality. When it comes to more specific cancers, for example, liver cancer, incidence in England is highest in people living in the most deprived areas of the country, with approximately 1,170 people diagnosed each year, a rate double that of those living in the wealthiest areas. Cancer Research UK (2025) also notes that many of the deaths are caused by preventable risk factors such as obesity and smoking.

I had been with my partner for about 18 months, both my parents had died and my girls were only seven and five at the time, so it was difficult. The schools were supportive because I was diagnosed in the summer, just before the girls were about to break up from school, they let them have some time off before my operation, so I could spend time with them. It was hard having to get used to the 'new' me, and difficult to explain that to the girls as well.

IMPACT OF POVERTY AND PARENTAL CANCER ON CHILDREN

Poverty negatively influences children's life chances and limits access to healthcare (Bidmead et al., 2024). Parental cancer causes major disruptions for children, particularly school-aged ones and adolescents (Inhestern et al., 2021).

Huizinga et al. (2011) found:

- Parental cancer is a family-wide stressor; adolescents (especially girls) are most vulnerable.
- Some children show post-traumatic growth, developing a greater appreciation for life.
- Key supports include:
  - School involvement, though often from the perspective of the parent, not missing the voice of the child.
  - Healthy co-parents, whose emotional stability helps buffer children, but lone parents face added strain.
  - Having both a social network and healthcare support, though barriers include the mutual difficulty of sharing emotions, lack of guidance and time pressures.
- Vital protective factors:
  - Family functioning, parenting quality, open communication, the child's own coping mechanisms and the children's appraisal of the parent's cancer.
- No firm conclusions could be drawn about the direct role of socioeconomic status, but the authors recommended tailored care with support provided by a multidisciplinary team.

When considering all the findings above, it is important to consider how all these factors are compounded with the impact of poverty. The added worries and concerns that come on top of the way your life has changed, and being terrified that you might lose your parent.

Challenges for lone parents (Inhestern et al., 2021):

- Parents with serious illnesses (especially single parents) face barriers to employment due to care demands or health constraints.
- Childcare costs and limited access to full-time roles exacerbate financial pressures.

Policy and Structural Issues

- UK welfare policies add stress:
  - The two-child benefit limit and benefit cap introduced in 2017 reduced support for larger families regardless of employment status (JRF, 2025). When this is lifted from April 2026, families with more than two children will be eligible for additional support. The government estimates that the change will mean 450,000 fewer children in poverty by 2029–30.

The Day-to-day Impact

At that time, I was struggling financially. This added a whole new level of stress. I remember, between appointments, visiting the food bank. I was not able to work, and I didn't know what the future held at all. I didn't have much money. I struggled to navigate a lot of the bureaucracy that is needed for receiving benefits. I was really lucky. There was a charity called Ashley's birthday bank, and they gave us a £100 food shop, like they ordered it all, and it just got delivered one day. Brilliant, that helped. I had quite a few friends help out with the children, picking them up from school, feeding them, etc. I had a friend who tried to work out a menu for the first week or so.

My grandmother was really kind and bought me some clothes, as I needed them for the hospital and afterwards. My body shape had changed, and it was difficult to physically put on some types of clothing. I was lucky, because I lived about a ten-minute walk from the hospital, so I did not have to pay for transport and parking, but even when I had sepsis, I walked there. I was just stubborn. I was on my own with my girls, and I kind of think, as a mum, you have to keep things together sometimes, for their sake, if nothing else. And so, I just had the mindset, I've got to do this.

Whilst I was looking after the girls, my partner was meant to be working but was between jobs. He hadn't been paid for his last job, and he didn't want to go on benefits. I think that was in part pride, and because he may not have wanted to share with the Government about what he had been doing. He lied and manipulated his way around a lot of things. We still had food and bills to pay for, so it was a difficult time, but I still made sure the girls always had what they needed and stuff.

He left after I was diagnosed, and I became a lone parent.

UK STATISTICS: POVERTY

- 44% of children in lone-parent families were in poverty in 2022/23 (Joseph Rowntree Foundation, 2025)

It was quite traumatic after he left, and I found out he had all sorts of debt. I had to contact the people who sent the letters to tell them he no longer lived at the address, having to say he cheated on me and he's gone. I didn't want a bailiff to knock on my door. So, it was more stressful. Actually, it was the best thing he did was leave me, as he was unreliable; he wouldn't be around at certain times, even when I had sepsis, I couldn't get hold of him. In terms of paying the bills, everything was down to me. I've always been quite savvy with money, and I can make it stretch, but it would have been more comfortable to have a buffer of a couple of 100 quid. At the end of the month, there was nothing in the bank, and I was living day to day. Even now, I know there are some more benefits available, but accessing them is still a challenge, for example: I do not receive disability living allowance benefits for my girls as I struggle to fill in the forms. I felt let down by the whole system.

The lack of money meant I could not make ends meet, and so I had to use the food bank and community pantries. I felt anxious walking in there, really ashamed. I kind of didn't really have much of a choice. The other weird thing that I found is I've always cooked with fresh ingredients, and I really struggled to learn how to cook with tins. I know that might sound really odd, but food banks don't carry fresh ingredients, because it's not cost-effective for them to do that. I was really lucky, that when I went in there, the very first time, there was a volunteer in there who ~~I~~ knew me from somewhere else, and that instantly made it a little bit better for me. I had a hug off him as soon as I walked in the door, and he's like, don't worry. It's interesting, because now I'm in a different place. Yet then and now, I still feel like I should be able to do stuff, and I should be able to keep a roof over my girls' heads. I should be able to feed them.

FOOD BANKS

The rise in the cost of living has seen an increased number of families accessing food banks. In 2023/24, the Trussell Trust supplied 3.12 million emergency food parcels, and 2.3 million people in the UK lived in households which had used a food bank in the previous 12 months in 2022/23 (UK Government, 2025).

Carrie-Anne shares how hard it was for her to access the food bank and the need she felt to provide for her children. The feelings of shame that come with accessing a food bank are well documented (Caplan, 2016; Brennan-Tovey et al., 2023; Beck and Gwilym, 2023; Douglas, 2023; Spellman and McBride, 2025), with many seeing themselves as failures, as they are not able to stand on their own two feet and need support. The feelings that we should provide for our children, whatever the circumstances, are grounded in the culture and society in which we live. Not being able to achieve this can impact our self-worth. Caplan (2016) argues that this sense of shame can be reinforced through the interrogative questions to prove that they are entitled to the benefits that people are asked as part of the claim process.

Reflective Exercise:

- What do you think about the reliance that society now has on those in poverty having access to food banks?
- How do you feel when you see a community food bank box in a supermarket?

The psychological impact: The physical and mental changes were fundamental, and I was in a deep, dark place for a long time. It is hard as a woman, and this is something I have struggled with over the years as well, because especially when he left, I felt like, who would love me? Another thing that impacted me was that my mum had breast cancer, and whilst I was having my test done, I realised that my mum's cancer was on the same side that mine was, and all of a sudden, I burst into tears because it hadn't really dawned on me until that point. It was hard, because my mum was quite a closed book. This made my diagnosis harder because it brought back memories of my mum as well. My mum's story hadn't ended well, but she had the added problem of having chronic kidney failure and other health-limiting conditions. So that's why I tell my girls, I will be alright. You know, I didn't have those problems like my mum did, and I'm willing to fight. My mum had lost her fight quite early, I think, from when my dad had died.

POVERTY AND HEALTHCARE

Twenty years ago, Whitehead and Bird (2006) noted the serious impact that poverty can have on health, with people's health putting them at greater risk of poverty and poverty impacting their health and suggesting that health systems were often part of the problem rather than the solution. Arguably, nothing has changed.

Cancer patients may experience poorer health and well-being than people without a diagnosis, self-reporting a lower quality of life (Williams et al., 2016). Receiving a breast cancer diagnosis can have negative impacts on mental health (Fortin et al., 2021), with patients experiencing anxiety, distress, depression and post-traumatic stress disorder (Dinapoli et al., 2021). Patients can also experience cognitive impairments such as memory loss during hormone therapies or chemotherapy (Dinapoli et al., 2021), as well as experiencing body image, deterioration of self-concept, difficulties in social relationships and sexual problems (Wang and Feng, 2022).

People who experience poverty face challenges in accessing services, with many finding that the cost of travel, the cost of medication (if ineligible for free NHS prescriptions) and the need to pay for internet access (as many information and services were accessed online) are prohibitive (Woodward et al., 2024). Navigating financial assistance, such as the application process for benefits, is challenging, and people often forego accessing potentially useful phone apps due to cost and cannot afford to go out with friends, due to prioritising funding for essentials (Woodward et al., 2024). Over and above the cost of accessing the treatments for the physical illness, there is also the cost of accessing treatment for those who experience psychological side-effects for which there are long waiting times. However, the cost of accessing these services privately is also prohibitive.

I think in life, you either follow what your parents have done, or you go the opposite way. And I try to be the opposite of all those things. I'm definitely more open with my children. Knowledge is power for them, and it helps them make informed decisions and understand. If when they're older and someone has a diagnosis of any kind, at least they can say, 'my mum did that. It might not be the same, but I understand. I've got some empathy'. Also, I know now that breast cancer can be genetic, and there is a chance that one of my daughters might develop it in later life.

A cancer diagnosis can be a frightening experience, and although there is support available through dedicated charities, this does not take away the overwhelming feelings that come over you and the worries that you have for your children. There are worries and fears throughout the journey, and many of these are exacerbated by additional challenges such as poverty.

What Helped?

A key help was an inheritance that enabled me to buy my house. Not everyone is so lucky. This has enabled me to have some security, which, as one of my children has special educational needs, has been a godsend.

Another really important part of my recovery and future has been the opportunity to engage in worthwhile initiatives that help others. So, I was involved in the first Bournemouth, Christchurch and Poole Poverty Truth Commission (BCP PTC), which has absolutely changed my life. I have even addressed MPs.

Doing the PTC helped me realise that I'm worth something because other people believed in me when I didn't believe in myself. One of the civic business commissioners knew me before and was with me during the process. He said to me at the end I can see how much this has changed you, and that meant the world to me. You know he's always been there, and for him to say that, to see how positive the change has been. It's really worth it.

I also contribute to the Poverty Truth Network, which works across the whole country. Helping people see the advantage of collaborating alongside people with lived experience of poverty. Having the opportunity to focus my life now on my children and work with organisations that are trying to make a difference for others in poverty has played a key role in my recovery journey.

What Would Make a Difference?

One of the questions to guide this chapter is, what needs to change? That's important, and I would say some financial assistance should be offered when you're diagnosed. With grants often means tested, you have people being intrusive into your ins and outgoings. Wouldn't it be amazing if you were given, I don't know, £100 gift card or whatever, for Asda, where you could buy clothes, or you could buy food, regardless of your circumstances. People would have the right to say no, if you were a multi-millionaire, you'd hopefully say no. I just think it's not a, 'oh, well, here you go', here's a cancer diagnosis. It's about people realising this is a difficult time for you and wanting to help make it easier.

Thinking bigger, what we really need is that every council has a Poverty Truth Commission and a Poverty Truth-style programme at a government level to bring MPs and people of lived experience of poverty into the same circle. We need our MPs to have a real understanding of what it is to worry about how you are going to ensure your child has good food, to understand the stress and worry that comes from having to prioritise which bill you will pay first, and the shame that comes with this.

Ultimately, people in positions of power need to learn to really listen to people's circumstances and offer support, not restrictions.

REFLECTIVE ACTIVITY

Part A: Poverty and Me

Reflect on your answers to the following questions:

1. Have you yourself experienced poverty?
   If yes....what was it like for you? What did others see?
   If no...How easy is it for you to imagine what living in poverty might be like?
2. Do you feel poverty is relative?

Part B: What If...?

Read the statements (PTC, BCP, 2025) below, and draw a picture of a world where all these are true...

What images would you include in your picture?
What If... Change is possible?
What If... Everyone can meet as equals?
What If... We could challenge the stigma of poverty?
What If... We listen to each other really well?
What If... We could change perceptions about poverty?
What If... We could unlock deep culture change?
What If... Local people who are struggling against poverty could be involved in influencing the decisions, policies and systems which directly affect them?
or you to imagine what living in poverty might be like?

Source: *What If...? – Poverty Truth Bournemouth, Christchurch and Poole*

Further Reading

The Wisdom Lab – sharing stories to educate people against the struggles of poverty. https://povertytruthbcp.org/wisdom-lab/
Let's End Poverty Campaign. https://letsendpoverty.co.uk/dearpm/
Church Action on Poverty – *12 inspiring anti-poverty stars and stories from 2020*. https://www.church-poverty.org.uk/12-inspiring-anti-poverty-stars-stories-from-2020/?gad_source=1&gad_campaignid=1655914314&gclid=EAIaIQobChMI0auV3t6xjQMV2JlQBh0AlRlfEAAYASAAEgIWJfD_BwE
Macmillan Cancer Support – cancer support and living experience stories. https://www.macmillan.org.uk/cancer-information-and-support/stories-and-media
NDRS – results of the *cancer quality of life survey*. https://digital.nhs.uk/ndrs/data/data-outputs/cancer-data-hub/cancer-quality-of-life-survey
Ashley's Birthday Bank – *gift and crisis service*. https://ashleysbirthdaybank.co.uk/sample-page/

References

Beck, D. J., & Gwilym, H. (2023). The Food Bank: A safety-net in place of welfare security in times of Austerity and the covid-19 crisis. *Social Policy and Society*, *22*(3), 545–561. https://doi.org/10.1017/S1474746421000907
Bidmead, E., Hayes, L., Mazzoli-Smith, L., Wildman, J., Rankin, J., Leggott, E., Todd, L., & Bramhall, L. (2024). Poverty proofing healthcare: A qualitative study of barriers to accessing healthcare for low-income families with children in northern England. *PLoS ONE*, *19*. https://doi.org/10.1371/journal.pone.0292983
Brennan-Tovey, K., Board, E. M., & Fulton, J. (2023). Counteracting stigma-power: An ethnographic case study of an independent community food hub. *Journal of Contemporary Ethnography*, *52*(6), 778–798. https://doi.org/10.1177/08912416231199095
Cancer MacMillian Support. (2025). Cancer prevalence. Available at: https://www.macmillan.org.uk/about-us/what-we-do/research/cancer-prevalence Accessed 20 May 2025.
Cancer Research UK. (2025). Cancer in the UK 2025: socioeconomic deprivation. 21 February. Available at: https://www.cancerresearchuk.org/sites/default/files/cancer_in_the_uk_2025_socioeconomic_deprivation.pdf
Caplan, P. (2016). Big society or broken society? Food banks in the UK. *Anthropology Today*, *32*(1), 5–9. https://doi.org/10.1111/1467-8322.12223
Dinapoli, L., Colloca, G., Capua, B. di, & Valentini, V. (2021). Psychological aspects to consider in breast cancer diagnosis and treatment. https://doi.org10.1007/s11912-021-01049-3
Douglas, F. (2023). What qualitative research can tell us about food and nutrition security in the UK and why we should pay attention to what it's telling us. In *Proceedings of the Nutrition Society*. Cambridge University Press. https://doi.org/10.1017/S0029665123003713
Fortin, J., Leblanc, M., Elgbeili, G., Cordova, M. J., Marin, M. F., & Brunet, A. (2021). The mental health impacts of receiving a breast cancer diagnosis: A meta-analysis. *British Journal of Cancer*, *125*(11), 1582–1592. https://doi.org/10.1038/s41416-021-01542-3
Huizinga, G. A., Visser, A., Zelders-Steyn, Y. E., Teule, J. A., Reijneveld, S. A., & Roodbol, P. F. (2011). Psychological impact of having a parent with cancer. *European Journal of Cancer*, *47*. https://doi.org/10.1016/S0959-8049(11)70170-8
Inhestern, L., Johannsen, L. M., & Bergelt, C. (2021). Families affected by parental cancer: Quality of life, impact on children and psychosocial care needs. *Frontiers in Psychiatry*, *12*. https://doi.org/10.3389/fpsyt.2021.765327

Moss, J. L., Pinto, C. N., Srinivasan, S., Cronin, K. A., & Croyle, R. T. (2020). Persistent poverty and cancer mortality rates: An analysis of county-level poverty designations. *Cancer Epidemiology, Biomarkers & Prevention,29*(10), 1949–1954. https://doi.org/10.1158/1055-9965.EPI-20-0007

Poverty and Truth Commission, BCP (2025). What if? Available at: https://povertytruthbcp.org/what-if/ Accessed 20 May 2025.

Spellman, C., & McBride, J. (2025). Gendering "The Hidden Injuries of Class": In-work poverty, precarity, and working women using Food Banks in Britain. *Gender, Work & Organization*. https://doi.org/10.1111/gwao.13237

The Joseph Rowntree Foundation. (2025). UK poverty 2025: The essential guide to understanding poverty in the UK. Available at: https://www.jrf.org.uk/uk-poverty-2025-the-essential-guide-to-understanding-poverty-in-the-uk Accessed 20 May 2025.

UK Government. (2024). House of Commons Library briefing: Cancer statistics for England. Available at: https://commonslibrary.parliament.uk/research-briefings/sn06887/ Accessed 20 May 2025.

UK Government. (2025). Food poverty: Households, food banks and free school meals. Available at: https://commonslibrary.parliament.uk/research-briefings/cbp-9209/ Accessed 20 May 2025.

Wang, Y., & Feng, W. (2022). Cancer-related psychosocial challenges. *General Psychiatry*, *35*(5). https://doi.org/10.1136/gpsych-2022-100871

Whitehead, M., & Bird, P. (2006). Breaking the poor health-poverty link in the 21st century: Do health systems help or hinder? *Annals of Tropical Medicine and Parasitology*, *100*(5–6), 389–399. https://doi.org/10.1179/136485906X97363

Williams, K., Jackson, S. E., Beeken, R. J., Steptoe, A., & Wardle, J. (2016). The impact of a cancer diagnosis on health and well-being: A prospective, population-based study. *Psycho-Oncology*, 626–632. https://doi.org/10.1002/pon.3998

Woodward, A., Nimmons, D., Davies, N., Walters, K., Stevenson, F. A., Protheroe, J., Chew-Graham, C. A., & Armstrong, M. (2024). A qualitative exploration of the barriers and facilitators to self-managing multiple long-term conditions amongst people experiencing socioeconomic deprivation. *Health Expectations*, *27*(2). https://doi.org/10.1111/hex.14046

5

POVERTY AND BEING A CARER

Val McKie and Kate Jupp

In 2005, out of the blue, my husband was diagnosed with stage 4 cancer and given just weeks to live. Like so many people, I suddenly fell into the role of a carer. John lived for a further two years; during this time, we relied on savings and credit. Devastated by his death and debt, I sank into the depths of poverty and despair. It would be ten years before I was freed by the power of hope and started to heal. This is my story.

Poverty and the fear of poverty had sat like a shroud over my home and family. My father was born in 1921. One of his earliest memories was not eating on Friday nights and Saturday mornings because his father didn't get paid until Saturday lunchtime. This was not uncommon; he lived in the North East of England, a place synonymous with poverty. To some degree, I believe we are, at least in part, products of our upbringing. Fear can be infectious, and my father's fear of poverty certainly infected me and would go on, at times, to act like a silent saboteur.

Unable to go to university as the family needed his wages, my father's first job was with the Inland Revenue. He wasn't happy there, and with war looming, he joined the RAF. He was in his element; was put on a navigator's training course in Canada and passed with flying colours. He met my mum in Canada; they married, and two years later, as war continued to rage, she came to England. It was a huge culture shock for her, coming from a relatively affluent home in Toronto to my grandparents' two-bed terraced flat without a bathroom or electricity. She was an alien in a war-torn country, and life was a struggle.

My brother was born in 1945, mum suffered preeclampsia and was ill for the first eighteen months of his life. Her concerned parents paid for her and my

DOI: 10.4324/9781003638476-6

brother to travel to Canada, with my father following once he was able to find work there. The fear of poverty continued to haunt my father, and he chose to stay in the UK and keep his secure job with the Inland Revenue. He managed to get a council house in his hometown, and my mum and brother returned. I was born in 1952, and my sister 22 months later.

Our family became a part of a newly forming middle class. My father rose through the ranks and in 1958, after a promotion and a move to the North West, my parents bought our first house, a four-bedroom detached house in a leafy Liverpool suburb. They had scrimped and saved, going without many things, but not food, to raise the deposit required.

Like many families in our area, money was always tight. My father hated his job, struggled with depression, and we all felt the burden of his suffering. My mum never had paid employment and was permanently homesick for Canada. She and her mum wrote weekly and all we could ever afford was one phone call a year, a three-minute Christmas call costing more than half my father's weekly wage. Mum died of cancer in 1979, aged 55, it broke us all.

My earliest memories were that money was always tight. Our prevailing belief was that there was just enough to survive, and that required getting a job you might hate, and not taking risks, just to keep going. Holidays, day trips and meals out happened once every three or four years, but there was always food; my father made sure of that, ensuring that we never went hungry as he had.

I got a job as a Saturday girl in a local newsagent and was puzzled that some of our customers who lived in beautiful, large houses struggled to pay their paper bill. Later, I helped in a store in one of the poorest parts of Merseyside and was shocked at the difference. In this store, people bought expensive boxes of chocolates and splurged out on all kinds of things that no one bought in my home store. It was my first experience of a different kind of poverty, one where there was no hope or belief that things could be better, where generations of grinding poverty had taken its toll, and small treats were an essential salve to wounds. I was only 18 but acutely aware of the disturbing narratives around the deserving and undeserving poor.

My life moved on, I loved my work in the newsagents, the interaction gave me confidence and after my A levels I went full-time. I became a store manager, got married and gained two lovely stepchildren. My husband had always dreamed of running his own store, so we saved and bought a lease on a small news agency of our own and purchased a house.

Money was tight, but something I was used to, but then mortgage rates went through the roof and the leaseholder on our news agency tripled our rent. It was a tough time. I took on an extra part-time job. After two years of deep struggle and pressure from the bank, we were lucky enough to sell the shop, and we re-mortgaged our home. My husband, who was 12 years older than me, struggled to find work, and money continued to be tight, but at least we were out of the mire of unaffordable and spiralling costs.

I started a part-time degree course and secured a job teaching on a youth training programme working in one of the poorest parts of Merseyside. I loved it. This work showed me just what deprivation does. The trainees and I had fun together, whilst we faced many challenges, we learnt so much from each other, and I watched them grow with pride. Being there during the Hillsborough disaster formed a bond between us, enabling us to achieve more together than had ever been expected. In time, I was promoted into the Management Training Department and designed programmes that tackled the core issues around conflict, physical and psychological safety. During this time, I became more involved in Urban Regeneration Initiatives, trying to bridge the divide between communities, businesses and local and national government. My professional life was good, but my marriage was falling apart, and eventually I walked away. A year later, I was made redundant and returned to self-employment, setting up my own training and consultancy business.

In 2003, I remarried. My husband, a New-Zealander and older than me, had a part-time job in a sports store, things were stable and the future positive. Then, in 2005, when I had just won a contract with a good client, out of the blue, my husband, John, was diagnosed with stage 4 cancer and given just weeks to live. Nothing had prepared us for this shock. Life as we had known it ended in the couple of minutes it took the doctor to share the diagnosis and prognosis. We knew in our hearts that nothing would ever be the same again. I immediately stopped working to care for John and allow us to spend as much time together as we could.

Becoming a carer was never part of my life plan. Caring, supporting and protecting those I know and love was just something I had done for much of my life. It wasn't a job; I had other plans, but it just seemed natural to care for people as part of being human and doing so aligned with my core values.

DEFINITION OF A CARER

An unpaid carer is someone who is providing unpaid care and support to a family member, partner, friend, or neighbour who is disabled, has an illness or long-term condition, or who needs extra help as they get older. This support could be a few hours a week, or it could be round-the-clock care (Carers UK, 2025a).

ECONOMIC VALUE OF UNPAID CARE

The Centre for Care has put the value of care in the whole of the UK at £184 billion. This is a 29.3% increase over the past decade (£119.4 billion in 2011).

Looking after someone who is terminally ill is the moment when the unspoken fears we have when someone we love is poorly become reality. It is not just about coping with the physical symptoms and the brutal nature of chemotherapy and radiotherapy; it is also the terrifying nights when you lie next to someone, wondering just how long you have left together; and the times you worry that their next breath is their last. It grips your very soul, but you know that you must hide how you feel and stay calm and upbeat. This is not the time to have wants or needs of your own; it is not you who is dying, it is the person you love lying next to you who must face that journey.

I vowed to do everything I could both to support John on his journey and to seek anything that might give us longer together. I made a conscious choice to go into debt to support my husband and give him the best possible end-of-life care. Like so many other times in my past, my decision was based on what I thought was best for others, with little thought of the impact on me. I now know that was a conditioned response, based upon my need to be needed and not seen as selfish. In an environment where sacrifice is often seen as a 'good thing', my need to be loved and do the 'right thing' was paramount. It paid off in a way, and John lived for two years longer than had been predicted. This enabled us, at least in part, to come to terms with his illness and to heal many of the emotional wounds he had gathered throughout his life.

HOW COMMON IS CARE, WHO CARES AND WHEN:

- In the UK, it is estimated that one in five adults are unpaid carers, typically family members or friends, and this equates to about 10.6 million people providing unpaid care (Carers UK, 2022).
- The 2021 Census found that in England and Wales, women are more likely to provide care than men. Fifty-nine per cent of unpaid carers are female, with the biggest proportion of people caring in England and Wales being from the 55–59 age group.
- 1.7 million people in the UK are providing 50 or more hours of care per week (Carers UK, 2025a, 2025b).
- The 2021 Census in England and Wales also found that the older age groups provide the highest hours of unpaid care per week. For women, it was those aged between 75 and 79 who were most likely to provide 50 hours or more of care. For men, it was those aged between 85 and 89 who were most likely to provide 50 hours or more of care.

More facts about carers (Carers UK, 2025a, 2025b)

During this time, we had no income, just savings to get us through. Many years previously, when my mum was facing the same end-of-life battle, my father, who out of necessity had always been very cautious with money, went out and bought my mum a portable colour television to have in hospital. It was the most, possibly only, impulsive purchase he had ever made. She never saw it. She died the following morning before he arrived with the television. There would be no watching afternoon programmes together. The memory of that haunted me for years, becoming a focus for the grief I felt on losing my mum. With this at the forefront of my mind, I made a second vow, no matter what, John would get whatever made him happiest. I couldn't bear the thought of facing the same regrets my father had.

Meeting John's ever-changing and considerable care needs and wishes was a constant strain on our meagre savings. Whilst there is no doubt that paying for extra travel to and from hospitals, keeping the heating on and buying good quality food and even extra medical care were necessary and added significantly to our outgoings, there was an additional expenditure that meant the debts skyrocketed. During John's illness, I spent what felt like a fortune on four return flights to New Zealand to support John to be with his family. On the last occasion, this necessitated a business-class journey back with an expensive stopover as John was too poorly to travel any other way. I needed, come what may, to grant John his long-standing wish to be at home in the UK to die.

ADDITIONAL COSTS ASSOCIATED WITH CARING:

- Many carers face extra financial challenges associated with their caring role.
- Carers are finding it increasingly difficult to pay for essentials. 28% of carers are cutting back on essentials like food and heating – an increase from 25% in 2022 (Carers UK, 2024a).
- Carers often struggle to afford utility bills, 60% of carers finding it hard to afford essentials reported struggling to afford electricity and gas (Carers UK, 2024a).
- Some carers are skipping meals or using food banks to cope with rising costs of everyday essentials such as food, heating and transport costs (Carers UK, 2024a).
- Many carers struggle to afford housing costs, with 21% struggling to afford rent or mortgage payments, and 38% worried about increases in these costs (Carers UK, 2024a).

Of course, despite my family's concerns about the money I was spending, I was locked into a loop I couldn't escape. Fuelled by my mantra 'you can never say no to a dying person', I just carried on racking up the debts, blind to the impact this would have on me down the line, and that would take me over a decade to clear. Being aware of the accumulating debt and being open to thinking about its possible consequences are very different things.

Like so many people, I had been brought up to believe that thinking about myself and my needs, especially my future needs, was selfish, a label I couldn't bear. I have come to recognise that it is foolish to ignore and deny my own needs, just as it is foolish to refuse to care for a car or home and get them repaired when needed.

FINANCIAL IMPACT OF CARING ON CARER WELLBEING

- The majority of carers are worried about their finances in the future. 61% of carers are worried about living costs and whether they can manage in the future, and over a third (35%) do not feel confident that they will be able to manage financially over the next 12 months (Carers UK, 2024a, 2024b, 2024c).
- Financial worries are affecting carers' health and wellbeing. Over half (51%) of carers said that their financial situation is having a negative impact on their mental health and wellbeing, and 61% feel stressed or anxious when they think about their financial situation.

I shared none of my mounting fears about this growing debt. I presented as outwardly strong and stoic, whilst inwardly I was dying. We had only started to access benefits when all our money was gone. Juggling and 'surviving' the debt occupied my mind, keeping my thoughts away from the overwhelming reality of a future without John. It was a strangely safe and familiar way to get through each day, after all, I had survived debt and poverty in the past.

FINANCIAL SUPPORT FOR CARERS

Navigating the benefits system is complex, and options vary depending on circumstances; many voluntary and charity sector organisations offer support with benefit applications.

- Carer's Allowance is a weekly benefit. Carers spending at least 35 hours a week caring for someone with an illness or disability may be eligible for Carer's Allowance. Carer's Allowance is paid at a rate of £83.30 per week (2025/26) (HM Government, 2025).

Ninety per cent of carers receiving Carer's Allowance do not think this benefit is sufficient (Carers UK, 2024a).

- Carers of working age may also be eligible for **Carers Credit**, to help maintain National Insurance contributions to secure a future state pension.
- Carers who have reached State Pension age may be able to claim **Pension Credit**.
- Local authorities have a statutory obligation to conduct a carer's financial assessment.
- Additional financial support might be possible through applications to specific grants, funds and charities (Carers Trust, 2025).

Many carers feel the process of claiming benefits could be improved: 67% would like more information and advice about what benefits they are entitled to, and 57% would like more support with understanding the rules for certain benefits (Carers UK, 2025).

John died peacefully at home in May 2007, a week after our fourth wedding anniversary. I was now on a new journey, living with the aftermath of the decisions I had made. I was no longer a carer, the sole focus of my recent life and identity gone. I was propelled into the vortex between regret and fear of the future, and pride at supporting John to die peacefully, knowing how much he was loved. Writing this down for the first time, I have cried in a way I haven't before. It has shown me how starkly we can walk in two opposing worlds with two very different voices playing out in our minds. There is the voice that says 'Well done you, you did the best you could', and the other, more familiar voice that goes

> What a miserable, selfish person you are moaning about facing a bit of poverty and homelessness when so many people have lives far worse than you. How could you even contemplate what might have been if you hadn't spent money on John being with his family?

I am now able to tell that second voice that I understand, and to have some compassion, recognising that I am only human. This second voice is still present in the darkest reaches of my mind, sneaking out occasionally when I am exhausted or distressed.

Devastated by John's death and debt, I quickly became a shadow of the person I used to be, bound by the shackles of hopelessness. My landlord, who had been wanting to sell the property but had kindly left it whilst my husband was alive, now asked me to leave. Wracked by grief, I couldn't get back to work as I had thought I would. It wasn't just the two-year career gap but also the trauma of what I'd been through, and being in my mid-fifties didn't help. I felt useless and a failure. My previous work was supporting people to identify and find solutions to their problems, and I didn't have the strength to work at that depth and intensity. The upheaval of trying to find a home with no income took its toll; I was really struggling. In the following ten years, I sank into a depth of poverty and despair like nothing I had ever known before.

IMPACT OF CARING ON EMPLOYMENT

- Census data show that around 3 million carers aged 16 and over in the UK are in paid employment, and 2.7 million carers are not in paid employment.
- WPI Economics reports that being out of work is the single strongest quantitative predictor of poverty for unpaid carers.
- Carers who are not in paid employment are even more likely to be struggling financially. 47% of carers aged 18–64 are struggling to make ends meet, and just under a quarter (24%) are in debt as a result of caring (Carers UK, 2024).

My lifeline at this point was a couple of friends, and the three of us managed to rent a house together as if we were students, I was 54! At 55, I could access a small private pension of £350 a month, and I started to get some work. It is said that things repeat themselves until we learn the lesson. I was clearly a slow learner. I had always found it difficult asking for help and was fiercely independent. It is also said that just as it takes a village to raise a child, it takes a village to free someone from the wounds of life; my sense of shame and failure meant I struggled to seek out that village.

The firm I had started working with again closed, and our communal home was sold. I moved in with a friend 50 miles away from my sister and hometown. I felt remote and isolated. I ploughed on, refusing to accept the help I so desperately needed. My vulnerability was hard to hide and was evidently more visible than I thought. I was scammed and terrified as the scammer knew where I lived. I had a breakdown – I didn't realise this at the time and just reframed my life as a series of consecutive tragedies.

Without hope, I felt unable to try anything new. Caring, debt and grieving had left me on my knees, my heart broken and all hope gone. I continued to move and became a couch surfer, lucky enough to stay with various friends around the country, and living on my £350 per month. I didn't access benefits as I had no fixed address. This lasted three years.

POVERTY AND THE CARING ROLE

- Research commissioned by Carers UK and conducted by WPI Economics found that 1.2 million unpaid carers live in poverty, and 400,000 live in deep poverty in the UK.
- Carers are more likely to face poverty than non-carers. A report by the Joseph Rowntree Foundation (Joseph Rowntree Foundation, 2025, UK Poverty 2025) highlights the link between unpaid care and poverty.
- Carers providing end-of-life care can face extra significant financial costs, and many carers whose caring role has come to an end can find it difficult to return to paid employment. People who said their caring role had come to an end said they had gained or improved skills in empathy (78%), resilience (75%) and advocacy (72%) (Carers UK, 2024b).
- In 2024, a quarter of carers (27%) surveyed by Carers UK were struggling to make ends meet, and 28% were cutting back on essentials like food and heating, reducing meal sizes or skipping meals.
- Some carers turn to unsustainable solutions to manage finances; 28% of carers said they were using credit cards, 22% had used their overdraft and 14% of carers were in debt because of caring (Carers UK, 2024).

At age 61, I just couldn't do it anymore and rented a room in a private house. I applied for benefits and started to live a little. Living with strangers was a bit of a challenge, but we rubbed along. In 2015, I became eligible for my State Pension and around the same time, a friend who now often worked away from home asked if I would like to be her lodger. It was great, I came off all benefits and finally had enough to live on.

The relief of having a guaranteed regular income, no matter what, and a less precarious roof over my head transformed my life. I felt safe and secure for the first time in a decade, and I started to see just how debilitating my grief, trauma and homelessness had been. I was, at last, freed by the power of hope and in a position to start to heal.

It was only when I started to write this chapter that I realised that my journey into poverty, accompanied by a sense of failure and shame, was all too common. Life for me now is all about finding balance. Most importantly, this means being honest with myself, ditching the protective mask that has allowed me to pretend everything is okay for so long, when it is not, and instead share my true feelings with others. Looking back, I can see how I was thinking of my husband more as a child during his illness, and not the adult he was. I had wanted to wrap him up in cotton wool and protect him at all costs. I now recognise that I would be appalled if someone I loved kept their pain and distress from me to protect me.

What poverty means to me

When we talk of poverty today, we tend to think of it in terms of money and material goods, but what about the poverty of spirit too? How is it for people who can't experience the joy of giving or sharing? Or those who live in criticism and judgement – are they not poor too?

I remember my mum regularly saving for weeks to buy the seven shillings and six pence (37&1/2p) Max Factor red lipstick she loved so much. We felt lucky, but seemed to be surrounded by families that had much more than us. I remember the shame of being laughed at for having a non-regulation cheap gym shirt at school. Now, when I hear people passing judgement on families living in poverty for buying expensive trainers for their children, I feel desperate at the lack of understanding that lies behind this. It is so easy for people to pass judgement without insight into the true meaning. So often it is our small experiences that hold greater significance.

Shame goes hand in hand with poverty. Not having enough money is many people's best kept secret. Some people reading this book will know exactly what I mean. When I was homeless and couch surfing (and even now), few people knew just how little I had to live on. They do not know that to this day, my last thought at night and first in the morning is 'do I have enough this week to balance the books and pay the bills?'

To many, I seem rich, and I am, but that richness is in friends and relationships, hope and faith. I am lucky because I have experienced not being poor and have some friends who are not poor, so I have access to resources that others don't. If you are born in poverty, have never experienced anything different and don't have the people around you, how can you realistically believe that life can be any better? It would require believing in a miracle, with the only way out a lottery win, or a long-lost rich relative; a reliance on something external to us that we have no power or control over and that happens by chance.

The narratives around poverty that I heard as a teenager still run like the writing through a stick of rock in our society. Poverty can apply to anyone, no matter what. Being in poverty is very frightening and can be life threatening. It can be much easier to think that someone in poverty is there because there is something wrong with them, that they are lacking in some way; psychologically distancing ourselves rather than facing reality. I suspect that this is the reason why people who sit just above the poverty threshold are often the most critical of those who sit below it.

How to support carers

Becoming a carer is something that can happen to any one of us. Sometimes it feels like a choice, and sometimes it feels like something that is thrust upon us.

For some, being a carer is a joy and a privilege, and for others it's a burden that can unleash a deep resentment. I think it is a spectrum that we journey on, often going backwards and forwards as we seek to find an equilibrium.

We all know what it feels like to have good days and bad days, days when we feel that we are coping really well and others when we feel overwhelmed, helpless and in deep despair.

What I feel that we need is understanding, acceptance and kindness to ourselves and the same from others. We need to know that what we are feeling is natural at any point and is nothing to be ashamed of. Supporters of carers need to be able to listen without judgement and help them reflect, and also guide them with patience through the system, being aware that what might work one day may not work the next. It is as much coaching as counselling.

The first step is for supporters to be their authentic selves to enable them to build trusting relationships. The people match is quite important. Carers who have been self-reliant doers often like things done quickly without a fuss, so small, quick wins of help really help. For people like myself, we may say very little, but a trained person will be able to read the clues we hide quite deeply.

Messages to my earlier self

What I wish I had known in 2005 at the time of John's diagnosis

- It's ok to cry (actually wished I had known that at 17).
- It's ok to be vulnerable, ditto the above.
- To trust that others would help if asked.
- I also wish I had known that I was about to embark upon a journey that would have been much easier if I had sought support from friends, family and external agencies, rather than not want to bother anybody because I thought there were so many people more in need than me and that I should just get on with it.
- I wish I had been kinder to myself and not been such a perfectionist, and I also wish that I had known then that perfectionism was a trauma response to unhealed childhood wounds.
- And finally, I wish that I had realised that as a carer I had valid needs too and that addressing them would have been the right thing to do.

What I wish I had known in 2007 (John's death)

- I wish I had grieved more rather than running away from the pain and busying myself with everyone and everything.

- I wish I had understood that I was not a failure and had not been ashamed of the financial situation I was in, and that so many people had journeyed into poverty as a result of being a carer.
- I also wish I had asked for help before my situation brought me to my knees.

So now in 2025

I am glad to know that I am human with faults, flaws and a sense of humour. I am grateful for all the challenges I have faced and quietly proud of how I have been able to use some of them to support others.

- I wish I knew that I had a financially secure future.
- I wish that those I love knew just how much I love them.
- I wish that you, the reader, have gained an insight that will help you be part of the solution. That you give yourself the opportunity to pause and reflect on all that you have read in this book, knowing that it is ok to be part of HumanKIND and especially to be KIND to yourself and others.

Solutions

We know the answers to so much material injustice lie in the better sharing of resources. It is simple enough, but an issue which has perplexed humanity for all our recorded history.

As we write new narratives about poverty based on our lived experiences, let's look for ways to tap into the human psyche from a perspective that breaches the divide and moves away from criticism and condemnation towards nurturing and thriving. We are, after all, just human beings; each with stressors and coping strategies – they may be different, but we all have them.

So often, people want the same thing. I doubt many people would argue against ending poverty, particularly if they felt ending it would also benefit them. Yet poverty has always been with us. It is not a resource issue, but rather poverty of spirit and polarity of beliefs that underpin and perpetuate poverty. One of these is that 'because we have never been able to fix it we never will'. Let's start by reframing that into 'We now have more knowledge, understanding and the tools and resolve to fix it'.

One of the things that we learnt as a result of Covid 19 pandemic was that the same slogan that was used to sell lottery tickets, 'It could be you', was also the strapline that led to major modifications in our human behaviour. Perhaps now is the time to reframe this message to 'it could be you, who, with a simple act of kindness can make a difference in someone's life'.

We might not be able to alter external factors like natural disasters and terminal illness, but we can build a society based on love and care and a healthy lifestyle. Let's look to end the toxicity of our thinking and judgement around poverty, remember who we really can be when we feel loved and not afraid. The writer Elisabeth Kubler Ross once said, 'If we could raise one generation with unconditional love, there would be no Hitlers'. Let us each become part of the village that heals the pain of poverty. Imagine if we each made it our mission to share love and kindness whenever we can; what a difference that would make to the world.

Let us remember that we each have a deep strength that may well have got buried by the trauma we have experienced. We are more than our emotions! We may feel bad, weak, etc., but it is not who any of us are. It takes great strength to be vulnerable and to trust; becoming a carer might well be the first step on a pathway from independence to interdependence. You might well be the one to make a real difference in a carer's life, not just by what you do but by how you do it.

Many thanks for reading this.

Val McKie

REFLECTIVE ACTIVITY – YOU WILL NEED THREE PIECES OF PAPER AND A PEN/PENCIL/CRAYONS.

We invite you to sit quietly and think of a time when you felt really great about your life, a time that made you smile. When you are ready, take a piece of paper and write down the key factors that made you feel this way.

Next, take another piece of paper and think about a time when you felt really down and unhappy. Please don't worry, we won't keep you there for very long. Again, write down the factors that made you feel this way.

Looking at the time you didn't feel so good, ***ask yourself*** this question:

'If a friend of yours was thinking, feeling and acting from that state of being, what would they have believed about themselves and their world?'

List all that comes to mind.

Looking at this list, have you unearthed any beliefs you hold about yourself?

Now please sit up straight with your feet on the floor and take five deep breathes, inhaling to a count of seven and breathing out to the count of 11. Now please stand up, shake your head, arms and shoulders. Smile as broadly as you can, lift your hands in the air and hum your favourite tune. You can do this for as long as you like.

When you are ready, take a look at your answer to the first question – **a time when you felt great**. Sitting comfortably, deeply remember the joy and love you felt and ***ask yourself:***

'Which of these thoughts can I keep to the front of my mind whenever I need to bring some love and light to my thinking?'

Take another piece of paper and express those happy thoughts in whatever way feels right for you, and place them wherever feels the best place for you.

Take a moment to relax

When you are ready, step back into your day, knowing that the world is a better place because of your smile.

Further reading and resources

Findings from a recent scoping review revealed the paucity of research specifically focused on unpaid carers' financial wellbeing and highlighted a significant gap around carers' understanding of the future financial implications of unpaid caregiving, or whether longer-term financial consequences are considered when making decisions about care.

The cost of caring: a scoping review of qualitative evidence on the financial wellbeing implications of unpaid care to older adults

Watkins M, Overton L. The cost of caring: a scoping review of qualitative evidence on the financial wellbeing implications of unpaid care to older adults. *Ageing and Society*. 2025; 45(7):1465–1492. doi:10.1017/S0144686X24000382

A briefing paper from the Centre for Care Evidence highlights the evidence supporting paid carers' leave as one measure that could improve carer financial wellbeing, and employee retention and productivity.

Centre for Care Evidence briefing: the Employment Rights Bill and the Case for Paid Carer's Leave (2025).

The Carer Poverty Coalition (formed in 2023) is a campaign organisation comprising over 130 organisations. Collectively, they campaign to end carer poverty through policy change, reform the benefits system, better support carers to continue in employment and raise awareness of carer poverty (Carer Poverty Coalition Manifesto, 2024).

Mobilise is a UK digital platform for unpaid carers used by local authorities and carer organisations. **Mobilise** aims to help councils uncover hidden carers and, through scalable digital outreach and dynamic assessments and is a digital provider of carer resources and support.

Carers in the Cost of Living Crisis (Bournemouth University PIER Partnership) – a short film sharing the experiences of six carers of the impact of the cost-of-living crisis that started in 2021, and looks set to continue beyond 2025.

Carers of persons with dementia and the social consequences of caring (2025) – caring affects the social relationships of unpaid carers and the families of those being cared for in multiple ways. Carers are also prone to care poverty. This article examines the social consequences of providing care for a person with dementia. Based on 21 diaries written by carers, and using the concept of ailment as an analytical lens, the analysis broadens our understanding of how unpaid care can have manifold social repercussions on a carer's life. L Van Aerschot, U Halonen, E Leinonen, T Kröger

Carers UK – three short videos in which carers share how caring has impacted their financial situations and their employment opportunities.

Matthew McKenzie – a video from Caring Minds on how poverty impacts unpaid carers.

Healthwatch England – a short video highlighting what support a carer can get.

References

Carers Trust (2025) *Help for carers: Grants and Discounts, available at Grants & Financial Support for Carers*. Carers Trust

Carers UK. (2022, November). *State of caring, 2022: A snapshot of unpaid care in the UK*. https://www.carersuk.org/media/p4kblx5n/cukstateofcaring2022report.pdf

Carers UK. (2024a, October). *State of Caring 2024 - The impact of caring on: finances*. https://www.carersuk.org/media/umaifzpq/cuk-state-of-caring-2024-finances-web.pdf

Carers UK. (2024b, October). *Unpaid carers under huge financial pressure are forced to cut back on essentials, heating and food*. https://www.carersuk.org/press-releases/unpaid-carers-under-huge-financial-pressure-are-forced-to-cut-back-on-essentials-heating-and-food/

Carers UK. (2024c, September). *Poverty and financial hardship of unpaid carers in the UK*. https://www.carersuk.org/reports/poverty-and-financial-hardship-of-unpaid-carers-in-the-uk/

Carers UK. (2025a, February). *Sate of Caring – The impact of caring on cares' mental health and the need for support from social services*. https://www.carersuk.org/reports/state-of-caring-the-impact-of-caring-on-carers-mental-health-and-the-need-for-support-from-social-care-services/

Carers UK (2025b, June). *Facts about carers* (last updated June 2025). https://www.carersuk.org/media/xajkldmo/facts-about-carers-june-2025final.pdf

HM Government. (2025). *Carer's allowance*. https://www.gov.uk/carers-allowance

Joseph Rowntree Foundation (2025) *UK Poverty 2025: The essential guide to understanding poverty in the UK*. https://www.jrf.org.uk//uk-poverty-2025-the-essential-guide-to-understanding-poverty-in-the-uk

6

POVERTY AND BEING CARE EXPERIENCED

Caitlin Turner and Tilia Lenz

This is a story of survival, institutional neglect, and abuse. It is a story about sadness, loss, and trauma, and a story of slow healing and hard learning.

I was failed by the system, but I am not a 'system failure'. I am enough. I am a survivor of institutional abuse and neglect, a victim of Child Sexual Exploitation (CSE) and Child Criminal Exploitation (CCE), and endured trauma that made me 'bat shit crazy'. And now I am a warrior. I fight back. I have a voice. And I am speaking to you, so you can learn, reflect, and challenge an unjust system in which poverty and neglect get mixed up and confused to the detriment of children and families.

I am a daughter with no mother to hug and a mother with no child to comfort.

Poverty makes you vulnerable. Puts you in a corner, makes you an easy target, and even easier to exploit. It makes it hard to trust and love.

WHAT POVERTY MEANS IN THE UK CONTEXT

Definition: Poverty is more than low income – it is also about limited opportunities, social exclusion, and insecurity.

Relative Poverty: In the UK, households are in poverty if income is below 60% of the national median.

Scale of Child Poverty: Around 4.3 million children (30%) in the UK live in poverty (Child Poverty Action Group, 2024).

DOI: 10.4324/9781003638476-7

Impact on Care-Experienced Young People: Poverty both contributes to children entering care and makes leaving care harder, as young people lack family financial safety nets.

What this means for social workers

Be cautious not to confuse poverty with neglect. Distinguish between harm caused by lack of parental care and harm caused by structural inequality. Poverty-aware practice helps prevent unnecessary family separation.

My name is Caitlin, which has Greek roots, stemming from the word katharos, meaning 'clear, clean, and pure'. Yet my story is messy, complex, and chaotic.

I am 25 years old, and I have two children, Lexi and Huntter. I am their mum, and yet, I am not there to put them to bed, to kiss them good night, to settle them if they have a nightmare, to get them ready for school, to jump around with joy when they do something amazing, or to gently wipe their tears away if they are hurt or sad.

My children have other mums now who do that for them.

I am a care leaver. Though that is a funny term, 'care leaver', as if I had a choice in any of this. I didn't really leave care – I was simply not able to live in the place where I was because of my age.

When I was a 'looked after child', no one really looked after me. When I was 'in care', no one really cared about me.

But let me start from the beginning to help you understand where I am coming from and where I am now.

I first grew up with my mum and got into 'care' when I was nine years old and stayed in Local Authority care until I reached adulthood – well, until I turned 18. But who really is an adult then…

I moved placements at least 30 times, so many times that I actually lost count. And again, 'I moved placements' sounds as if I had a choice in this; I did not. I got told from one day to another that I would need to pack my stuff and get to another place. More new people, more stress, more working out my place and where I belong in the world. More feeling lost and not knowing whom to trust.

I have Complex Post-Traumatic Stress Disorder (CPTSD), a diagnosis of bipolar disorder, am autistic and have ADHD – I see the world very differently than you, have a really strong sense of justice and indeed injustice. And whilst my mind is working in funky ways, my body carries its own battle scars and holds physical trauma that will probably never heal, so I now have fibromyalgia.

With all of those labels and the fact that the world around me can be just really scary, overwhelming, and painful, it is tricky for me to have a job, a 'proper job' where you are required to function every day for eight hours.

POVERTY AND MENTAL HEALTH IN CARE LEAVERS

- **High Prevalence**: Over half of care leavers report significant mental health difficulties.
- **Intersection**: Poverty and trauma increase risks of depression, PTSD, and long-term physical health problems.
- **Mortality Risk**: Care leavers are up to seven times more likely to die by suicide than peers (ONS, 2020).

What this means for social workers

Securing income, education, and housing is a mental health intervention. Advocacy that reduces financial stress can directly improve well-being and resilience.

My body and my mind just can't do that. I am too broken. Broken by the system that was supposed to look after me. Care for me. When the 'Corporate parent' was no better than my birth parent and just put me in really dangerous situations, so all I learned was to survive – but never to live.

Corporate Parenting is the legal and moral duty of local authorities and certain public bodies to act as a parent for looked-after children and care leavers.

Legal Basis (England):

- Children Act 1989, Section 22: Local authorities must safeguard and promote the welfare and education of children in care.
- Children and Young Persons Act 2008: Strengthened duties around care planning, health, and education.
- Children and Social Work Act 2017, Section 1: Introduced seven Corporate Parenting Principles, including acting in the child's best interests, promoting health and well-being, supporting education, ensuring safety and stability, and preparing for adulthood.

Corporate parenting duties apply across services – social care, education, health, housing – requiring all to act with the same commitment as a 'good' parent would.

I am not sure if my mother deserves to hold the title 'mother' – mothers are supposed to care, protect, and love. She didn't do that, and I endured a lot of trauma and abuse as a young child, yet she told me it was all my fault, and it was down to my own behaviour that I got into care, and told me that I was a risk to my little brother. Children's Social Care had been involved since I was about four years old because my stepfather was cruel – he used force and physically abused me by grabbing me by the ears and dragging me up the stairs to then dangle me out of the window by my ankles. My 'mother' just stood by. I was often grounded in my room when I was naughty, but I had no door on my room, no wardrobe, and very few clothes apart from my school uniform. My brother, on the other hand, had toys, clothes, and a bed with a slide on it!

Sometimes I lashed out at my mother. I guess it was learned behaviour – I had seen my stepfather do it! But also, the ADHD, the autism and my very young age meant that I actually could not control my emotions and they just burst out. All I craved for was a space where I felt safe and be recognised for who I was, someone to love me. But all I was told was that I was 'Satan's spawn'.

My mother had her first child adopted, and I can see now that there is an intergenerational cycle of trauma and abuse. I can see that there is a lot of brokenness in my family, but my mother still cannot accept my experiences as true.

THE CYCLE OF POVERTY AND CARE

- **Poverty as a Cause**: Children from the most deprived 10% of areas are 11 times more likely to enter care than those in the least deprived.
- **Poverty as a Consequence**: Early independence without resources leads to 'accelerated adulthood'.
- **Intergenerational Poverty**: Many care leavers' children enter care due to systemic poverty, not parental intent.

What this means for social workers

Adopt a poverty-aware practice approach – seeing poverty as structural, not individual failure. Work in partnership with families to reduce financial hardship and advocate for systemic change.

When I got into care first, when I was a little 9-year-old girl, I really struggled. I could not contain my feelings of hurt; I could not label them and I could not make sense of them. I was an explosive ball of pain that no one could hold, so I never felt safe – ever. So, I started to run away from my foster carers and became quickly labelled as 'unmanageable', so I ended up in residential care at the age of 11. But a 'children's home' is not really a home for children (Table 6.1).

TABLE 6.1 Placement Types

Placement Type	*Description*	*Usually Proposed For*	*Level of Support*
Foster Care	Child lives with approved foster carers in a family home.	Children needing stable attachments in a family setting.	High emotional support; carers present daily.
Residential Child Care	Child lives in a group setting, staffed by trained professionals.	Young people with complex emotional and behavioural needs.	24/7 staff care; structured and therapeutic.
Independent Living	Young person lives alone or in semi-supported housing (e.g. supported lodgings).	Older adolescents (16+) preparing for adulthood.	Limited; support is often outreach-based.

It was a place where lots of broken kids, who were hurting on the inside, were put together. Kids who had not learned to manage their pain in any other way but to hurt others and themselves. I got beaten up by the older girls a lot and learned to stay quiet, cos no one was listening and nothing was gonna change anyway. And guess what – when you don't feel safe in your 'home', you might as well not be there, so I ran away again…

Social workers tried to stop me from 'putting myself at risk' and making 'risky lifestyle choices' and put me in a residential unit 'out of county' – from Bournemouth to Worthing, away from everything I knew, everything that was familiar, everything that made sense to me. I was 11 years old!

In one of the 'homes', staff locked all the food away in the office, which led to me having a very unhealthy relationship with food. The only things available were bread and pasta, but there was no support to manage and control a healthy diet and learn how to look after yourself. I got really, really fat and developed body dysmorphia – I could not feel myself or see myself, just the pain and hurt inside me. And just imagine you get your period when you have no idea where your body starts and where it ends. When your hormones play havoc with your mind, you get depressed and anxious and snap back at anyone. Just imagine there is no one who 'cares' enough to be there with you to explain and make sense of what is happening. Just imagine…

Would you stay in such a place? Would you really? Well, I didn't.…So when you run away a lot, and you are as young and vulnerable as I was, there are people who look out for you and pick you up – it feels like they care for you. But looking back, they didn't really; they exploited me, and I now realise that I am a victim of CSE and CCE.

CHILD SEXUAL AND CRIMINAL EXPLOITATION (CSE AND CCE)

CSE and CCE are both forms of child abuse that involve the coercion, manipulation, or grooming of children and young people into exploitative situations, often for the benefit of others. Whilst they differ in form – CSE involving sexual abuse and CCE involving criminal activity such as drug trafficking – they frequently overlap, particularly in contexts such as county lines, where both sexual and criminal exploitation may co-occur.

Both are recognised in statutory safeguarding guidance as forms of significant harm. The updated *Working Together to Safeguard Children* (DfE, 2023a) outlines multi-agency responsibilities to identify, respond to and prevent these forms of exploitation.

Legal frameworks

- **Sexual Offences Act 2003** (Sections 47–51): Criminalises CSE, including offences related to child prostitution and pornography.
- **Modern Slavery Act 2015** (Section 2): Applies to cases of trafficking for exploitation, including both CSE and CCE.
- **Children Act 1989 and 2004**: Place duties on local authorities and partner agencies to safeguard and promote the welfare of all children.
- **Serious Violence Strategy (Home Office, 2018)**: Provides a framework for understanding and responding to CCE, especially in the context of serious youth violence and gang exploitation.

Though CSE is more clearly defined in legislation, CCE is increasingly recognised in national policy and safeguarding practice. Both require multi-agency, trauma-informed, and contextual safeguarding approaches to address the complex power dynamics and systemic vulnerabilities that enable exploitation.

When I was placed in Worthing, a lot of older people were hanging out with us young kids in care – I was not even a teenager yet when I was first sexually assaulted and exploited by them, and when I told care staff what had happened, they wondered if it was rape, as I was so young and could not have consented. Yet no police got involved, no safeguarding processes were followed, and my abusers got away with it, and the abuse just escalated. I ran away a lot from the 'home' with some of the other girls, and it essentially became a game of tag with the staff who tried to catch us – it was a manhunt, catch me if you can. The adrenaline became the driver, and I did more and more risky stuff.

Anything but to feel the pain inside, anything to numb it, anything to distract. But the pain never went away. And it wasn't just my pain but a collective grief of what happened to all the kids in care – the girls who shared a house with me. Some became wonderful friends, we probably had a trauma bond… we all hurt so much, maybe the only feeling we actually knew and understood was pain. Maybe I should not be surprised that my best friend self-harmed so severely that she ultimately committed suicide. And you should not be surprised that I feel guilty for not having helped her, for not being able to take the pain of the gang rapes, the beatings, the abuse away from her.

And yet this is an experience that we all somehow had in common and endured over and over – adding to the layers of scars that never heal. When I tell you, I am a survivor, that is what I mean. I defeated all the odds to still be here. At the age of 25, I have been to more funerals of my friends than any birthdays and weddings combined.

All I wanted was to be loved and love someone else – so yes, at 16 I got pregnant because I wanted a baby. A human to love and love me back. I was a child who had a child, but unfortunately, the support that other young parents may get from their families was not what I got – instead, I was assessed on how I could care for my daughter. Instead of being taught and helped to develop as a mum, I was observed and scored. And guess what… I was told that I failed, that I was not good enough at being a mum because sometimes I still needed to be a child, sometimes the hurt and the pain bubbled up, and I needed time out. They took Lexi away from me, and the court decided that she needed to be adopted. I was still a child.

Then I met Matthew through my cousin, he was 6 years older than me and seemed a proper adult, stronger than me, bigger than me – someone who could hold me. He moved into my flat as he was homeless. And then he raped me in my sleep, and I got pregnant, but I was so scared to endure it all again. I did not know how to access abortion services, otherwise I would not have had him. But I was vulnerable and alone, pregnant from a registered sex offender, trying to come to terms with the loss of Lexi. I was in a mess, so I did not tell anyone that I was pregnant until 20 weeks. Matthew was violent, beat me up, and continued to sexually assault me. I was 17. Still a child. Still, no one cared. And I was so scared!

So, the process started again, and social workers assessed me and concluded that I was in an abusive relationship with a registered sex offender – poor lifestyle choices of a promiscuous child. A child indeed, I was 17. Yet no protection, no support, no recognition that all I needed was safety, love and care. Instead, Huntter was removed, and the courts decided again that he should be adopted.

I have sold my soul to the devil more often than I have met angels since then…

And what has this all to do with poverty, you may wonder… Poverty means that you are trapped, lack freedoms and are low on expectations. As I did not really finish school with great GCSEs and then had my babies, I have few qualifications to show for. Whilst I am now in a much better place with my physical and mental health, I cannot access further education, even if I wanted to, just because I cannot afford to pay the college fees. At 25 years, I need to fund any course myself with no family who could back me up financially.

I am on benefits and get by, but really, to have a fulfilled life means you have stuff to do, like work.

CARE LEAVERS AND POVERTY – KEY STATISTICS

- **Education and Employment**: Only 26% of care leavers aged 21 are in education, employment or training (compared to 57% of all young people).
- **Homelessness**: Around 25% of young homeless people have experience of care.
- **Reliance on Welfare**: By age 30, over half of care leavers rely on state benefits.
- **Financial Pressures**: Care leavers face bills (rent, council tax, utilities) earlier than peers, without family support.

What this means for social workers

Transition planning should include financial literacy, benefits advice, and advocacy for fair entitlements – going beyond housing to sustainable income.

But my health conditions mean that I cannot do a 9–5 job, and I can only do a couple of days a week to manage my physical pain and chronic fatigue. So, I am stuck with unqualified bar work that pays the minimum wage, and I have to be careful not earn too much to have my benefits reduced. I do not have the privilege of earning more than pocket money.

To have a fulfilling life, people have hobbies, do something they enjoy, balancing the dull and difficult stuff in life. I loved horse riding and dancing as a child, but can you imagine someone on benefits having a hobby like that? A hobby that requires you to have the kit and go to places? No, nor can I.

My dogs mean the world to me; they love me, and I can love them, but they need to eat, and sometimes I go without food, so they get theirs. But without them, without love, I might as well just not be. They get me up when I cannot move for all the pain. They get me out when I cannot face the world. I cannot let them down.

There are people who have left this world and could not stand the pain any longer. You cannot hear their voices anymore, but they are still in my heart. I need to speak on their behalf and ask you to take action:

Give us a chance. Give us the resources to build a life after care. But not just tokenistic 'support' that is half-arsed and laden with blame and shame. What we – the children who have been let down by our parents and society need, is kindness and compassion without question or return. We need to be able to access services that can help us heal and make sense of our experiences. Not just a six-week course of 'steps to wellbeing' – that ain't gonna cut it with 25 years of trauma.

We need systems that allow social workers to see children as children and not as small adults with a bad attitude. That may be what we present as, but it is not what we are.

We need society to understand that social work and care work are important and valuable, and we need the government to fund this work to enable children to grow into adults who can be responsible for their own lives.

Foster Carers need to be paid for the job they are doing and the emotional labour they undertake to help children heal their broken hearts.

We need the educational system to change – from primary to secondary and beyond. Care leavers need to have access to education post 25, free of charge – because sometimes, often, it takes so much longer to heal those wounds and for us to be able to sit and listen and learn. Only then can we take on skilled jobs and step out of the cycle of poverty.

We need you to hold the system to account and speak up for the kids in care. Advocate for them, fight for them, and keep them safe. Stop blaming us when we seek out the wrong people to love. Stop blaming us when we make mistakes, when we don't even know what we did wrong. Stop holding us responsible for 'poor lifestyle choices' when we had no options.

We need support when we are trapped in abusive relationships with no way out – we need real options for safety and not tokenistic, budget-strapped, volunteer-run support groups.

We want you to fight the injustice in the system, and when children in your care get pregnant, you need to still see them for what they are: children! We need you to support them to make choice that is right for them and right for their baby. They need support, care, and teaching on how to be a parent. We need you never to forget that we do not want to make the mistakes that our parents made – but we need you to help us with that.

We want you to rethink if semi-independent living is really adequate, because let's face it, we cannot even get a tattoo at the age of 16, let alone live pretty much on our own. We are literally set up to fail by the system and then blamed when it doesn't work! Give us the support, guidance, and nurturing environment that kids need at that stage in their lives, especially if they have experienced trauma – as all kids in care have.

HOUSING IN THE CONTEXT OF THE CHILDREN (LEAVING CARE) ACT 2000

Purpose of the Act is to improve outcomes for care leavers by delaying the transition to independence and ensuring appropriate accommodation is in place, to prevent homelessness and housing instability.

Who does it apply to?

- *Eligible* and *relevant* children (aged 16–17 in or recently left care) and former *relevant* children (aged 18–21, or up to 25 if in education/training).

Key housing responsibilities of local authorities

1 Pathway Plan, which includes a detailed housing plan that is regularly reviewed.
2 Personal Adviser (PA) who supports the care leaver in:

   - Finding and maintaining accommodation.
   - Understanding tenancy rights and budgeting.
   - Accessing practical support services.

3 **Suitable Accommodation**
   Local authorities must:

   - Ensure placements are safe, stable, and appropriate.
   - Consider proximity to education, employment, and support networks.
   - Avoid Bed and Breakfast placements except in emergencies.

4 **Staying Put**

   - Enables young people to remain with foster carers after turning 18.
   - Provides a gradual transition into independent living.

What this means for social workers

Begin housing planning early (ideally well before age 18) and advocate for care leavers' housing rights by collaborating with housing teams, leaving care services, and external providers.

Legal reference

Children (Leaving Care) Act 2000 (amending the Children Act 1989)
See also: DfE '*Care Leaver Strategy*' and local authority guidance.

And what I want for myself, you may wonder… I would love to work in a place that is supportive. Where I could take a break if my body or my mind hurt too much. Where I am valued for my skills and wits, where I can grow, learn, and be strong.

I would love to be in love. The kind of love that fills your heart with joy and makes you content with yourself. The kind of love that makes you feel hopeful for the future, a future in which I could be a mum again.

Bibliography

Legislation

Children Act 1989
Children Act 2004
Children and Young Persons Act 2008
Children (Leaving Care) Act 2000
Children and Social Work Act 2017
Sexual Offences Act 2003
Modern Slavery Act 2015

Government guidance and statutory policy

Department for Education. (2018). *Applying corporate parenting principles to looked after children and care leavers*. https://www.gov.uk/government/publications/applying-corporate-parenting-principles-to-looked-after-children-and-care-leavers

Department for Education. (2023a). *Working together to safeguard children*. https://www.gov.uk/government/publications/working-together-to-safeguard-children--2

Department for Education. (n.d.). *Children Act 1989: Transition to adulthood guidance*. https://www.gov.uk/government/publications/children-act-1989-transition-to-adulthood-guidance

HM Government. (2013). *Care leaver strategy: A cross-departmental strategy for young people leaving care*. https://www.gov.uk/government/publications/care-leaver-strategy

Home Office. (2018). *Serious violence strategy*. https://www.gov.uk/government/publications/serious-violence-strategy

Statistics and data sources

Centrepoint. (n.d.). *Youth homelessness databank*. https://centrepoint.org.uk/youth-homelessness/databank/

Child Poverty Action Group. (2024). *Child poverty facts and figures*. https://cpag.org.uk/child-poverty

Department for Education. (2023b). *Outcomes for children looked after by local authorities in England*. https://www.gov.uk/government/collections/statistics-looked-after-children

Office for National Statistics. (2020). *Deaths of care leavers: Mortality analysis*. https://www.ons.gov.uk/

Policy frameworks/practice models

Firmin, C. (2017). *Contextual safeguarding framework*. University of Bedfordshire.

Academic sources

Bywaters, P., Brady, G., Sparks, T., & Bos, E. (2016). *The relationship between poverty, child abuse and neglect: An evidence review*. https://www.jrf.org.uk/child-poverty/the-relationship-between-poverty-child-abuse-and-neglect-an-evidence-review

Recommended reading/viewing/listening

Caitlin's podcast: Through the looking glass https://www.instagram.com/ttlg_care_experienced_podcast/?igsh=eXR2d3lqY3Rubjkw&utm_source=qr#
Firmin, Carlene. (2020). *Contextual safeguarding and child protection: Rewriting the rules*. 10.4324/9780429283314.
Sissay, L. (2019). *My name is why*. New York.
Winfrey, O. & Perry, B.D. (2021). *What happened to you? Conversation on trauma, resilience, and healing*. Flatiron Books.

Websites

https://www.contextualsafeguarding.org.uk/
https://brenebrown.com/podcast/brene-with-oprah-winfrey-and-dr-bruce-d-perry-on-trauma-resilience-and-healing/
https://thecareleaders.com/
https://www.contextualsafeguarding.org.uk/blog/the-contextual-safeguarding-young-people-s-podcast-series/

7

POVERTY AND DISABILITY

Steve Huxford and Sally Lee

My name is Steve, and this chapter is about living with disability and my experience of poverty. As you will read, disability and poverty are closely connected.

Looking back, I don't remember being aware of poverty when I was growing up in Cornwall in the 1980/90s. Even as an adult, I thought poverty was only in housing estates amongst people who didn't work. My view was stereotypical and influenced by television programmes like Benefit Street. Since then, my view has changed, and I now understand that poverty is a live issue for anyone, whether they live in rural parts of Cornwall or a big city.

POVERTY IN RURAL AREAS

The lived experience of poverty in the UK is diverse; it's not just different from person to person, but also informed by geography and location. For people living in rural areas, poverty can be caused or exacerbated by low wages and the lack of access to essential services and opportunities such as education, health, employment or transport. In rural areas, lack of affordable housing, precarious employment and inadequate services may be factors leading to poverty. This underlines the importance of practitioners understanding the characteristics of the location in which they work and being alert to the impacts those characteristics may have on the local population.

To further explore the diversity of poverty in the UK in 2025, the House of Commons Library has published the report 'Poverty in the UK: Statistics'.

Also, the Joseph Rowntree Foundation publishes up-to-date information and has published their 2025 report 'UK Poverty 2025'.

DOI: 10.4324/9781003638476-8

I learnt about the reality of poverty when I was injured at work in 2014, followed by years of poor physical and mental health and extreme self-medicating with alcohol. During that time, I faced poverty, found help at a food-bank and learnt to navigate the complexities of the benefits system. I was finally diagnosed with fibromyalgia in 2016 and have come to accept the likelihood that I won't be able to work again. There is a common misconception that people on benefits don't want to work, but most people with disabilities or long-term health conditions would love to be able to do a full-time job. For me, I struggle with fatigue, which means that all of my muscles wear out quickly and affect all the senses as my eyesight varies massively over the day. This also means that repetitive movements are exhausting, so typing, chopping food, walking and even things like holding things steady are challenging.

I am also in constant pain, which affects all the nerves, muscles and also joints. So any kind of exercise is problematic as I can't walk for long, have muscles tensed and even the lightest of touches can be agony! One of the few things that does help me is regular massages with a trained sports massage therapist, as he can get the muscles relaxed, although the experience is torture. I use a pair of sticks when I'm walking, as that helps with both balance and spreading some of the load away from my legs.

My brain doesn't work as quickly as it used to, either. I can rapidly get brain fog when I'm trying to concentrate, so writing this chapter has taken a long time and has needed my co-author to help take my thoughts from conversation and written text and turn it into a coherent and hopefully a very useful part of this book to ensure you can understand some of my life and experiences.

There are many other symptoms and effects that are common with fibromyalgia, and we'll look at more of that later in the chapter.

When you've been an active and hard worker for many years, then this takes a lot of getting used to. It involves going through the grief cycle for the life that you thought you would have and then learning to accept the new life, where finding a new purpose is vital for wellbeing. Today I am at a point where I can help others by sharing my story – I hope you find it helpful too.

My background

In the distant past, I studied computer science at university, and whilst I quickly discovered that computer science was not for me, I did find that I loved spending time around people and especially helping them. Those years at university, helping with Nightline (a student-led, confidential listening service), enabled me to find my passion and purpose in life: making a difference to those around me. It's something I've reflected on since my injury and later diagnosis, as it can be difficult to accept what your new life is like and to learn whether your purpose in life is something new or an adaptation of your previous purpose. I am glad to say that my purpose is the same: to help people, but just in different ways.

After university, I moved to London and started stewarding for events, gigs and high-end retail. I love music, so it was great to be paid to go to concerts even though we would sometimes be stuck outside in the cold and wet for 16 hours per day! This work was my first exposure to vast differences in wealth (people spending thousands of pounds on basic items, which blew my mind!) as well as the poor treatment of low-paid workers. Cleaners, caterers and stewards were looked down on, and we were made to feel like we were unimportant and expendable.

INCOME AND WEALTH INEQUALITY

Steve's experience of inequality is borne out in research. For example, the Office of National Statistics (ONS) regularly undertakes the Wealth and Assets Survey and show that (when it was last updated in 2020) the bottom (in terms of wealth and income) 50% of the population own 14% of the wealth, whereas the richest 10% of the population owns 44% of the wealth.

Further research by the House of Commons Library suggests that if trends seen since the 2008 financial crash were to continue, then the top 1% will hold 64% of the world's wealth by 2030. The research was reported in The Guardian.

Poverty is often associated with unemployment, but increasingly, people with jobs are experiencing poverty too. This may be due to unstable or 'gig' employment or low pay such as that experienced by the workers Steve mentions.

Working in security means there's always the risk of injury, and unfortunately, an incident resulted in a back injury, which was probably the trigger for my fibromyalgia. The type of work I was doing meant I didn't have much sick leave and so had to go back to work before the injury was healed. I then couldn't understand why I had lots of pains in different areas of my body – which I now know was the fibromyalgia. I tried to push through the pain with painkillers and a drink or two after work. At the same time, I developed severe insomnia and found that alcohol was one of the few things that numbed the pain enough for me to get some sleep. Over time, I started having a couple of drinks alone at home, then a bottle or two of wine, and then I moved on to spirits. Much later, I learned that this was a coping strategy. Eventually, I was having so much to drink each night that I was incapable of working. I knew this situation wasn't sustainable and had been seeking help, and in 2014, I went to rehab.

Undergoing rehab meant I learnt about my mental health and the coping strategies I had been using – I had to retrain myself to use more useful strategies.

> Here are links to some sources of information and techniques I have found especially helpful:
>
> Calm – 10 mindfulness exercises to include in your daily routine
> Mind – mindfulness exercises and tips
> Patient – relaxation exercises
> NHS Inform – benefits of breathing exercises

Because I had both addiction issues and mental health needs, the services were limited as mental health services tend not to work with people until their active addiction is addressed. A lot of people find themselves in this dilemma, which I discovered during my rehab, and it is described by the term 'dual diagnosis', specifically for people who have addiction and poor mental health. Working with people with a dual diagnosis is a specialist service, and it took me a whilst to find the psychiatry team that I felt really understood me and treated me holistically.

For me, I needed mental health support in order to tackle my addiction. Being in rehab was also the first time I applied for welfare benefits, and I managed to get the basic rate of Employment Support Allowance (ESA), as it was back then, but would now be Job Seekers Allowance or Universal Credit. When I started claiming ESA, I was living in a flat which had been just about affordable when I was working. However, the Housing Allowance cap was about £40 per week less than my rent. This had to come out of the £75 ESA. Bills quickly took up the rest of the ESA, and my savings rapidly disappeared. My financial situation became increasingly dire, and I was forced to cut back on heating, food and getting out of the flat. I had to make hard choices every day, and I was living the description frequently used in the media about having to choose between heating and eating. I felt desperate as I couldn't afford the flat (which was very small), but nor could I afford to move, and I was not well enough to move either due to the cumulative effects of the injury and the anxiety, depression and panic attacks. For me, what made the difference between becoming homeless or surviving was that I am very fortunate to have a supportive family who helped me, but I am very aware that lots of people are not so fortunate.

REFLECTIVE ACTIVITY

Imagine you are in your local supermarket doing your regular shopping. As you mentally browse the shelves, are there items you automatically don't buy? Are there items your hand edges towards, and you would like to buy but don't? List the factors that inform your decisions about what you do and don't buy – you will be asked to use the list in reflective activity 3.

It took over a year of being on the basic rate of ESA until I had a Work Capability Assessment to decide if I should be job seeking or assessed as unable to work. As I was still getting panic attacks and crippling anxiety along with severe depression, in 2015, I was placed in the latter category, which enabled me to get treatment. But throughout the waiting period, I was struggling mentally, physically, emotionally and financially. It was my mum who discovered my dire financial state and, although she doesn't like me saying that she dragged me to the local foodbank, that's definitely how it felt to me, and I am so glad that she did because it completely transformed my life!

INFORMATION ABOUT FOODBANKS

Foodbanks provide emergency food and practical advice for individuals and families experiencing food insecurity and other forms of poverty. The number of foodbanks in the UK has rapidly grown over the last 15 years, and in 2025, there are approximately 2,800 foodbanks run by the Trussell Trust (the main provider) and other independent organisations, including churches and charities, with almost 3 million food parcels distributed in 2024/25. Hunger is a live issue in the UK, exacerbated by the cost-of-living crisis, unaffordable housing and low wages, find out more by reading the Trussell Trust report Hunger in the UK.

Most UK foodbanks need a referral. There are a lot of referrers, so it is easy to find somewhere to go for help (go to your local foodbank's website to find information about their referral system or go to their webpage). For example, the Trussell Trust (get a food voucher).

As I was accessing my local drug and alcohol service, I asked my keyworker, and she was able to discreetly provide me with a referral.

When we arrived at the foodbank, we were greeted at the door by someone who immediately put us at ease. A volunteer chatted to us and gave me some choices for the food parcel that I was getting. When someone is at the point of needing a foodbank, they often don't have too many choices left, and there is something empowering when the choices they do have are simple and without big consequences! Choosing between pasta or rice, tea or coffee is a positive option rather than having to choose which bill is going to be left unpaid that month.

REFLECTIVE ACTIVITY

Do you know your weekly/monthly budget and what you spend on essentials such as housing, bills, transport and food?

What would you consider to be essential or be prepared to sacrifice if you had a monthly budget of £316.98 (current Universal Credit allowance for a single person under 25), and what factors would you consider when making your decision?

Compare these factors with the ones you identified in the previous exercise – how much does budget inform your decision-making?

Lots of foodbanks also have advice services that can discuss your situation and help direct you to the most useful places or even help fill out some of the benefit forms for money you might be entitled to.

The stigma of going to the foodbank that first time quickly dissipated, and they weren't judgemental about my being there. This is something that I know people can fear when attending foodbanks and I would like to reassure readers that if they are struggling, it's okay to ask for help.

It was during this time that I realised I wasn't able to do much walking, and a combination of extreme fatigue, lots of different aches and pains, brain fog and forgetfulness led doctors to investigate. This led to a diagnosis of fibromyalgia in 2016. I'd never heard of it before, but connected up these different symptoms plus others that I had no idea were part of the same issue!

Soon after my diagnosis, I found an online support group which helped me make some good friends who understood the condition and, over time, helped me understand my adapted purpose. This was a very difficult time for me as I felt so unwell, isolated and in mourning for the person I had been. I could no longer fulfil the socially expected role of full-time worker and provider. Experiencing social poverty as well as financial poverty was devastating to me, but I can thank my nieces and nephews for helping me rediscover myself as a role model for them and regain my sense of purpose.

FIBROMYALGIA AND LINKS TO HELPFUL INFORMATION AND SUPPORT GROUPS

Fibromyalgia is a long-term condition that causes pain and tenderness all over your body. Unlike arthritis, this isn't because you have problems with your joints, bones or muscles. It's thought to be caused by your nervous system in your brain and spine not being able to control or process pain signals from other parts of your body.

The condition is also linked to:

poor sleep
feeling you can't concentrate or remember things
extreme and constant tiredness that doesn't improve with sleep or rest – which is known as fatigue.

There can be many other symptoms that affect different parts of your body, and the following links will give you more information:

NHS – Fibromyalgia Overview
Arthritis UK – Fibromyalgia
FMA UK – Patient Booklet
FMA UK – Support Group Map

With fibromyalgia, it's uncertain about who it affects and all the different symptoms and impacts that come with it. One of the likely routes to getting it is having a genetic predisposition and then some kind of trigger, which might be physical, emotional or mental trauma. For me, the incident at work might have been a trigger, but then the additional anxiety, stress and rollercoaster ride I had with alcohol and self-medication added further pressure, compounding the impact. I have found that sorting my use of alcohol has helped me feel more stable and secure mentally, and this has helped with my fibromyalgia. I've noticed that people get uncomfortable about the idea of counselling or CBT and therapies being used or recommended as treatments for conditions like mine, but I find these types of treatments give me a bit of headspace by helping with the anxiety, and they also help me to understand what's going on around me. So now I'm more aware of myself and how to manage my health, including recognising the signs of getting worn out or pain levels getting too high when I have to say, *'OK, that's it, have a rest'*. But rehab and adjusting to disability are not one-off events but are instead journeys that are not always smooth. I started rehab in 2014, and it took years of struggling with poor mental health and addiction up to 2018 before I got through it and finally learnt my purpose and value for myself and others, which helped me to get and stay sober.

One major impact of disability can be social isolation; for example, with fibromyalgia, it is sometimes unpredictable how much energy a person may have. Also, because fibromyalgia affects the nervous system, the senses can become amplified, confused and overwhelmed, and this makes things like socialising or using public transport difficult. For me, I sometimes think that I'll just stay in and shut myself away to rest and manage symptoms. For me, it's about listening to my body and my mind. This is something I have had to work hard to accept, as we all seem conditioned to be very busy all the time, and the idea about having a rest is often considered being lazy. I was always incredibly busy and felt that if I wasn't working, I wasn't making money and then couldn't cover rent and bills. Poverty furthers this isolation because you can't afford to get out, use transport or attend events when there is cost involved. To avoid falling into depression, it is important for me to have a few things in my diary each week.

The fibromyalgia support group and Citizens Advice service at the foodbank mentioned Personal Independence Payment (PIP), and they have helped me with applications, appeals and tribunals several times since then. PIP has been a lifeline.

INFORMATION ABOUT DISABILITY-RELATED BENEFITS

Over the last 15 years, there have been major changes made to disability-related benefits, including their eligibility criteria. This can make it complex for individuals to navigate as old and new systems of benefits overlap, as well as the outcome of an application depending on the individual, evidencing the impact of their disability on their health and wellbeing, which can be distressing and stressful as Steve describes later in the chapter. Other factors, such as work history and financial assets, are considered in assessments of benefit entitlement, which can further add to the complexity.

The main disability-related benefit for adults of working age is currently the health component of Universal Credit, which is means tested, and PIP.

PIP is made up of two components, daily living and mobility. Applicants are assessed and awarded points according to the level of need in relation to activities such as getting washed and dressed, cooking or getting about. People with all types of disabilities, neurodiversity or mental ill health may be eligible depending on the impact on the individual. The number of points awarded in an assessment determines both eligibility and whether PIP is paid at the lower or higher rate.

As an indication, in 2025 the rates were £73.90 (lower weekly rate) and £110.40 (higher weekly rate) for the daily living part; and £29.20 (lower weekly rate) and £77.05 for the mobility part.

There is more information on the PIP website.

Getting PIP is a slow and stressful process; initially, you have a month from when you request the form to fill it out and get it back. It then takes a couple of months to process, followed by an assessment, which takes a few more months before you get the result. You then have a month to go through a mandatory reconsideration, which is made by another decision maker in the same department. You may then have to go to an independent tribunal or appeal the decision. Altogether it takes around a year from application to conclusion, but if you are successful, it may be backdated to when you started the application. I don't know anyone that the process has run smoothly for, and I know some people decide not to appeal a negative outcome because of the associated stress and uncertainty. At my last review, I was dropped two points under the standard award, which reduced my allowance, but the subsequent mandatory reconsideration put me back into the standard and higher payment. This was very stressful to me and impacted my health.

NEW LEGISLATION

There has been extensive debate and controversy over the Universal Credit Bill that, at the time of writing, is passing through the UK Parliament (BBC News). The bill implements cuts to the health-related element of Universal Credit for some claimants and had sought to make it harder for people to claim PIP; however, lack of support from some MPs, as well as extensive campaigning by disability organisations, has led to this being abandoned. The bill and the related debate reflect long-standing arguments about the affordability, purpose and helpfulness of benefits. Different sides of the debate are informed by political perspectives, with more pro-benefits arguments tending to be from left-leaning sources. To gain a balanced perspective, it is helpful to compare news from different sources, and one way that Steve does this is by using the Ground News app. For example, look at this comparison of news sources reporting on the Universal Credit Bill.

For further information and help with applying for PIP, go to Citizens' Advice guidance or Scope's advice.

Applying for PIP can also be depressing because it focuses on what you can't do, and you have to repeatedly state, *'I can't do this, I can't do that'* to prove you are eligible. I work hard at trying to look at things in a more positive light, but having to then think, well, actually I can't do this and I can't do that, is really frustrating and distressing. But PIP makes a massive difference to me as the mobility part helps me manage to get around – if you get awarded a certain number of points, you are then entitled to things like a bus pass, and a blue badge and there's also a taxi discount card. Receiving the daily living element of PIP allows me to get a specialist massage that helps maintain my basic mobility, plus the type of food that I can manage is expensive so that uses up big chunks too.

EXTRA COSTS OF LIVING WITH DISABILITY

Scope researches the additional costs of living with disability incur and their latest Disability Price Tag research for 2025 found that disabled households with at least one disabled adult or child face extra costs of £1095 a month on average. This is just to have the same standard of living as non-disabled households. Just as Steve describes, medical equipment, higher energy bills, and specialist support all add up. PIP is meant to help disabled people afford the additional costs, but as Scope (2025) explains, PIP is falling short with the average PIP payment being £465 a month across households, not enough to cover the extra costs of £1,095 per month. This leaves a £630 shortfall.

Volunteering

I said at the start of this chapter that I believe my purpose in life is to help others. I now do this by volunteering at my local foodbank one day a week. I've been doing this since 2015, after I first used it. Back then, I was physically able to help move stock around and go out to collect items and helping with the sorting. As the effects of the fibromyalgia have increased, I've become more involved in the advice side of the foodbank work. I now sit at the door and say hello to people coming in, helping to put them at ease, just like the person did for me the first time I went to the foodbank. I check referral details, and I'll often give some advice or refer people on to other services. One of the strengths of the team is recognising the different areas that people have experience and knowledge in, and these strengths are used to help people – I'm especially good at talking to people about disability and chronic pain. Saying I'm good at something doesn't come naturally to me, so my saying this is evidence of all the personal development I have had! I realise that I love hearing people's stories, but also people can relate to mine and having realised this, I started sharing my living experience with the stories team at Trussell. This is a team of experts by experience who are put in contact with the media if somebody is wanted to share their experience. Recently, I have been involved in campaigning where I've met MPs and Peers and shown them the value of having people with lived experience involved in discussions and decision-making, rather than just people with power trying to make decisions on their own.

The Trussell stories team is not about telling the worst stories of poverty, which seem to be the ones often picked out by the tabloids. Instead, these are relatable stories that readers/audiences might identify with. This is important because people are good at thinking '*that's not going to happen to me*', but poverty can happen to most of us simply because life happens. As I have shared with you in this chapter, I had an incident at work which led me into poverty; other people might have some other injury, disability or ill health – it's important for us all to recognise that our circumstances can change very quickly and lead us to poverty.

REFLECTIVE ACTIVITY

Steve never thought this would happen to him, and he has needed to make very difficult decisions to keep going. Through all his experiences, when Steve has faced change and disruption, he has found renewed purpose. Research around wellbeing highlights the importance of having a sense of purpose. Would you agree, and if so, what do you think is your sense of purpose? Has this changed over time, and if so, what has led to the change?

What needs to change?

People in positions of power and decision-makers need to listen to people with lived experience, like the people in this book. They need to say, '*OK, I want to hear more about your story so that I can help improve the situation*'. I know that changes might cost money and that can be difficult, but it's vital that policy decisions that have long-term impact are made; things like investing in the health service and education to improve earlier treatment. Life can be stressful for most of us, and especially for younger people who are struggling to find the help they need.

Also, it would be beneficial if the different agencies, like social services and the benefit system, were to feel supportive and that they are genuinely trying to help. I expect most people who go into that kind of work are trying to help people, but somewhere along the line a disconnect happens, and they lose that sense of care. This is especially true with the way that PIP is assessed and processed; we meet people for the assessments, but the decision makers are usually separate and do not meet the people they're trying to make a difference for. This makes the system feel like it's just marking points and totally removed from the person.

My message

As a society, I believe we need to have better, kinder conversations that move us past the stigma of poverty, mental health, addiction and disability. If we can just say to somebody, *'I'm really struggling today'* and have a meaningful conversation that doesn't blame or judge. This would take off so much pressure to conform to a socially prescribed and unrealistic view of perfection, which is communicated through social expectations to behave, look and think in a certain way.

I hope you have found this chapter helpful and interesting, and thank you for reading my story.

Further reading, viewing and listening

BASW and CWIP. (2023). *Anti-Poverty Practice Guide for Social Work*. Second Edition. Birmingham: British Association of Social Workers

Disability and Poverty Research by Scope. https://www.scope.org.uk/media/disability-facts-figures

Fibromyalgia NHS Information. https://www.nhs.uk/conditions/fibromyalgia/

Fibromyalgia Support Groups. https://fmauk.org/

Marmot, M., Allen, J., Boyce, T., Goldblatt, P. and Morrison, J. (2020). *Health Equity in England: The Marmot Review 10 Years On. Institute of Health Equity*. Available from: https://www.health.org.uk/publications/reports/the-marmot-review-10-years-on

Media, Poverty and Public Opinion Rreport. https://www.jrf.org.uk/narrative-change/the-media-poverty-and-public-opinion-in-the-uk

Research into Public Attitudes to Poverty. https://www.kcl.ac.uk/policy-institute/assets/attitudes-to-poverty.pdf

Scope (2025). What You Need to Know About the New Bill to Change Disability Rights 23 June 2025. Available at What you need to know about the new bill to change disability benefits. | Disability charity Scope UK

Trussell End of Year to March 2025. https://cms.trussell.org.uk/sites/default/files/2025-05/EYS_factsheet_UK_2025.pdf

Wilkinson, R. and Pickett, K. (2009). *The Spirit Level: Why Equality Is Better For Everyone*. London: Penguin.

8
POVERTY AND HOMELESSNESS

Sam and Kate Parker

In April 2007, I left my family home, with my four children, not realising that I was walking away from financial and housing security I would not regain for nearly 20 years.

My father got my children and myself out of the marital home. He knew that I couldn't stay with my abusive husband any longer. Enough was enough. But I left a four-bedroom home, which we owned, with only four years left to pay on the mortgage, to stay with my parents in their two-bed semi-detached house.

I assumed that I would be able to get back on my feet. I had business acquaintances who offered for me and my children to stay with them. That worked well until they needed to sell that property, and I returned to my parents. We shared with those friends again, but they were also not financially stable, and as their marriage broke down, we had to leave, and we were back to square one.

In January 2009, I approached the local authority for help. They assisted us into private rented accommodation. This was temporary, but from there, we moved to a housing association property, which should have given us the stability we needed. Instead, we faced a permanent battle with mould and disrepair. My daughter became ill with acute asthma due to the mould.

I was not sure how my life had got to this point. I had a very traditional upbringing, which was steady and boundaried. I felt confident and wanted to do well. I had moved to London, and my dream was to be an interior designer.

In some ways, I was naïve when I met my husband. I had just turned 21 and did not see the warning signs. I was flattered by him and overwhelmed by the intensity of him wanting to be with me all the time. He seemed to really

DOI: 10.4324/9781003638476-9

love-bomb me, and I thought he truly loved me. In contrast to my family life, he seemed more exciting. He was one of four children, and his parents' marriage had ended in a bitter divorce. His mother was a strong character who focused all her energies into my husband; he was her golden boy. They had moved around a lot compared with me, who had lived most of my life in one place. His three siblings were lively and seemed adventurous. I was not aware, at that time, that my husband's sister was being abused by her husband. Similarly, I was taken in by my husband's charm and didn't realise as he gradually took control. The coercive control was happening slowly and gaining momentum throughout our relationship and marriage.

It wasn't until we had been married for over 20 years that I realised how bad things had become. On Christmas Day 2006, I'd experienced verbal abuse all day. His moods switched between extremes of happiness and anxiety and stress. This affected the way he was towards me, and I was always caught off-guard. He would think nothing of making comments about me in public about how I looked and what I was wearing, but then could be overbearingly attentive. I'd had enough, but I realised there was nowhere for me to escape to. I used to hide away in the bathroom to get away, but he would follow me and kick the door.

My children and I hid the truth. I learned to disassociate from what was going on. It was important to me not to let my family know what was happening and for the outside world to think that we were a perfect, successful family.

On my son's birthday in March 2007, there was the usual verbal abuse and accusations and then physical violence from my husband. Within a month, I had left. It felt against all my principles as, following my parents' example, I thought marriage was forever and that, by leaving, I'd failed. It takes both one moment and years to decide to leave. As a mother, I questioned my right to make that decision.

I was on my own with my children, with no home and no income. I felt vulnerable but knew I had to keep going.

3.8 million (7.8%) people over 16 experienced domestic abuse in the survey year ending March 2025 (ONS, 2025)/Domestic abuse prevalence and trends, England and Wales: year ending March 2025

In the year up to the end of June 2025, '25,990 households were owed a relief duty after being made homeless due to being a victim of domestic abuse'. Source Statutory Homelessness England level time series 'live tables'.

'A person is homeless if it is not reasonable to continue to occupy their accommodation because of the probability of violence or domestic abuse' (Shelter).

My husband and I had built up a successful business, but I felt I had to let this go when I left. I didn't think it was fair to take that away from him. He didn't continue, but his response was to dissolve the business.

I was told that in leaving my marital home, I had given up the rights to the property. I had to sign a contract for a Barclay loan to pay for representation in my divorce. Towards the end, my ex-husband represented himself, which made the process longer and more expensive. He harassed me while attending court for the eighteen months of proceedings, so much that, on the final day, I suffered an acute panic attack and an ambulance was called. The marriage was legally ended, but my share of the sale of the house went to pay for the costs of my solicitor and barrister.

My husband stopped paying for anything. He paid child support for less than a year, a total of £4000. All the bills were in my name. He said he was a victim, that he needed protecting from me, he said that I had an affair and accused me of fraud, even though he moved a new partner into the family home during the divorce. It was as if he wanted me to lose everything, including contact with our children. But I kept going and didn't give up. I was awarded full custody of the children, but he paid me nothing towards them.

I maintained as normal a family life as possible and prioritised making sure that the children's education was not disrupted. I am pleased that I always managed to keep them in their school. My focus was on providing a safe and consistent environment for my children. This is where the housing system let me down.

ENGLISH HOUSING SURVEY (EHS) ON EXPERIENCES OF THE 'HOUSING CRISIS'

'Housing Crisis' refers to the collection of social and market conditions that result from a shortage of affordable housing, including increasing house prices, households waiting until later in life to purchase their homes and difficulty getting on the housing ladder, longer wait lists for social housing, independent children living with parents for longer, a rise in rough sleeping and families and renters living in overcrowded, substandard and insecure homes.

A large proportion of certain groups, such as **low-income private renters, are spending more than 30% of their income on housing costs.** With fewer private renters expecting to buy a home compared with ten years ago.

These findings suggest a **growing disparity across households in England**, with a smaller but **substantial proportion of households**

struggling with finances, particularly housing costs, and increasingly exposed to risk, and others who are more comfortable in their living situations, with savings or equity in housing.

Source: English Housing Survey 2023 to 2024: experiences of the 'housing crisis'

Years of housing insecurity

Technically, we were made homeless in 2007 when I left the marital home. We moved so many times, living in overcrowded conditions, with no home of our own and no long-term solution in sight. From 2007 to 2009, we moved between temporary homes and friends' houses. Sometimes we had to return to my parents' two-bed semi-detached house, where all five of us shared one bedroom. In January 2009, we were again technically homeless – living in overcrowded conditions, with no home of our own and no long-term solution in sight.

ENGLISH HOUSING SURVEY (EHS) – OVERCROWDING

Households are said to be overcrowded if they have fewer bedrooms available than the notional number needed according to the bedroom standard definition. **The proportion of households living in overcrowded homes remained stable over the past ten years at 3%.**

In 2023–24, over 800,000 households were overcrowded and over half of those had at least one person with a health condition.

Private renters in overcrowded homes were more likely to have a health condition than those not in overcrowded homes.

Source/reference: English Housing Survey 2023–2024: health and housing – fact sheet

The council eventually placed us in private rented accommodation, which felt like a lifeline – but it wasn't permanent.

We were then offered a housing association property, but it was riddled with mould. Her bedroom and the rest of the house had mould, so I had to keep trying to keep it dry and aired. I ended up repainting all the time, and it was ignored by the council and the housing association despite the health issues it caused. One of my daughters became seriously ill with acute asthma. A medical consultant confirmed it was not a historic condition; the asthma had been triggered by exposure to the mould in that property. Environmental Health and a representative from the council came out to inspect, but despite the Consultant's evidence, they said the home was safe. We were left to remain in a property that was harming my daughter's health.

FROM 27 OCTOBER 2025, SOCIAL LANDLORDS HAVE NEW DUTIES UNDER AWAAB'S LAW TO DEAL WITH EMERGENCY HAZARDS AND SIGNIFICANT DAMP AND MOULD WITHIN FIXED TIMEFRAMES.

After two-year-old Awaab Ishak's death, the coroner concluded he had fallen ill due to prolonged exposure to mould at his parents' housing association home. His family reported the damp and mould numerous times, but their landlord did not take the necessary steps to resolve the problem.

In response, the government announced it would introduce major changes to the law on hazards in social housing, to be known as Awaab's Law.

Eventually, the council took over the housing association property and we were moved out, but not into a permanent home; we were forced back into the private rental market again.

This time, the property was close to my parents, and we finally had six years of relative stability. Those years felt like a gift, even though we still experienced many ups and downs.

In 2017, we had to move again when the landlord of that home passed away. Unfortunately, our next experience of renting privately was not as good. The property was not in good condition; there were cracks in the ceiling and, once again, mould. We stuck with it despite the problems, but in 2020, I received s21 notice that we had to leave. We had two months to find somewhere else to live.

SHELTER BRIEFING (2022): POOR QUALITY CONDITIONS AND DISREPAIR IN THE PRIVATE RENTED SECTOR HOUSING

In 2023, 21% of homes in the PRS were non-decent, with 10% having a Category 1 hazard.

Source: Chapters for English Housing Survey 2023 to 2024: Headline findings on housing quality and energy efficiency

PRS homes, on average, also have the worst energy standards. This means private renters will, on average, have to pay more in heating bills due to poor insulation, inefficient heating systems or lack of double-glazing. Private renters are already paying **higher housing costs than any other tenure**, with average private rents being higher than mortgage repayments or social housing costs.

Private renters who complained to their landlord, letting agent or local council in the last three years were two and a half times (159%) more likely to be handed an eviction notice than those who had not complained.

Source: Shelter analysis of YouGov survey of 1,006 private renting adults in England, 2023

I had no savings, no guarantor, because my parents were the only people who could support with this, and they were already guarantors for my daughter so that she could go to university. This meant that the private rented market was no longer available to me, and there was nowhere for me and my two daughters (my sons had left home) to go. I was facing homelessness again with my two dogs and realised that I had no option but to stay in my car.

I was only on bronze band on the housing register at the time. This meant I was not likely to be successful in bidding on the housing register. I spoke to the local authority housing team, but I had no contact from my housing officer, and I didn't know what to do.

SHELTER LEGAL WEBSITE CONTENT – LOCAL AUTHORITY ALLOCATIONS SCHEMES

All local housing authorities are required to set up and maintain an allocations scheme under Part 6 of the Housing Act 1996.

The procedure by which a local authority allocates accommodation must be clear from the scheme. Most allocation schemes give applicants for an allocation either a certain number of points or place them in a group or band, depending on their circumstances.

Just two weeks before the end of my tenancy, I was once again facing homelessness. There was no housing offered to me by the council – no support, no communication, and no clear understanding of my situation. It was retraumatising. The fear of having nowhere to go reawakened every vulnerability I had carried for years. I no longer felt safe, or stable, or seen.

My wellbeing spiralled. The lack of secure housing broke me down emotionally, mentally, and physically. After so many years of trying to survive, it felt as if the ground had disappeared beneath me once again.

SHELTER CONTENT – LOCAL AUTHORITY HOMELESSNESS DUTY

You can apply for help from a local council if you are homeless. This is called a homeless application. What help you get depends on your circumstances. The council must give some help to anyone who is homeless or at risk of becoming homeless and meets immigration and residence conditions.

You can apply if you are homeless or facing homelessness in the next eight weeks.

The council must arrange emergency housing immediately if it thinks you might be homeless, meet immigration and residence conditions and have a priority need. Priority need includes if you have children, are pregnant, or are vulnerable, for example, because of a disability.

It was at this point that I was finally able to get advice. I heard about Shelter through the local foodbank. I contacted Shelter, and they advised me that the notice I had been given was not correct and therefore I could not be evicted – yet. The landlord issued the notice again, but it was done incorrectly several times. No energy performance certificate was ever issued to me, which legally delayed the move. This situation of facing possession went on for nearly three years.

SHELTER CONTENT – WHAT A S21 NOTICE IS

A landlord can end an assured shorthold tenancy by serving a valid section 21 notice in writing on the tenant. They do not need a reason or ground for possession. The standard minimum notice period for a section 21 notice is two months.

Note: At the time of writing, the Renters' Rights Act has received Royal Assent. The Act introduces significant changes for private renters and local authorities from 2026, including an end to no-fault eviction.

Impact on my wellbeing

Although I worked throughout COVID at a garden centre, I was permanently stressed with the threat of losing my home.

In 2022, my GP recognised that I was no longer able to work. I had been stressed and struggling for so long that I was depressed and unable to function. I had been strong for so long, but now I felt that everything was gone. I had no money, no job, no home. I needed to use foodbanks to survive.

Impact on my children

When I think about the impact on my children, these were the effects:

- No childhood stability
- Not able to take part in school trips and activities
- No financial stability
- Changing environments
- Loss of confidence
- Limited toys and belongings
- Nowhere to have friends to play
- Emotional strain from instability, even though we stayed close, communicated openly and remained a strong team throughout.

SHELTER REPORT – THE IMPACTS OF HOMELESSNESS ON CHILDREN, SEEN THROUGH THE EYES OF TEACHERS AND EDUCATION PROFESSIONALS

Children affected by homelessness often felt an overwhelming sense of displacement, having lost a place that felt like home. This led to a number of practical, emotional and behavioural challenges.

Homelessness could also cause severe emotional trauma leading to emotional stress, anxiety and problematic behaviours. Negative impacts were particularly influential at critical points in a child's educational journey – e.g. when a child was nearing exams, making it difficult for them to catch up irrespective of capability and potential.

Impacts could also be more pronounced in areas of mixed levels of affluence and deprivation, as children experiencing homelessness 'stood out' more to peers and teachers, leading to feelings of alienation and self-consciousness.

Source: Kantar Public (2017): Shelter report, Impacts of homelessness on children – research with teachers

Experiences with statutory services

After leaving my marriage, I felt that the agencies meant to provide safety often became instruments of further control. Social workers interviewed my parents, my two eldest children and me. I was told not to speak negatively about my ex-husband in front of the children. Meetings focused on arranging his contact rather than understanding the abuse the children and I had endured.

He did not play by the rules. Through charm and manipulation, he convinced many of the very professionals I believed would protect us that he was the victim. His calm, persuasive manner contrasted with my visible exhaustion and fear, which worked in his favour. The police, social services and other agencies often accepted his version of events, allowing his control to continue through official channels.

He remained in the marital home and had already moved another woman in. Despite this, I was repeatedly summoned to court and forced to defend myself against false accusations. What should have been a process of protection became another cycle of humiliation and coercion.

I was advised by a solicitor to ask my doctor for antidepressants, saying, 'most women take them' during divorce and domestic abuse. The response was equally disheartening from health services. Instead of being offered trauma-informed counselling or support, medication was the only suggestion, reinforcing the message that my pain was something to suppress rather than understand.

These experiences revealed how easily systems can be manipulated by perpetrators and how urgently professionals across social work, policing and health need to recognise post-separation abuse, listen without bias and respond with compassion, curiosity and trauma-informed care.

No one listened beyond the surface, and no one thought to ask the most human questions:

How are you? How are you feeling? Is he still using controlling behaviour? Is the abuse continuing?

Finances

In 2007/08, I had a sudden financial collapse stemming from the aftermath of the divorce proceedings. I needed to get a loan before I could be legally represented.

I struggled financially as a single person with four children. I did not understand fully about the benefits system as I had never claimed. I only had Child Benefit for a year and was going back and forth for help from my parents.

When I was helped into accommodation by the local authority, I was not able to claim Housing Benefit because I was deemed to have an asset in the family home, despite not being able to live there. All the utilities and the car were in my name, and until the divorce was finalised, I was liable for them and the existing debts we had. I became more and more in debt.

There was no help; the divorce solicitors were focused on the divorce proceedings, and I did not get the wider advice I needed. I became incapable of managing my financial stability because I was overwhelmed.

In 2012, my marriage debt became too much. I contacted a debt line, and they helped me apply for a Voluntary Arrangement. I finally managed to pay this off in 2019. The last £1000 was a joint gift from my adult children and my parents.

Cash flow was difficult. I had Housing Benefit, my salary and Child Tax Credits. If there were any hiccups in my Housing Benefit, I would need to get a loan from QuickQuid with massive interest rates, which made the situation worse. I had always been good at managing money and was able to save, but when I was at my lowest, when I was already struggling, I had to battle systems I didn't understand to try and keep afloat. Someone to advocate for me at this time would have been invaluable because I had lost the ability to do this for myself. When I explained my difficulties to a Housing Benefit adviser, I was advised to go to the foodbank!

My partner never took any financial responsibility for the children (even now). He paid £400 a month contribution for ten months, and that was all. He left the UK after our divorce and ended up working abroad, and there was no way I could pursue him for payment. He came back after a few years, and although he was working, he did not declare this, and no one from the Child Support Agency pursued him.

I went to work in the evenings and had to leave my 14-year-old child with his younger siblings from 6 to 10 pm each evening. My thoughts were food, rent and bills at all costs.

This lack of finances underpinned my homelessness. Every time we moved, we lost our possessions; every time there was damp and mould, we lost our possessions. There was no way that I could save or get credit or prepare for the next period of homelessness. I was stuck and could see no way out. I realise now that for years I was in survival mode, and I am only just coming back to life.

Rebuilding

My salvation finally came when, in 2023, my parents asked me to move in with them, as their carer. Both of them had become unwell and were no longer able to look after each other. If it weren't for this, I would have become homeless. I was lost in the system and was contacted by the council, but this was long after I had first approached them.

Today, my life is totally different. Living with my parents finally gave me the stability that I needed and that I had not had. I have had the opportunity to rebuild myself. I look back at the confident young woman that I was and realise

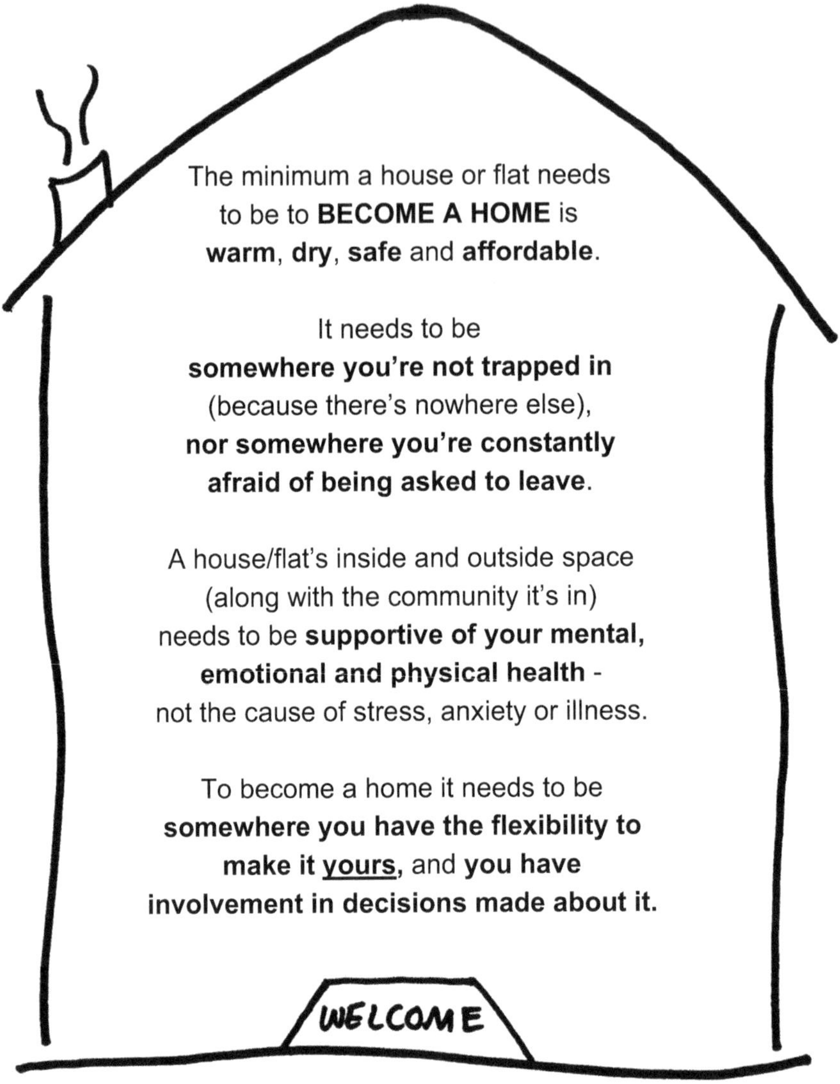

The Poverty Truth Community Commissioners shared their experiences of housing and home, and together explored what makes a house a home. They created this baseline that they would like to become the vision for homes in Bournemouth, Christchurch and Poole, a vision that provides residents with a comfortable and dignified quality of life.

POVERTY TRUTH
BOURNEMOUTH • CHRISTCHURCH • POOLE

FIGURE 8.1 What makes a house a home.

that my relationship took away my life plans. There were good periods, and I was really committed to my marriage and my family life, but the relationship with my husband and the divorce took away all my confidence. I no longer recognised myself; somewhere I had lost my identity. My feelings of insecurity and fear never went away, no matter what I did or where I was. At a couple of points during my journey, I had a complete breakdown where my body and mind could no longer cope. I felt that I had completely shut down.

The foodbank had an important part to play in helping me rebuild my confidence. They were there for me and seemed to know what I needed even when I didn't know myself. They suggested that I could volunteer at a local domestic abuse charity, helping in the café. I thought this was an opportunity for me to give back; it was also the start of me being able to heal. I was part of a team, and we supported each other; the team checked in with me all the time about how I was. I felt safe and accepted there. I regained the ability to talk to people, which I had lost through lack of confidence and trust in everyone and everything. There were classes, such as pattern changing, which I was able to participate in. For the first time since I was 20 years old, I felt that I could be me.

Looking ahead, I can see that I have a role to play in helping people who have been in similar situations to me. I am a trustee of the local domestic abuse charity; I am involved in making changes to the local housing system and strategy. My church continues to be a big part of my life. I can accept what has happened, and nothing was in vain, if I can make a difference for other people. This is my driving force and gives me hope for the future (Figure 8.1).

References

Office for National Statistics, released 11 June 2025, ONS website, article, Homelessness in the UK: 2004 to 2024

Public K (2017) Shelter report - The impacts of homelessness on children, seen through the eyes of teachers and education professionals. Available at www.shelter.org.uk

Shelter analysis of YouGov survey of 1,006 private renting adults in England (2023). Available at www.shelter.org.uk

Shelter Briefing (2022) Poor quality conditions and disrepair in private rented sector housing. Available at www.Shelter.org.uk

Recommended reading/viewing/listening

Useful Websites for information on advice, campaigns and policy relating to housing and homelessness:

- Crisis www.crisis.org.uk
- Government Gateway www.gov.uk
- Homeless Link www.homeless.org.uk
- Shelter www.shelter.org.uk

Films

1. *I, Daniel Blake* (2016) – Directed by Ken Loach
   This film follows the story of Daniel Blake, a man struggling to navigate the UK's social welfare system. The film poignantly addresses issues like housing insecurity, poverty and the challenges of being a single woman and mother in such a system.
2. *Someone's Daughter, Someone's Son* (2022) – directed by Lorna Tucker
   Now a successful filmmaker, Lorna was once a teenage runaway sleeping rough on the streets of London. For this frank, forceful and inspiring documentary, she returns to her former haunts and speaks to current and former homeless people about why, twenty-five years later, record numbers of people are still reduced to living on Britain's streets.
3. *A Street Cat Named Bob* (2016) – Directed by Roger Spottiswoode
   A British biographical drama film that tells the heartwarming true story of James Bowen, a recovering drug addict, and his bond with a stray ginger cat named Bob.
4. *Cathy Come Home* (1966) – Directed by Ken Loach
   The catalyst for political and social change, this film remains relevant today with its themes of poverty, homelessness and social injustice.
5. *Sorry We Missed You* (2019) – Directed by Ken Loach
   Another film by Loach, exploring the gig economy and its devastating impact on families. It follows Ricky, a delivery driver, and his wife Abby, a home care worker, reflecting the challenges women face in low-wage, insecure work and the housing issues tied to this.

Podcasts

1. 'Housing Britain' – *BBC Radio 4*
   Rocketing prices and rents, a new homes shortage and a homelessness crisis. Vicky Spratt travels across Britain, asking what went wrong with our housing and what can we do to fix it.
2. 'Homelessness Matters'
   This podcast by Emmaus has people who have experienced homelessness sharing their stories, as well as exploring the causes of homelessness beyond individual situations.
3. 'Going beyond' Homeless Link's practice podcast for people working in the homelessness (and related) sectors. Includes episodes on barriers homeless people face in accessing essential services such as local authority housing and social care.
4. 'The Hidden Homeless' – BBC documentary podcast highlighting the crisis of homelessness for families in Britain.
5. *Invisible Women: Exposing Data Bias in a World Designed for Men* by Caroline Criado Perez

This podcast, based on the book *Invisible Women*, discusses the gender data gap and the ways in which women are often marginalised in policy and planning, leaving women more vulnerable to issues like overcrowding, poor housing conditions and domestic violence.

6 *'The Housing Podcast'*
Hosted by experts in social housing and the housing crisis, it explores the key issues in housing today. It touches on issues like homelessness, affordable housing, and the gendered impacts of housing policy.

Books

1 *Our Country in Crisis: Britain's Housing Emergency and How We Rebuild* by Kwajo Tweneboa. This is a call to action to resolve the housing emergency.
2 *No Fixed Abode: Life and Death Among the UK's Forgotten Homeless* by Maeve McClenaghan
Maeve McClenaghan has spent years investigating the crisis on Britain's streets. These are only some of the stories of struggle, loss, survival and courage she has heard. *No Fixed Abode* will change how you think about homelessness and show you that this crisis is not impossible to solve.
3 *The Gendered Society* by Michael Kimmel
While this book is broader in scope, it addresses how different social policies – including those related to housing – affect men and women differently.
4 *The Routledge Handbook of Homelessness*, edited by Joanne Bretherton and Nicholas Pleace
With contributors from around the world and editors from the Centre of Housing Policy at the University of York, this handbook provides a groundbreaking and authoritative guide to theory, method and the primary interdisciplinary debates of today on homelessness.
5 *The Estate: My Life Working on the Front Line of Britain's Housing Crisis* by Charmain Bynoe
As a Council Housing Officer, Charmain shows how, with humanity and consideration for others, we can make things better in ways that don't have to cost a fortune but can deliver results that are truly priceless.

Documentaries and news

1 *Evicted: The Hidden Homeless (BAFTA-winning documentary) – Real Stories*
The story of three families who have endured the emotional trauma of being evicted.
2 *Prince William: We Can End Homelessness – ITVX*
Documentary about the launch of Homewards, his five-year programme to show it is possible to end homelessness, working with six locations across the UK.

9

POVERTY AND HOUSING

Dominic Watters and Julia Armstrong

Extreme insecurity

I moved onto the council estate with my daughter when she was 18 months old; we had to bid for a property and then got offered this flat, where I still currently live. This was after I was in court to get full custody of my daughter as a single dad. During that time, I was just learning how to be a dad, as a young man. We got offered our place to call home, which was not in a liveable condition, including an unusable kitchen and asbestos in the flat.

I remember calling the repair company that worked on behalf of the council to get my floor fixed. I had been placed in a council property with a young child that was not fit for purpose, but I felt like I should be grateful for what I was given, as the support to make the place liveable wasn't forthcoming, and I was laughed at and mocked by services. It's a different power dynamic and a lack of care given to a single parent who is trying to help their small, little family flourish.

I feel that it was my unquenchable drive to make my situation better for my daughter that led me to start using my platform to make changes for me in my flat, but also for other residents in the blocks. It has taken me 15 years to get the flat to the current liveable standard with little to no support from the council. I came from an unheard, invisible place, but was able to use my platform to get to a position where my voice started carrying a certain amount of weight to affect change. In the beginning, I had to ask for support from friends and family, and it took a long time to make the place a physically safe environment for my child.

It's a different level of resilience you have to show; the need to overcome every little step that people take for granted. You have to fight for every little

DOI: 10.4324/9781003638476-10

thing just to be in a safe space where your daughter can run around on the floor in the front room. Other people might have given up on certain aspirations and the idea of being able to have a life outside the estate. The estate, however, becomes your community, and outside of that bubble, you feel like you don't fit in, are not accepted, and are not understood.

Living in a council property means you have to ask permission for everything; the repairs I had managed to do, I was told off for during an inspection, even though I had made the place better and more liveable. Living in a council property also means that you live with extreme insecurity. Years after moving into my property, I wanted to be able to start studying for a career in social work. However, I had to move from Job Seekers Allowance (JSA) to Universal Credit (UC) to be able to start the course. There was a lack of information and support in relation to the Housing Benefit element, and UC was a brand-new system then (roughly 2018–2019). So, 6 months into my master's course to become a social worker, while on placement in the local authority, I came home to find a Notice to Seek Possession (NSP) stuck to my front door.

> **A Notice to Seek Possession** (NSP) applies to all social housing tenants, including those renting from local councils. An NSP informs social tenants that their landlord intends to repossess the property due to breach of tenancy or other legal grounds.
>
> (UK Government, 2025b)

This highlights the depths of extreme insecurity; I was desperately trying to create a career for myself to bring about change, to empower, to be 'deserving' and have a place in the world, and I came home to an NSP of my property due to rent arrears I didn't know I had, due to the change in benefit process that they didn't communicate to me.

There is also extreme insecurity in being able to provide food for my child, as the local shop doesn't stock fresh food and is expensive. The public transport is terrible, so you can't access a larger, cheaper shop with fresh, healthier food; it's like a food desert on the estate, as our place is so neglected. I would be feeding my daughter with not enough food to feed myself. My gas and electric would be on emergency due to a pay-as-you-go meter, and if it went off in the middle of the night, the food in the freezer would go bad. We would turn our boiler off to save money, and it would cost £2 just to turn it back on again. I have since lobbied to get new, condensed boilers for everyone in the block; our bathrooms weren't designed to have showers. The front doors were never fire safe, and we have only had proper fire doors since Grenfell. We didn't have recycle bins; we didn't even have bins outside. There was no fence, so people would just park on the little bit of grass we have.

The Grenfell Tower fire occurred on June 14, 2017, in London, killing 72 people. It was fuelled by flammable cladding on the building's exterior. The tragedy exposed severe safety failures, regulatory negligence, and social inequality, prompting public outrage and an ongoing inquiry, which has now concluded, into accountability and housing safety reforms.

(Grenfell Tower Inquiry, 2025)

You are constantly in fight/ battle mode, and this constant trauma impacts how you function in society. When I was on the social work course, I would leave home, get on a coach to a social work session at the university, and you would be having in-depth conversations about anti-discriminatory practice (Thompson, 2020) and when you're actually living and going through these things that people are talking about from a place of comfort, it feels like there is no way to express your trauma; or your trauma kind of freezes you. I didn't really know how to interact with others because of how it would be viewed.

Fifteen years ago, the idea of being a single dad wasn't even an established concept to consider. There was no acknowledgement, but that was something I had to overcome, too. On so many levels, there were different elements of struggle I had to overcome. It also totally changes the dynamic from being a single male to a single dad. My daughter was my first priority, and you can feel like you're failing if you're not able to, for example, provide a safe floor/shelter, when you have so little resources and so many obstacles. Being a single parent, I kind of found a superhero power inside myself. Where we have got to now is amazing; my daughter is now 19.

The housing inspector doesn't come for years on end, and then they just turn up. We had some plants in my hallway which I put out, and an elderly retired neighbour would look after them. It is the only green thing we have in our control in the block. The inspector said it was a fire risk, so we had to remove it, so now the plants are no longer there, and my elderly neighbour can't look after it. They control everything [council housing inspectors], even the way they talk to you in your own home brings it all back, that feeling of insecurity. There's a real lack of acknowledgement, there is a total power imbalance. They have all the power, and we don't have that. I still don't feel secure in my current place, but I am currently trying to buy it. Once I have bought my property, I will be drinking champagne to celebrate; it will be different then as they can't just come in.

I feel like they [society] don't want the poor to own anything; we're not even meant to own our own experiences; they have to be translated through an academic who is thought to be able to articulate it better. Being poor isn't a protected characteristic under the Equality Act 2010, but I think it should be. It just shows the lack of recourse we have due to the oppression we experience.

The Equality Act 2010 is a law that protects people from discrimination, harassment, and victimisation based on protected characteristics. The protected characteristics are age, disability, gender reassignment, marriage and civil partnership, pregnancy and maternity, race, religion or belief, sex, and sexual orientation. (Equality and Human Rights Commission, 2021; UK Government, 2025)

In 2022, a United Nations report identified 'povertyism' as a negative stereotyping against the poor, realising that socioeconomic rights depend on people in poverty being protected from discrimination. The UN report concludes that anti-discriminatory frameworks should effectively prohibit direct or indirect discrimination on the grounds of socioeconomic disadvantage. (De Schutter, 2022)

It could be argued that poverty should be a legally recognised form of disadvantage that deserves protection, and the current legal framework fails to address that, leaving people who are living in poverty without a way to challenge systems, which in itself is a form of oppression.

Sometimes it has been difficult, living in times of extreme insecurity, not knowing if I have somewhere for me and my daughter to live, something to eat, and I would be asked to write about being a single parent coming from a council estate and talk about my lived experience. But this isn't my lived experience, this is my living experience, I am still living it.

LIVING EXPERIENCE

In social work practice, recognising living experience encourages practitioners to engage with people as active agents in their current realities, fostering responsive, real-time support rather than relying solely on retrospective narratives. While lived experience remains valuable for understanding a person's history and context, focusing on living experience allows social workers to better align interventions with people's evolving needs, emotions, and choices in the present.

(Ali et al., 2024)

In order to describe your experiences, to be understood, to be heard, you need to make yourself vulnerable to address the inequality to people who don't understand your living experience. You have to expose yourself to highlight the oppression and discrimination. These things should be addressed, as it is the right thing to do, without you having to tell your story, but people who are able to make a difference don't, as they don't recognise it due to their privilege. It's inviting you to speak somewhere, but not expecting that you need to be paid. When I have finished talking about the hard things about my life, I then have to go back to that, but they go home to their comfort. Safe shelter should be a basic human right, but because we live in a capitalistic world, it's not like that. We talk about 'service users' or 'people who are known to services,' but these people are my neighbours. I know what they are going through. Reflecting back, it makes me realise a bit more the intensity of the disadvantage and the hardships we went through, but also how I have managed to flourish.

Visual deprivation

Visual Deprivation signifies poverty; it's what poverty looks like. My four blocks look like poverty. There has, however, been a polarisation of urban environments in series and films. My blocks are not as high as you might imagine from films or stereotypes, but they don't differ too much from that. My estate's quite big, and there are a lot of houses, but I go to different estates as part of the research I do, and not all estates look the same; some are less visibly deprived than others. There are lots of stereotypes of estates, but I would like people to remember that we are just families trying to get by, and it is our home. People are often facing challenges that disproportionately affect people in deprivation than people in affluent areas.

Around four years ago, the local MP and her team were canvassing the area, and I could see her and her team from my window. We saw them walk towards our blocks, and they looked around, stayed still for a minute, talked, and then they just turned back; I guess it is for us to try and pull out and highlight what that means. It could have been for a variety of reasons, but for me, as a single dad and my daughter who were struggling to get the help we needed, for them to not be interested in communicating with us, hearing our voice, or even considering our vote, has stuck with me ever since. The MPs say they plan on helping the area, and on many levels, this area signifies neglect, so it makes you question the purpose of their job as MPs. It speaks to the broader issues around who votes and who doesn't. But when the person who represents you isn't willing to talk to you, it doesn't feel great. But they have never visited our blocks, the MP's as representatives, but also the local authority, local governments, neglect our area, and they aren't even interested in hearing our views.

In a way, this has made me keep on trying to speak up, but I know my neighbours and my community; there is a lack of value given to their voices, and it crushes their aspirations. Even when I have done so much to create a career from a place of poverty, to address my rent arrears, the uncertainty around housing, to provide for me and my daughter, I have not been able to practice social work in my local authority, as they said it was a conflict of interest with me speaking out about poverty publicly. They felt I was talking specifically against them rather than about systemic oppression and discrimination. So now I train teams all across the country, including social work teams and managers, but I can't work for a local authority and complete my Assessed and Supported Year in Employment (ASYE) due to speaking out. I would say that I am upholding social worker values in speaking out.

SOCIAL WORK CODE OF ETHICS

The British Association of Social Work (BASW) outlines in the code of ethics that social work values are about upholding human rights (2.1), social justice (2.2), and having professional integrity (2.3). This includes challenging oppression and unjust policies and practices as well as upholding and promoting human dignity and well-being, and respecting people's right to self-determination.

(BASW, 2021)

To challenge our lack of open space, me and my daughter tried to redesign the balcony during COVID to have some plants and some vegetables growing. The block is all concrete and raw brick, and no greenery. We have no real green space to use, but the grass patch outside now has a fence up, and people use it to meet and talk. It's hard to get off the estate due to buses and local transport. There are people who live in an affluent area just a mile and a half away, but they don't know we exist, and we are aware they exist. We used to have a pub in the estate where people would meet, socialise, play games in the garden, and spend time in the garden, as they had a big garden space, but that has since been knocked down. We don't have anywhere in the community now to gather; it ripped the heart out of the community. There are people trying to do good things for people, like community fridges, but we would have to try and get to them; they never come to us here on the estate.

Urban green spaces are vital for community well-being, particularly in low-income areas, where access to nature can significantly improve mental and physical health. Urban green spaces help address environmental inequalities by reducing air pollution, lowering urban heat, and providing safe, free spaces for recreation and social connection. In communities that live on estates, green spaces can also promote social cohesion, support youth engagement, and offer relief from the stresses of poverty, while contributing to long-term neighbourhood stability and resilience.

(Bao et al., 2023; De Haas et al., 2021; Mell and Whitten, 2021)

Me and my experiences are not even on the map

There's a connecting thread, and that is often overlooked, at least in my story. But when I say overlooked, I mean in broader society around being a single dad. I don't know how it is for other single parents, but I would passionately say that single dads aren't recognised. There seems to be an assumption that single dads somehow get treated better; however, I would strongly, and from my experience, say that this is wrong.

Even with court cases, to have full custody of your child, it took four years, rather than in mirroring cases where the roles are reversed. I think the legal system is more directed against the dad. When I contacted child maintenance, they would ask me how I wanted to pay, as they could tell it was a man on the phone. It is hard when you're financially insecure and struggling, and you have no support. When you reach out for some support or justice, you're met with a position that puts you at odds.

The trauma of living in poverty is a position of being unseen and unrecognised, and it makes you doubt yourself. It makes you question what you have done wrong to be here and question why no one is listening to you. It makes you wonder why these disadvantages are not being recognised by broader society. It's an extra level of discrimination, of marginalisation and inequality.

Carrying the pain of poverty

Carrying the pain of poverty is the daily traumas of living in poverty that are everywhere you look; not being able to provide the necessities for your child in terms of safe housing, amenities, healthy food, etc. When you are brave enough to try to access some help, you are often treated with such disregard. For people who have experienced this trauma, it is covered in shame, stigma, and snobbery.

I was trying to elevate myself in terms of education, and I would be sitting in a social work classroom, and people were speaking about anti-discriminatory approaches and anti-oppressive practices (Tedam, 2020; Thompson, 2020), but it felt like these were not the approaches I was met with when I needed support. These approaches are meant to support you, but they left me feeling like I was not even meant to be there.

Anti-discriminatory practice involves actively challenging inequality and promoting equity by recognising and addressing discrimination based on race, gender, disability, age, sexuality, or other characteristics. It tries to ensure that all individuals are treated with dignity, respect, and equal access to services (Thompson, 2020).

Anti-oppressive practice focuses on challenging power imbalances and structural inequalities that marginalise individuals or groups. It aims to empower people by promoting social justice, inclusion, and equal participation in decision-making (Tedam, 2020).

It can sometimes feel like there is a juxtaposition to the values, principles, and ethics of social work when in practice, particularly when based in local authority social work, due to the statutory duties sitting in systemically oppressive processes. It can feel like the focus is on the service and not the people who are accessing the service for support.

Activity

Begin to reflect on how Dominic's book, 'Social Distance in Social Work: Covid Capsule One' (Watter, 2021), can be analysed as an example of the obstacles faced in anti-discriminatory practice (BASW PCF 3)

- Who is included in the book?
- Is the concept of home explored in the front cover, or anywhere else?
- How is a deeper understanding of poverty demonstrated?

I felt like I was a person sitting in that classroom, trying to create a career, learn a profession, and become a social worker, and these topics that are championed can be at odds with what you're actually going through and what you're going home to. It's intersectional (Crenshaw, 1989) and multidimensional, and it leaves you feeling hopeless and like giving up on the whole system.

My voice has been a vehicle for change, as painful as it is, and despite the many obstacles I have faced, I have spoken up about my experiences, used my voice, and raised awareness to build understanding, even if it is on a micro level. This has progressed to working with different local authorities running training on poverty, and it feels like there is a legacy that lives on. When people think about how they can harness living experience to influence policy and practice, especially around poverty, housing, and food, they talk to me. That is a real honour; that position I hold is dear to my heart because I know I am speaking directly about people who live next to me. It has taken a long time and a lot of commitment; I started talking to one or two people, and I now talk to hundreds and thousands of people, and I have kept going when others may have given up.

I had never heard of the term imposter syndrome (Clance and Imes, 1978), but I was definitely experiencing it on a trauma-based level when in social work classrooms. The impact it has on your voice when you actually come from a place of living in pain is a different dynamic, but struggling through is what has given my voice that authenticity and the weight it carries. I certainly feel imposter syndrome when I attend events, and they won't let me in. Or when I am allowed in, they are handing out packets of biscuits, and I am aware that at one time, that was the only thing I had to feed my daughter. It was hard standing there surrounded by people who are mobilising the experiences that we've actually gone through; they have so-called authority in the space of food poverty, then there's me, not even being allowed into the room.

I think that the authentic voices can actually be the agents of change. Authentic voices should at least impact on practice and policy, from living experience. However, sometimes your voice can be seen as not fitting the agenda, or you don't present in a way that fits the space. Carrying the pain of poverty is where every time you speak, you're speaking from a place of persecution and oppression. I have spoken up for where I live, but there might be some people where I live that don't even want people to know they live there due to shame, maybe because of the snobbery they would experience from family or wider society; that can shut down voices. Also, some people don't know any different from where they live, so they have an acceptance of this is where they are, so why would they try to challenge it? They internalise their experiences and just accept them, and wouldn't fight or strive for better or challenge the policy of systemic issues, as it is an acceptance of the status quo. If it were just me and I didn't have my daughter, I probably would have given up. However, because of having my daughter, I knew it wasn't right, even if I didn't have the words, so that was the fuel that kept me going.

This is controversial, but there are people in positions of influence or power who live in some level of comfort in society and/or in their profession, where they actually get a level of pleasure hearing about the suffering of others or people who live in a lower socioeconomic status, as it makes them feel better about themselves. It is a concept called 'poverty porn' (Beresford, 2016; Jensen, 2014; Mooney, 2011).

'Poverty Porn' was initially researched as a concept in relation to media content that exploited people's struggles to evoke sympathy or guilt. This was often for fundraising or to increase views on media rather than to drive meaningful change. This approach reinforces stereotypes, removes people's dignity, and does not focus on ethics but on emotional impact for capitalist gain. It could be argued that in society, we have moved away from living in communities and society has become more focused on looking out for themselves as individuals. 'Poverty Porn' can be used to reinforce the rhetoric that people living in poverty are 'scroungers' and do not deserve support, which is also reinforced by the British media. It becomes a battle between the 'deserving and undeserving' rather than addressing systemic oppression and discrimination.

(Beresford, 2016; Jensen, 2014; Mooney, 2011)

I write this closing comment with what I have shared in mind. All I can ask is that what I have overcome somehow helps you to find your voice. Harness the pain of your experiences to interrogate and grapple with the power imbalances that are purposefully designed to destroy our hopes on a daily basis. The poor are prone to exploitation: the University of Kent has prospered from appropriating my experiences, and elites have tried to capture my concept of 'living experience' (Watter, 2021). I was let go during my ASYE due to speaking up for the unheard. I was included only as a tokenistic display of alignment with poverty by leading organisations, and after it all, I was thrown back to the job centre. But my little estate block, my home, has created a voice for my community. Actually, invisible communities just like mine exist across the country. I can only pray that my words inspire some change.

REFLECTIVE ACTIVITIES

Mapping home and housing insecurity

Objective

To explore personal and societal understandings of home and reflect on the emotional, social, and structural impacts of housing insecurity.

Instructions

1 Draw or Map Your Concept of 'Home':

- On a blank sheet of paper, draw or create a mind map of what 'home' means to you.
- Include physical aspects (e.g., shelter, bed), emotional aspects (e.g., safety, belonging), and relational elements (e.g., family, solitude).

2 Reflective Prompts (Write 5–10 minutes for each):

- What does home feel like to you? How do you know when you are home?
- How might these feelings or meanings be disrupted or denied by housing insecurity?
- Can someone experience 'home' without stable housing? Why or why not?

3 Perspective Shift (Empathy Exercise):

- Having read Dominic's story and experiences of housing insecurity and poverty, reflect: How does their concept of home compare to yours? What structural or societal barriers shape their experience?

4 Group Discussion (if in a group setting):

- Share insights and consider:
- How do dominant narratives about housing shape our assumptions in practice?
- What role should social workers play in advocating for housing as a human right?

Outcome

This activity helps deepen awareness of how housing and home are socially and emotionally constructed, and challenges social workers to consider both personal bias and systemic responsibilities when addressing housing insecurity in practice.

What can you do?

List of suggested actions to take

1 Donate to your local foodbank or go along and see if they need volunteers.

2 Write to your MP about what's happening in your local area.
3 Share your experiences or speak to people about their experiences. Be empathic and curious about the people around you.

Further reading, viewing, and listening

- *Four Pillars of Food Insecurity* – **House of Commons launch (2025)**
- 'Dominic Watters gave one of the most powerful presentations seen in Oxford in its near 90-year history.' – *Farmers Weekly* (2025)
- Estate2 Plate (Dominic Watters) – GoFundMe
- A council estate single dad helps start a paradigm shift in policy development – **Recipe for Health: a plan to fix our broken food system (2024)**
- 'I'm a single Dad' – House of Lords
- 'I was silenced by snobbery' – *New Statesman*
- 'It feels like an attack on the poor' – *BBC Newsnight*
- Impact of food price rises for the poor – *ITV News w/* Chris Choi
- *Hackney Community Food Hub & me* – Associated Press w/ Sylvia Hui
- 'Our aspirations are being dimmed daily' – *BBC Radio 4* live interview
- Cost of Living Crisis – Sky News w/ Kay Burley
- Westminster Reimagined Podcast – Full Interview: Armando Iannucci and the New Statesman
- 'To me, "lived experience" suggests that we are now heard.' – Oxford University Press
- My first book where I coined the concept of 'living experience' – *Social Distance in Social Work: COVID Capsule One*
- 'This book is a mark of respect to everyday people' – Book review: *Social Work in Action*, Routledge Journal
- 'Dominic notes it is not the "lived" but the actual everyday "living experience" of so many of those involved in social work' – *Book review: British Journal of Social Work*, Oxford University Press
- *Research Briefing*, Food Poverty: Households, food banks and free school meals – House of Commons Library (2025)
  The Food Foundation

References

Ali, N., Flestead, K., Mohamed, O., McIvor, A., Wilkes, J., and Watters, D. (2024). Why is it important to ensure the voice and influence of people with lived experience in social work research and practice? *British Journal of Social Work*, 54 (4), 1391–1401.

Bao, Z., Bai, Y., and Geng, T. (2023). Examining spatial inequalities in public green space accessibility: A focus on disadvantaged groups in England. *Sustainability*. (15), 1–22

BASW. (2021). *BASW code of ethics for social work*. Available from: https://basw.co.uk/policy-and-practice/resources/basw.code-ethics-social-work (Accessed 19 July 2025)

Beresford, P. (2016). Presenting welfare reform: poverty porn, telling sad stories or achieving change? *Disability & Society*, 31 (3), 421–425.

Clance, P. and Imes, S. (1978). The imposter phenomenon in high achieving women: Dynamics and therapeutic intervention. *Psychotherapy Theory: Research and Practice*, 15 (30), 1–8.

Crenshaw, K. (1989). Demarginalizing the intersection of race and sex: A black feminist critique of antidiscrimination doctrine, feminist theory, and antiracist politics. Available from: https://scholarship.law.columbia.edu/faculty_scholarship/3007/ (Accessed 19 July 2025)

De Haas, W., Hassink, J., and Stuiver, M. (2021). The role of urban green space in promoting inclusion: Experiences from the Netherlands. *Frontiers in Environmental Science*, (9), 1–11.

De Schutter, O. (2022). Report of the Special Rapporteur on extreme poverty and human rights. Available from: https://docs.un.org/en/a/77/157 (Accessed 18 June 2025)

Equality and Human Rights Commission (2021). Protected characteristics. Available from: https://www.equalityhumanrights.com/equality/equality-act-2010/protected-characteristics (Accessed 18 June 2025)

Grenfell Tower Inquiry (2025). Grenfell Tower Inquiry. Available from: https://webarchive.nationalarchives.gov.uk/ukgwa/20250319155650/https://www.grenfelltowerinquiry.org.uk/ (Accessed 18 June 2025)

Jensen, T. (2014). Welfare commonsense, poverty porn and doxosophy. *Sociological Research Online*, 19 (3), 1–7.

Mell, I., and Whitten, M. (2021). Access to nature in a post Covid-19 world: Opportunities for green infrastructure financing, distribution and equitability in urban planning. *International Journal of Environmental Research and Public Health*, (18), 1–16.

Mooney, G. (2011). Stigmatising poverty? The 'Broken Society' and reflections on anti-welfarism in the UK today. *Oxfam GB*. Available from: https://policy-practice.oxfam.org/resources/stigmatising-poverty-the-broken-society-and-reflections-on-anti-welfarism-in-th-146557/ (Accessed 19 July 2025)

Tedam, P. (2020). *Anti-Oppressive Practice in Social Work*. London: SAGE

Thompson, N. (2020). *Anti-Discriminatory Practice*. 7th ed. London: Red Global Press.

UK Government (2025). Types of discrimination ('protected characteristics'). Available from: https://www.gov.uk/discrimination-your-rights (Accessed 18 June 2025)

UK Government (2025b). Guidance. Understanding the possession action process: A guide for social rented tenants in England. Available from: https://www.gov.uk/government/publications/understanding-the-possession-action-process-guidance-for-landlords-and-tenants/understanding-the-possession-action-process-a-guide-for-social-rented-tenants-in-england-and-wales (Accessed 18 June 2025)

Watter, D. (2021). *Social Distance in Social Work: Covid Capsule One*. Kent: Social Distance Writers

10

POVERTY AND MENTAL HEALTH

Sarah and Christopher Ademuwagun

My name is Sarah. I'm 45 years old. I live in a city in the north of England, in a quiet, slightly crumbling house that I rarely leave, except for essentials or the rare walk to nowhere in particular. I'm here to tell you my truth. What it's really like to live with autism, PTSD, complex trauma, and poverty in today's Britain. I'm not here to tug at your heartstrings. I'm not interested in performing some sad little monologue for sympathy. What I want, what I need, is for you to listen with your whole self. To not just hear my words, but to *feel* them. To sit in my shoes, just for a little while, and understand the world as I experience it.

You might imagine poverty as a lack of money. A hole in your bank account. But for me, poverty is a heavy, ever-present fog that clings to everything. It's not just economic. It's emotional. It's physical. It shapes your posture, your breathing, your hope. Poverty is fear, plain and simple. And the worst part? It's silent. It's hidden. It thrives behind closed doors. You could pass me in the street and never know. People don't see poverty when they look at me. They see someone articulate. Someone who can "pass" in middle-class circles. I speak well. I write well. I was taught grammar before I was taught how to ask for help. But speaking doesn't mean coping. It means surviving. It means performing normality well enough to be denied the help I desperately need.

I grew up clever, quiet, and hurting. My first memory of self-harm is from when I was six. No one noticed. Or if they did, they never said. Maybe they thought I'd grow out of it. I didn't. The pain became part of me. Not because I liked it, but because it made the noise in my head quieter. School was a battlefield. I was the weirdo. The one who didn't understand sarcasm. Who cried too easily. Who didn't know how to make eye contact. I learned early on that

DOI: 10.4324/9781003638476-11

being good at schoolwork didn't protect you from cruelty. If anything, it painted a bigger target on your back. I spent lunchtimes hiding in the library. Not reading, just hiding. I'd crouch in the gaps between shelves, counting the minutes until the bell. Praying not to be seen. Because being seen meant being mocked. Being pushed. Being laughed at. Sometimes being hurt.

AUTISM AND SELF-HARM

Autistic people in the UK face alarmingly high rates of mental health challenges, not because of autism itself, but due to the relentless pressure to navigate a neurotypical world without appropriate support (Price, 2022; Beardon and Worton, 2011). Approximately 70% of autistic individuals experience co-occurring mental health conditions such as anxiety and depression, while over 66% have considered suicide. Autistic adults are up to nine times more likely to die by suicide than the general population (Cassidy et al., 2014; Mind, 2020). These figures are not inevitable; rather, they reflect systemic failures—from inaccessible health and education services to rigid and exclusionary employment structures (National Autistic Society, n.d.).

Only 16% of autistic adults in the UK are in full-time employment, a statistic largely attributed to workplaces that fail to accommodate neurodivergent needs (National Autistic Society, n.d.). Self-harm is also prevalent among autistic individuals, but is frequently misunderstood or dismissed. It is often misinterpreted as challenging behaviour, rather than recognised as a distress signal or a coping mechanism in response to overwhelming sensory or emotional stimuli (Mind, 2020).

Despite clear and significant levels of need, 80% of autistic adults report struggling to access appropriate mental health support (Mind, 2020). This lack of access is frequently due to professionals' limited understanding of autism, as well as the inaccessibility of mainstream services. These statistics highlight the urgent need for mental health and social care services, as well as wider society, to become genuinely inclusive, affirming the rights, voices, and lived experiences of autistic people.

I thought university would be different. I had this idea, this dream, that I'd finally find my people there. People who were weird like me. People who thought deeply, felt too much, struggled to belong. But I arrived, and the loneliness hit like a punch to the stomach. Everyone else seemed to float through it so easily, pubs, house parties, loud communal kitchens. I lasted three months before I made my first serious suicide attempt. There was no drama. No note. Just despair. Utter, hollow despair. A desire to stop existing without fanfare. To disappear so quietly that no one would have to bother missing me. Physically, I recovered. Emotionally, I didn't. No one asked why. No one offered long-term help. I was expected to get on with it. So, I did. Because that's what women like me do. We get on with it. We survive. Even when surviving feels like dragging yourself through barbed wire with your teeth.

Eventually, I carved out something resembling a life. I got a degree. I got a job, several, in fact. The last one was the best: project manager in the NHS. I was earning more than I'd ever imagined. I remember the first time I checked my payslip and cried, not out of fear, but out of sheer relief. I thought maybe I've made it. Maybe this is what normal feels like. But it wasn't normal. It was borrowed time. Because my stability was dependent on external scaffolding, mental health services, prescription refills, a GP who knew my history and believed me. When I moved to another area, all of that disappeared. My referral to mental health services got "lost." I called. I emailed. I walked to the clinic in person. They apologised. They'd get back to me. They never did. Three and a half years later, I'm still waiting.

That's when the cracks became canyons. I stopped leaving the house. I stopped answering calls. I lived on cereal and rice. I let my prescription lapse. I tried, again, to end it all. Not because I wanted to die, but because I didn't know how to live like that anymore. The system that was supposed to catch me didn't just fail; it wasn't even looking. I turned up at A&E, shaking and exhausted, clutching a plastic bag with a few belongings. I hadn't eaten in two days. I hadn't slept in four. I was wearing pyjamas and no shoes. I waited six hours to be seen. When I was, the nurse told me I seemed "too aware" to be admitted. "You've got insight," she said. "That's a good sign." No, it isn't. Insight is not protection. It's a cruel joke. I'm fully aware of how ill I am. And fully aware that no one's going to help.

They gave me a leaflet. Told me to go home. "Try to get some rest, Sarah." I remember walking out into the freezing air, feeling like I'd died already. I sat on my kitchen floor and stared at the wall. Not crying. Not screaming. Just… numb. That's the kind of story you never see in textbooks. You see graphs. Budgets. Statistics. But you don't see a woman with PTSD walking home from the hospital in January because there's nowhere else to go. After I lost my job with the NHS, everything unravelled. It didn't just knock the wind out of me; it collapsed the whole structure I'd so carefully, so desperately built. I went from being someone respected, salaried, and seen, to someone pitied, dismissed, and ignored. That fall was brutal. It wasn't just the money, although losing that income was devastating. It was the loss of identity. I wasn't "Sarah, the project manager" anymore. I was "Sarah, the claimant." "Sarah, the one who used to be something."

MENTAL HEALTH AND EMPLOYMENT

People living with mental health conditions in the UK continue to face significant disadvantage in the workplace. Fewer than half are in any form of employment, and just 30% of people with more severe mental health problems are in paid work (Mental Health Foundation, 2022). Many find themselves in precarious, low-paid, or part-time roles that offer little security or flexibility, often the only viable options when attempting to manage fluctuating health conditions (Mind, 2021).

The risk of poverty is disproportionately high: individuals with mental health difficulties are three times more likely to be in problem debt and twice as likely to experience housing insecurity compared to the general population (Mental Health Foundation, 2022). Mental ill-health remains the leading cause of sickness absence in the UK, with more than 17 million working days lost in 2022 alone (NHS England, 2023). Despite this, support for staying in or returning to work is often limited, fragmented, and poorly integrated with wider health and social care systems (Mind, 2021).

This is not merely an employment issue; it is fundamentally a matter of social justice. With reasonable adjustments and inclusive workplace policies, meaningful and sustainable employment can be accessible to many. However, systems and benefits frameworks frequently penalise people for their needs, rather than accommodating them in ways that promote recovery, stability, and dignity (Mind, 2021; Mental Health Foundation, 2022).

Eventually, I found part-time work as a cleaner at a centre for autistic adults. It's a strange sort of sanctuary. I clean in silence. No one expects me to talk. No one crowds me. I put my headphones in and scrub floors, toilets, and walls. And in those hours, I'm okay. I can breathe. I'm not judged. I'm not expected to explain myself or prove anything. I'm allowed to just exist. But two hours a day, four days a week, on minimum wage, doesn't come close to covering the cost of living alone in a city like mine. My rent is £750 a month. My wages barely scratch that. I survive, just about, on Personal Independence Payment (PIP). But it's always temporary. Always uncertain. Every envelope through the letterbox feels like a threat. Every brown letter carries the weight of collapse. And this week? I got the one I dread most. The PIP reassessment.

Reapplying for PIP is like being forced to relive your worst memories in bureaucratic bullet points. They want you to measure your pain. Score your trauma. Quantify your exhaustion. And God help you if you phrase something slightly wrong. Because that one sentence might be used to say, "You seem fine." That's what they always say. "You seem fine." I had an assessor once ask me why I didn't bring a support worker. I told her I didn't have one. She raised an eyebrow and scribbled something down. That's when I learned: it's a trap. If you have support, you're seen as less independent. If you don't, you're seen as coping. There's no winning. Just layers of judgement from people who don't know you, deciding your fate based on a one-hour meeting and a checklist that doesn't account for nuance.

MENTAL HEALTH AND ACCESS TO WELFARE PAYMENTS

Accessing welfare support such as Personal Independence Payment (PIP) is notoriously difficult for individuals living with mental health conditions. Although mental health is now the most frequently cited primary reason for new PIP claims, these claims remain disproportionately likely to be rejected (Mind, 2023). In 2023, over 60% of PIP decisions that went to tribunal were overturned in favour of the claimant, indicating systemic flaws in the accuracy and fairness of initial assessments (Disability Rights UK, 2024; Department for Work and Pensions, 2024).

Claimants with mental health difficulties frequently struggle to evidence the impact of fluctuating symptoms or so-called "invisible" impairments within a system that privileges observable, physical limitations (Mind, 2023). The use of standardised forms and rigid eligibility criteria often fails to reflect the complex realities of mental distress, trauma, and cognitive barriers that can prevent people from accessing or engaging with support in the first place. The application process is widely reported to be retraumatising, with many individuals describing how they are forced to repeatedly justify their suffering to strangers in order to retain essential income (Mental Health Foundation, 2023).

Sarah's experience is not isolated. It is illustrative of a broader systemic failure to recognise, accommodate, and respond compassionately to mental health within the UK welfare system. Until assessment processes are reformed to reflect the lived experience of mental ill-health, the welfare safety net will remain inaccessible to many of those who need it most.

Let's talk about housing. Because "technically housed" is a phrase that should win awards for cruelty. I live alone. I have to. My autism means I can't cope with people in my space. I need silence. I need an order. The idea of sharing a flat with strangers makes me physically ill. My skin itches at the thought. The thought of someone cooking in the kitchen while I'm trying to regulate after a meltdown is too much. But because I live alone, I'm told I'm not a housing priority. Never mind that the rent is unsustainable. Never mind that I'm teetering on the edge of eviction every month. "You have a roof," they say. "That's enough." But having a roof doesn't mean having a home. And being technically housed doesn't protect you from homelessness. It just delays it.

Then there's the physical health stuff. I've got surgery coming up—a hysterectomy. It's necessary. It's been a long time coming. But I've been putting it off for months, maybe years, because I know what it means. It means eight weeks of recovery. Eight weeks where I can't clean. Eight weeks without income. There's no sick pay in poverty. There's no compassionate leave for people like me. So, the choice becomes cruelly simple: pain or homelessness? How do you make that decision? How do you look at a calendar and say, "This is the day I'll stop working and hope the world doesn't fall apart while I heal"? It's not a decision. It's a gamble. And every time I think about it, I feel a knot in my stomach, tight and burning. Because I know this system doesn't care. I could bleed on the floor, and the DWP would still send a letter asking for proof I was ill.

The simple things become impossible under poverty. Shopping, for instance. I can't go to supermarkets. They're too loud. Too bright. Too unpredictable. I can't cope with the crowds. The constant barrage of noise. The fluorescent lighting that hums like a threat. So, I do online groceries. But there's a catch: you have to spend £40 minimum to place an order. So even if I only need bread and milk, I have to find enough items to reach that threshold. And most of what I buy has to be frozen, because it has to last. There's no room for waste. No fresh fruit unless it's on clearance. No treats. No spontaneous cravings. Every item is calculated. And every time I stim in public, I feel the weight of judgement settle around me like smoke. Stimming, those repetitive movements or sounds autistic people use to regulate, is a lifeline. It calms me when I'm overwhelmed. It's not a show. It's survival. But people stare. I've been mocked, filmed, and laughed at. Once on a train, a man moved seats because I was rocking and muttering to myself. He thought I was dangerous. I could see it in his eyes. That's the thing. People think autism looks a certain way. Usually male, usually young, usually white. And when you don't fit that image—when you're a middle-aged woman flapping her hands in Tesco, they don't know what to do with you. So, they judge. Or ignore. Or worse, they call security. I've been verbally abused in public for simply existing. For wincing when someone brushed my arm. For stepping back in a queue because the person behind me was too close. I've been called rude, stuck-up, and dramatic. All because I have a nervous system that interprets proximity as threat. I'm not trying to be difficult. I'm trying to breathe.

This is why I can't share housing. Why I live alone. Why does every letter from my landlord send me into panic? Because my autism isn't something I can turn off. It's not an inconvenience. It's my reality. And this reality doesn't make room for me. It punishes me for needing what others take for granted: quiet, space, safety. And let me tell you about loneliness. Not the "oh I haven't had a text all day" kind. I'm talking about deep, bone-heavy loneliness. The kind that wraps itself around your chest and makes it hard to breathe. The kind that makes you doubt whether you're real. I can go days without speaking to another person. Weeks without touch. I once realised I hadn't heard my own name spoken aloud in over a month. I said it to myself in the mirror, just to remember what it sounded like. People talk about "getting better" as if it's a straight line. As if recovery is just a matter of finding the right therapy, taking the right meds, thinking the right thoughts. But healing isn't linear. It's messy. It's circular. Some days, I feel strong enough to cook a proper meal. Other days, just brushing my teeth feels like climbing a mountain. And yet, I'm expected to prove my illness, over and over again, to strangers with clipboards and tick boxes. There's this belief in Britain that benefits are a luxury. That people like me are somehow "getting away" with not working. Let me be clear: there is nothing luxurious about begging a stranger for enough money to survive. There's nothing comfortable about detailing your trauma to justify a £62-a-week payment. And there is nothing easy about living every day with the knowledge that one bureaucratic error could leave you homeless. What I want you to understand, what I *need* you to understand, is that poverty isn't an event. It's a trap. It's not a chapter of my life. It *is* my life. Not because I chose it. But because everything around me was built without me in mind. Systems don't bend for the neurodivergent. They snap. And we're the ones who get cut on the edges.

There's one song I come back to over and over: *Floating in the Forth* by Frightened Rabbit. Scott Hutchison, the man who wrote it, knew what it felt like to be on the edge. To be held together by threads so thin they barely counted. "I think I'll save suicide for another year," he sings. That line haunts me. Because I've said it too. Quietly. To myself. To the sky. To the walls. "Not today. Maybe tomorrow."

Scott didn't survive. And every time I listen to that song, I cry. For him. For me. For every person who begged the world to notice and got silence in return. That lyric, though—it's become a mantra. Not because I want to die. But because sometimes, living feels like an act of rebellion. Like holding on is the only thing I can control. Sometimes I go to the sculpture park and just sit. I let the wind move through me. I let my thoughts unravel. It's one of the only places where I don't feel like a problem. No form to fill in, no appointment to be late for, no adviser judging whether I'm sick enough to be helped but not so sick as to be unhelpable. That's the cruel paradox of being "too well for support, too unwell for independence." And I've fallen through that crack so many times, I've stopped counting.

I think about how different my life could be if someone had just noticed earlier. If, at six years old, when I began self-harming, someone had said, "Are you okay?" and meant it. If someone had seen past the good grades, the perfect attendance, the quiet compliance, and realised I was drowning in plain sight. But I was the clever girl. The polite one. The one who never caused trouble. So, no one looked deeper. And that silence became the soundtrack to my life. University should have been a fresh start. A new chapter. But instead, it was the place I broke hardest. Within three months, I tried to take my own life. I don't remember much from that night. Just the cold floor of my student flat and a feeling of unbearable aloneness. No one followed up. No one called. I was discharged into nothing. And I learned, once again, that my pain had to be quiet if it was to be tolerated. So, I buried it. I built a life out of masking. I learned how to say the right things, wear the right clothes, and hold eye contact just long enough. I got jobs. I paid rent. I looked "normal" enough to blend in. But inside, I was screaming. Every day was a performance. And the cost of that performance was exhaustion so profound I could barely move. I've sat across from GPs who told me, "You're doing so well." As if being clean, dressed, and coherent meant I wasn't crumbling. I once tried to explain that the energy it took to attend the appointment meant I wouldn't be able to function for the rest of the day. They smiled politely. They didn't get it.

And how could they? The system doesn't train people to see nuance. It trains them to tick boxes. To assess risk. To manage caseloads. And I don't blame individuals; I know many are doing their best. But the system is broken. And when you're autistic, traumatised, and living in poverty, broken systems aren't just inefficient. They're lethal. I've learned not to ask for help unless I'm on the brink of collapse. Because if you ask too soon, you're not desperate enough. And if you ask too late, you're too chaotic to be supported. There is no right time to be vulnerable in this system. So, I've become my own case manager, support worker, and advocate. I've filled out forms with shaking hands. I've sat through PIP assessments with my heart in my throat. I've appealed decisions I barely understood. I've spent hours researching legislation just to make sure I wasn't being gaslit.

LEGISLATION

Under UK law, disabled people, including those with autism and mental health conditions, are entitled to specific rights and protections. The *Equality Act 2010* makes it unlawful to discriminate against someone due to a disability and places a legal duty on public bodies and service providers to make reasonable adjustments. For example, this means benefits assessments, healthcare appointments, and housing services should be accessible and adapted to individual needs. The *Care Act 2014* also requires local authorities to assess and meet eligible care and support needs, including for people experiencing substantial mental distress. Under the *Human Rights Act 1998*, individuals have the right to dignity, safety, and respect in all public services. These are not privileges; they are legal rights. When Sarah is denied appropriate support or asked to repeatedly prove her worthiness for help, it is not merely poor service delivery. It is a breach of the law. Knowing your rights is the first step towards challenging injustice.

And all of this, *all* of this, is just to survive. Just to keep a roof over my head, food in my freezer, and medication on my shelf. Survival isn't a life. It's a full-time job that pays nothing and costs everything. Let me tell you about one of the darkest moments. There was a night when I stood on a bridge, looking down at the water. I wasn't planning. I was just… wondering. Wondering what it would feel like to stop trying. To just let go. The river looked peaceful. And I was so tired. So, so tired. But then, a lyric floated into my mind. Scott's voice, from *Floating in the Forth*. "I think I'll save suicide for another year." And somehow, that was enough. Not hope. Not purpose. Just delay. And that delay saved my life. It's strange, isn't it? That a song can do what services fail to. That music can hold you in a way a crisis team never did.

So here I am. Still here. Still flapping. Still stimming. Still fighting for space in a world that keeps trying to erase me.

Still running.

Still breathing.

There are days when breathing feels like an act of defiance. When getting out of bed is a revolution. These aren't small things. Not to me. Not when everything in my body tells me to give up. Not when the world I'm trying to survive in was never made for someone like me. Because let me be clear, this isn't just about autism or trauma. This is about the way society treats people who don't fit. The way poverty isolates, marginalises, and dehumanises. The way the systems meant to support us are so entangled in red tape and targets that they can't see the individual in front of them. I am not a number. I am not a case. I am not a tick-box. I am a person. And all I've ever wanted is to be treated like one. Do you know what it's like to walk into a DWP office, clutching your evidence, terrified? To rehearse answers in your head, knowing that if you cry or get flustered, they might think you're unstable—but if you stay too calm, they'll say you're not unwell enough? To know that the outcome of that assessment could determine whether you eat next month?

I've sat across from assessors who didn't even look at me. Who typed while I spoke? Who smiled when they said, "Unfortunately, we don't think you meet the criteria." I've walked out of those appointments shaking. Dissociating. Feeling like I had to convince someone I was broken enough to be believed. And it doesn't stop there. Try applying for housing support. Try explaining why you can't live in shared accommodation when you "seem fine." Try putting into words the sheer panic you feel at the thought of someone cooking in your kitchen, knocking on your door, and hearing you stim. Try explaining that the sound of footsteps in the hallway makes your skin crawl, that the smell of someone else's food can send you spiralling. Try saying that and not being dismissed.

Autism isn't cute. It isn't quirky. It's exhausting. It's navigating a world full of noise and touch and unpredictability with a brain that registers everything at once. It's about needing routines and predictability, but living in chaos. It's flinching at kindness because your nervous system doesn't know what to do with safety. It's remembering everything and feeling it all, all of the time. And trauma doesn't fade. Not when it's complex. Not when it's been layered over decades. It weaves itself into your bones. It sits behind your eyes. It whispers in your ears when you try to rest. "You're not safe," it says. "Don't relax. Don't trust. Don't feel." So, you don't. You stay alert. You stay hyper-aware. And it's no way to live—but it's the only way you've ever known.

People talk about "resilience" like it's a badge of honour. Like surviving a broken system is something to be proud of. I don't want resilience. I want rest. I want ease. I want to wake up one day and not feel afraid. Every brown envelope is a potential eviction notice. Every knock at the door makes my stomach turn. Every time I see a letter from the council or DWP, my hands shake. Because I know that one wrong word, one missed appointment, one misunderstanding—and it all crumbles.

And still, I fight. I write. I speak. I run. I find moments of joy in the middle of the mess. I sit by the canal and watch the ducks. I listen to Frightened Rabbit and cry. I paint my nails bright colours because screw it—if I'm going to be seen, I'll be seen on my terms.

I am not a tragedy. I am not a hero. I am just trying to live.

Still here.

Still standing.

Still not asking for pity—just understanding.

There's something else I want to say—something most people avoid because it's uncomfortable. But we need to talk about how trauma intersects with poverty, how it feeds off it, and how being poor makes healing almost impossible. We need policies that reflect lived experience, not assumptions. We need services designed *with* us, not *for* us. We need benefits systems that are humane, housing that is accessible, and healthcare that listens. We need compassion. And more than that—we need change. Because survival shouldn't be this hard. Dignity shouldn't be this rare. And understanding shouldn't be optional.

I'm still here. And I'll keep speaking. Because if my voice can make even one person feel seen, one person who flaps, who freezes, who falls apart silently, then maybe it's worth it. When I say I live in poverty, I don't just mean financial poverty, though that's very real. I mean the poverty of connection. The poverty of time, of rest, of being understood. The poverty of comfort. The poverty of space, both physical and emotional. Poverty is the absence of choice. Of safety. Of freedom. When you live in poverty long enough, it becomes a mindset. You second-guess everything. You shrink. You apologise for existing. You avoid things you used to enjoy because joy feels dangerous. Because of the crash afterwards, the reminder that joy is temporary is too painful. You start to feel like you don't deserve anything more than this.

But that's a lie. A lie poverty tells you to keep you small.

And I'm tired of being small.

So I speak. I share. I risk being misunderstood. I risk the judgement. Because maybe, just maybe, someone out there will read this and feel less alone. Maybe someone will read this and say, "I didn't realise. I see it now." And maybe a student—a future social worker, support worker, policymaker—will remember my words when they sit across from someone who reminds them of me.

I hope they do.

I hope they look beyond the surface. Beyond the articulate words and the clean clothes and the forced smile. I hope they understand that survival doesn't always look like struggle. Sometimes it looks like functioning. Until it doesn't.

And I hope, above all else, that they bring compassion into the room with them. That they remember we're not statistics. We're not service users. We're people. Complicated, messy, brilliant, hurting, hopeful people.

And we deserve better.

So, no—this story doesn't have a happy ending. But it has truth. It has strength. It has survival. And for now, that will have to be enough.

Because I'm still here.

Still trying.

Still hoping.

Still human.

And maybe, after all this, you finally see me.

Not a diagnosis.

Not a deficit.

Not a drain.

But a person.

A life.

A voice.

Mine.

A REFLECTIVE ACTIVITY: A DAY IN MY SHOES

This activity is an invitation to step into Sarah's world, if only for one day, and to reflect on how that shapes someone's relationship with poverty and society.

Instructions

1. Choose one day this week where you'll spend time out of the house—doing everyday things like travelling, shopping, attending appointments, or going to work.

2 Your challenge is this: For the full day, do your best to ensure that no one comes within six feet (or two metres) of you. This includes in shops, public transport, on pavements, in queues, in offices, and in social settings. Imagine that proximity is not just uncomfortable—it is unbearable.
3 No shortcuts. Try not to stay at home all day to avoid the task. The aim is to live a "normal" day, just under this new constraint.
4 No explanations to others unless absolutely necessary. If someone steps too close, find a way to move away discreetly. Do not rely on others adjusting for you.

After the Experience

Once you've completed the day, spend some quiet time reflecting. You can write your thoughts down, record them as a voice note, or just think deeply. Use these questions to guide your reflection:—What did you notice about how people responded to you?

- Which situations were the most difficult to manage?
- Did you feel judged, anxious, excluded, or misunderstood?
- Were there any things you simply couldn't do because of the distance rule?
- How did this affect your sense of safety, connection, and confidence?

Then, take your reflection one step further:

- What if every day of your life was like this?
- How would it affect where you live, the job you do, or your ability to socialise or shop?

Can you see how this kind of experience could lead someone into poverty, not by choice, but because of circumstance?

My Hope for You

I don't want pity. I am asking for empathy. My goal with this activity is to help others understand the invisible barriers that make life harder for people like me—not because we lack motivation, but because society isn't designed to accommodate difference. By walking just one day in my shoes, I hope you'll think differently. More kindly. More justly. And with a greater awareness that poverty is sometimes born not of laziness or failure, but of simply not fitting into a world that was never built for you.

To Learn More, We Recommend These Resources

Listen

- ♫ Floating in the Forth—Frightened Rabbit (YouTube)

Read

- Aspies on Mental Health: Speaking for Ourselves—Beardon & Worton
- Autism and Mental Health—Mind
- Mental Health Hub—National Autistic Society
- Unmasking Autism—Devon Price

Watch and Learn

- TED Talk: How Autism Freed Me to Be Myself—Rosie King
- Strong Female Character by Fern Brady (Memoir)

Practical Tools and Support

- Reading Well Books on Prescription—UK Libraries Scheme
- Mental Health and Autism—Mental Health Foundation

References

Beardon, L. and Worton, G. (2011) *Aspies on Mental Health: Speaking for Ourselves*. London: Jessica Kingsley Publishers.

Cassidy, S., Bradley, L., Robinson, J., Allison, C. and Baron-Cohen, S. (2014) 'Suicidal ideation and suicide plans or attempts in adults with Asperger's syndrome attending a specialist diagnostic clinic: A clinical cohort study', *The Lancet Psychiatry*, 1(2), pp. 142–147. doi:10.1016/S2215-0366(14)70248-2

Department for Work and Pensions (2024) *Personal Independence Payment: Tribunal Outcomes and Decision Statistics – 2023 Release*. London: DWP. Available at: https://www.gov.uk/government/statistics/pip-tribunal-statistics-2023 (Accessed: 8 July 2025).

Disability Rights UK (2024) Flawed Assessments Continue to Fail Disabled People. Available at: https://www.disabilityrightsuk.org/news/2024/april/pip-assessments-overturned-tribunal (Accessed: 8 July 2025).

Mental Health Foundation (2022) Mental Health and Work. Available at: https://www.mentalhealth.org.uk/explore-mental-health/a-z-topics/work-and-mental-health (Accessed: 8 July 2025).

Mental Health Foundation (2023) Welfare, Mental Health, and the Benefits System. Available at: https://www.mentalhealth.org.uk/policy/welfare-and-mental-health (Accessed: 8 July 2025).

Mind (2020) Autism and Mental Health. Available at: https://www.mind.org.uk/information-support/tips-for-everyday-living/autism-and-mental-health/ (Accessed: 8 July 2025).

Mind (2021) Mental Health at Work. Available at: https://www.mind.org.uk/workplace/mental-health-at-work/ (Accessed: 8 July 2025).
Mind (2023) PIP and Mental Health: Challenges and Reform. Available at: https://www.mind.org.uk/news-campaigns/news/pip-assessments-unfair-mental-health (Accessed: 8 July 2025).
National Autistic Society (n.d.) Mental Health Hub. Available at: https://www.autism.org.uk/what-we-do/help-and-support/mental-health (Accessed: 8 July 2025).
NHS England (2023) Mental Health and Sickness Absence: Annual Report 2022–23. Available at: https://www.england.nhs.uk/publication/mental-health-and-sickness-absence-2022-23/ (Accessed: 8 July 2025).
Price, D. (2022) *Unmasking Autism: Discovering the New Faces of Neurodiversity*. New York: Harmony Books.

11

POVERTY AND PRISON

Gary Lee and Mel Hughes

My chapter is presented as four stories:

- What's the point of dreaming
- Stickman Saints and the System That Failed Us
- Homelessness by Design
- When the System Finally Listened

I then share a little more truth.

What's the point of dreaming?

I'm 57 years old, but I still feel like a traumatised 20-something. That's what poverty does—it traps you in a version of yourself you never chose.

When I was a kid, I didn't know we were poor. It was just life. I remember crying from hunger while my older brother rummaged through the kitchen cupboards like a magician. He'd mix curry powder with a lone fish finger from the freezer, sugar, flour, hot water—anything he could find. He'd pretend he was doing magic, trying to make me smile. Trying to make me eat.

Real meals were worse. Cabbage, swedes, potatoes. If you didn't eat what was on your plate, you got a beating. So you sat there, gagging, stuck between a rock and a hard place. Violence or vomit.

Poverty was in the bones of that house—but so was chaos. Some nights, money would appear out of nowhere. My dad would be flashing cash, passing out fivers, and carrying bags of drinks into the kitchen. Like we'd hit the jackpot.

DOI: 10.4324/9781003638476-12

Then next week, the fridge would be empty, and the police would be knocking. We'd be back to cold fish fingers and silence.

I remember being jealous of other kids' lives. Their homes felt safe. Full. Normal. I'd go to Andrew's house and steal his toys. Later, I started nicking sweets from the shop, then climbing through windows, kicking in doors. I wasn't just stealing stuff—I was trying to steal their lives.

By the time I left middle school, I was already spiralling. I didn't know how to live with the pain at home, so I used Class A drugs intravenously from an early age. My brother and I ended up in care because of the abuse. And by 15, I was in prison. That became the pattern. In and out for twenty years. Misery. Humiliation. Addiction. I was certain the drugs would kill me.

But they didn't.

I've been clean for ten and a half years. I've just started trauma therapy. It's not easy being me. My childhood wasn't one thing—it was too twisted to explain in simple terms. I was loved, and I loved my parents and my brother. But I was beaten and terrified of them, too. I was protected and neglected, fed and starved, hugged and hit. My parents cared, but their priority was always money—schemes, scams, survival.

There was no space for nurturing. No room to be a child.

So yeah—poverty's got a lot to answer for.

I scraped a life together in the end. I'm intelligent. I make a good, honest living now. I'm married. I've built something stable. But I still wonder, sometimes, what would've happened if I'd been born into a family like the Waltons. One of those gentle, well-fed households where people love out loud and money isn't a constant question mark.

What if I'd had that?

I kill time in the field behind our local Community Centre. I set plastic bags alight on the ends of sticks, watch them melt into black, toxic smoke, and drip like angry tears onto the dry dirt path. I think about setting the long grass on fire. I've done it before, you know. Then I kick cans and stones all the way home.

Outside the house, I can already see the front room light's on. Chintz curtains wide. He's there. Waiting. Brewing. Stewing.

I knock. My mum answers.

"Don't you feckin' smile at me ye cunty bollox. Get inside—your dad wants a word."

He's not my real dad. But Mum likes to pretend.

He's on the sofa. Doesn't even look at me. Just sits there. Belt coiled on the armrest like a sleeping snake.

"Yeah, Dad?"

"You wee bastard, I'm only going to ask once. Who took your mum's fags?"

"I don't know…"

He's up quick. Too quick. He always was. Grabs me by the hair, yanks me across the room. Mum's shouting "Leave it, Reg!" and then whack, she goes flying too.

"Get to fuck! Who took 'em? Whack! Tell me the truth and it stops."

Problem is—I don't know what the truth is. I don't know wrong from right. So I lie. Or maybe I don't.

Later he says he only did it because he loves me.

"Love you too, Dad."

That night, they think me and Rob are asleep. Their cab picks them up for work in Soho. Soon as it drives off, I'm up. Superman pants, threadbare carpet, creaking floorboards. Bathroom mirror catches my bruises—stripes up and down my thighs, arms, shoulders. I light a No.6 under the gas heater, blow smoke like I'm James Dean.

Back in the bunk, Rob sees me.

"I'm telling," he whines.

"Shut your mouth or I'll let the witch out the cupboard and feed you Shitabix."

He whimpers and counts teddy bears on the wallpaper until he falls asleep.

Then it begins. Glass smashing. Screaming. The soundtrack of our house.

I pull him into my bunk and hold him tight.

"You've wet yourself," I hiss. He starts counting again. One, two, three teddy bears…

Patsy Cline crackles through the radio. Crazy… crazy for feeling so lonely…

Mum stumbles upstairs, sobbing on the toilet. Makeup smeared, bruises bleeding through. Rob hugs her. She sings along through slurred breath: "Crazy… crazy for loving you."

"Go on then, good boys. Get dressed for school."

She tries to smile. I kiss her on the cheek—she smells of ashtrays and gin.

I cover her with a blanket and sneak Rob downstairs. The key in the back door's too loud.

"Gary. Robert." His voice cuts through us.

"Yeah?" we answer in unison.

"Put the kettle on."

Robert's sobbing because he can't find his shoes. I make the tea just how he likes it. He smashes the cup off the table anyway.

"You're useless. Just like your dad."

When he goes to belt Robert, I grab his arm.

"Fuck off. You ain't our real dad."
We bolt. Run across the fields. I'm holding Rob's hand tight.
"You're hurting me!" he squeals. I let go.
"Why can't we be a normal family?" he asks through tears.
"We are," I lie. "He ain't your dad and he ain't mine."
Rob reaches for my hand. I slap him. My hand stings. It feels good.
I walk him to the school gates. "Go on. Get lost."
Later I arrive late at school and run into Mr. Double. Reeking of stale beer, barking orders.
"Where's your uniform?"
"Don't know, sir."
"Office. Now."
He tells me to drop my trousers. Wants to see the marks. I won't. I'm not a grass.
"Fuck you, you fat cunt."
He lunges. I grab two canes, snap them over my knee, scarper out of the building.
I set fires. I nick chocolate. I cut my arm just to feel something.
When I get home, he's waiting again. Mr. Double's called. There's a meeting.
At the school, Mum and Stepdad are acting posh. Mr. Double's waving broken canes. Then comes the line:
"You're expelled, Krishna."
Reg's got me by the ear before the sentence is done. Here we go again. The bruises ain't even yellow yet.
Was that the tipping point? That day? The start of the spiral?
Soon after, I'm in care. Glue sniffing. Rolling joints. Fighting. Learning what "nonce" means. Learning what "maladjusted" means. Special school. Bars on the windows. Short sharp shocks. Detention centres. Homelessness. Prison.
Learned everything except how to be.
More than half of kids in care end up inside. I became a statistic. I deserved it, right? Little shit should've respected his elders. That's what they said.
But sometimes I wonder. Just wonder. Not dream.
What if I'd been one of the Waltons?
Night, John Boy. Night, Krishna.
What if I'd had a real dad? A gentle one.
What if I'd been encouraged? Nurtured?
What if I'd never known the taste of hunger or the burn of a belt?
But that's dreaming. And I don't do that anymore.

CHILDHOOD POVERTY AND DOMESTIC VIOLENCE

Recent UK data show that around 4.5 million (31% of all children) are living in relative poverty (Joseph Rowntree, 2025; End Child Poverty, 2025; Department for Work and Pensions DWP, 2025). 70% of children living in poverty have at least one parent in paid work. Children in the UK are even more likely to be living in poverty if they are from Black and Asian communities (49% compared to 24% of white children), if living in lone-parent families (43%), or living in a family where someone is disabled (44%). The Child Poverty Action Group (CPAG) reports that all of these figures are projected to rise.

There are proven links between poverty and domestic violence. Intimate partner violence has been consistently reported as highest in the poorest neighbourhoods with the poorest mothers, most likely to experience domestic abuse (British Association of Social Workers 2025). In a study by BASW and the University of Edinburgh in 2024, children of mums who had experienced domestic abuse had poorer scores on different measures of social and emotional development. The impact on children living in poverty and in a violent household, as described by Gary, is significant.

Stickman saints and the system that failed us

It was summer, 1978. Back when summer really meant something. West London. Neighbours out washing their cars—Morris Minors, Ford Escorts—waving at me like I was just another cheeky lad bunking off school. "Howdy, cowboy," they'd say, ruffling my hair. I'd ask for money or sweets, then disappear up Westcott Hill before they could ask questions.

I spent hours in the fields near a local Community Centre, setting fire to carrier bags on sticks, watching black smoke curl up into the sky. I was eight, maybe nine. Thinking about lighting the grass just to see what would happen.

I didn't go home unless I had to. And when I did, I knew what waited for me. My mum's partner—he wasn't my real dad, but that didn't matter much when the belt was on the arm of the sofa. He was quick, always quicker than you expected. If something went missing, it was always my fault. Even when I didn't know what the truth was, I'd deny it. And the beatings would come all the same.

Later, he'd say it was because he loved me. "Love you too," I'd say. What else can a kid say when no one's coming to help?

By 13, I was expelled from school for refusing to let the headmaster cane me. I'd seen the cane marks on other lads, but mine weren't from school—they were already there, from home. I didn't want him to see. I didn't want to give away what was going on behind our front door. No one talked about that sort of thing back then. What happened at home stayed there.

So when he told me I'd be punished, I panicked. I grabbed two canes from the pot in the corner and snapped them over my knee. I wouldn't let him touch me. He came at me, and I kicked over his bin—saw the empty cans in it as I backed away. I wasn't the only one with something to hide. I got expelled. No one asked why.

That was the start of the slide.

I found glue sniffing helped numb things. Not just the pain—but the noise in my head. The panic. The loneliness. By 14, I was in care. I told social services what had been going on at home. They believed me enough to move me, but not enough to really protect me. I learned to roll joints there. Lost my virginity. Watched other boys fall apart and figured I was meant to do the same.

By 15, I was in and out of youth custody. The short, sharp shock. By 17, I was doing 12-month stretches. And the truth? It felt safer in there than outside.

Outside, I had no permanent address. I slept in squats, under stairwells, on floors. I started injecting heroin before I had any idea what a future was meant to look like. There was never a plan. No long game. I'd learned early: the world doesn't plan for lads like me.

Me and my mates—my brother Robert, Dukes, and PJ—we got matching stickman tattoos with a needle and some stolen Indian ink. We were 14 and thought we were invincible. We called ourselves the Saints. A little gang of our own. Something to belong to, even if no one else wanted us.

One by one, they all went. PJ was found dead after falling from the roof of the local hospital. Dukes took his own life in prison while we were both on remand. And my brother Robert—he was found in an alley in Harrow, overdosed, his pockets turned out.

Three Saints down. Just me left.

YOUTH OFFENDING

Gary is not the only one to get caught up in the criminal justice system, and recent figures show that this number is rising. Government figures for 2022/23 showed that arrests of children increased for the second consecutive year in 2022/23 to around 59,000, 9% higher than the previous year, 2021/2022. Around one in three of these are for violent offences, and around 8% each for theft/handling stolen goods, drugs, or criminal damage. For those who are proven to have committed an offence, 32.5% go on to re-offend within 12 months (Gov.UK).

Official figures also show how children and young people are the victims of violent crime. While many incidents go unreported, a 2023 survey of 7,574 teenage children found that 16% of children had been victims of violence in the past 12 months (UK Parliament 2024).

Homelessness by design

These days, homelessness is a headline. But what they show you on the telly—the tents on Oxford Street, the lad curled up in a Greggs doorway—that's just the surface. That's the bit people can see. The real problem runs deeper. Quieter. And in most cases, it starts long before the street.

Today, you've got whole families living in one-bedroom flats. Parents sleeping on the sofa so the kids can have the mattress. Damp climbing the walls. No heating. No garden. No safety. Mould that makes the kids cough. Broken boilers. Rats. You name it. And the landlord? They're getting full rent—sometimes more—because the council's paying it directly.

Private landlords aren't just part of the problem—they are the problem. Most of them don't fix a thing. And why would they? They've got tenants on Universal Credit with nowhere else to go. No other options. No voice. The landlord holds the key—literally.

Social housing used to be a lifeline. But that rope's been cut. No one's building homes anymore. Not homes you can actually live in. The waiting lists are miles long, and even if you do get a place, it's often already falling apart. There's no pride in it. Just survival. Get in, lock the door, try and make it feel like something more than just four walls and a fire risk.

Then there's immigration. You can't talk about housing without mentioning it. It's not about blame—it's about numbers. The system is stretched beyond capacity. People coming here to escape war, torture, hunger—they need homes too. And instead of building more, the government just keeps shuffling people around, stacking them on top of each other, and hoping no one notices. But people do notice. They just don't say it out loud.

The truth is, every public service is on its knees. The NHS? Gone to bits. A&E waiting times are a joke. GP appointments are like gold dust. People with serious mental health needs are stuck in limbo, waiting for callbacks that never come. And that's if they even get assessed in the first place. The workers? Overloaded. Burnt out. Doing their best in a system that's set up to fail.

And don't get me started on prisons.

I tour prisons now. Spoken word, creative writing, helping lads find a way to say what they've been carrying for years. Most of them are just younger versions of me—care kids, sofa surfers, trauma survivors. No real place in the world. They're not bad lads. They've just never been given a proper shot.

The prison officers? Half of them are barely older than the prisoners. No experience. Just out of school, thrown onto the wings. Paid peanuts to manage chaos. And some of them are scared. You can see it in their body language. There's no control anymore. No trust either. It's every man for himself in there, and that's not rehabilitation—that's survival with a time limit.

And what happens when these lads get out? Same as it always was. They get handed a travel warrant and dumped into hostels that are full of dealers and users. They come out with hope, maybe. But hope can't beat trauma without backup. Without wraparound support, it's just a word.

I've met men inside who are more stable in prison than they ever were outside. Because at least they know what to expect. Food. Routine. Rules. They don't want to stay there, but they don't know how to survive anywhere else. That's not justice. That's a system that's lost the plot.

I sit with these lads and hear their stories. And I see it all happening again. The same cycle I got caught in. Only now, it feels worse. Because everything's more expensive. More hostile. More chaotic.

And the safety nets we used to fall through? They've been ripped out completely.

LIFE AFTER PRISON

As of June 2024, there were 87,726 inmates in England and Wales, 95.8% were men. 22,812 were serving sentences for violence against the person (Government Justice data). As Gary describes, life after prison is challenging. Prisons are required to support offenders to prepare for their release by working together with probation services, but in 2024, 41 out of 111 prisons did not meet their targets of releases with accommodation on their first night of release (Government Justice data 2024). 56 prisons did not meet their target for numbers in employment at six weeks following release. This is a significant number of people being released from prison with nowhere to go and no employment.

When the system finally listened

By the time I was 35, I wasn't just lost—I was running on empty. Four kids I barely knew. The mother of my children, gone. My brother, found in an alley in Harrow, overdosed, pockets turned out. My best friend died in a prison cell. And I was still trying to disappear into whatever I could get in a needle.

I couldn't make a doctor's appointment, let alone follow through on a housing application. I didn't even have an ID half the time. I was sofa-surfing if I was lucky, squatting if I wasn't. Some nights I'd sleep upright in stairwells. Others I'd walk all night just to stay warm, waiting for the morning shopfronts to light up. I wasn't really alive—I was just surviving between fixes and close calls.

That's when the fear finally caught up with me. Not fear of dying—that had followed me for years. It was the fear of dying without anyone knowing. The fear of being found like my brother, cold and gone, with nothing in my pockets but a busted lighter and some burnt foil.

But this time—somehow—someone heard me. Not a form. Not a tick box. A person. Someone who looked me in the eye and didn't flinch. Someone who didn't ask me for a five-year plan or a clean urine test. They just asked me what I needed.

And I didn't even know how to answer.

What I got was wraparound support. That phrase gets thrown around a lot, but I can tell you exactly what it meant to me: it meant having someone in my corner *before* I relapsed, *after* I relapsed, and again when I was ready to try. It meant getting into rehab *and* having somewhere to go after. Not a hostel. Not a crack den with curtains. A real space. A room with a door I could lock. A kettle. A bed.

Recovery wasn't magic. It was messy. Ugly. There were days I wanted to walk back into the old life just because it was easier. At least I knew the rules there. But something had shifted. I wasn't alone anymore. That's what made the difference.

People think addicts just need to "want it more." That's not how it works. You can want it and still fall. You can want it and not know where to start. You can want it and still get crushed by the weight of your past. I didn't stay clean because I was stronger. I stayed clean because people didn't give up on me—even when I gave up on myself.

I had support workers who called me just to ask how I was feeling. Probation officers who didn't treat me like a statistic. Recovery group leaders who'd been where I'd been. That mattered. They weren't reading from a manual—they were speaking from the same pain. That kind of honesty keeps you tethered. It kept me tethered.

Six months in, I looked in the mirror and barely recognised myself. I had colour in my cheeks. I was making my own bed. I was brushing my teeth without being told. That might sound small, but for someone like me, it was a mountain.

Bit by bit, I rebuilt. I got my kids back in my life. I got clean and stayed clean. I met someone. I got married. I got a flat on the south coast. I got dogs. And I started working in care—residential, with young people caught up in the same mess I came from. County lines kids. Forgotten boys who remind me of myself every single day.

I don't tell them everything. But they can see it. The way I listen. The way I look at them without judgement. They know I've lived it.

That's the power of real support. It doesn't just save lives—it gives them back.

WHAT WORKS

There are many reasons as to why people re-offend, and like Gary, many offenders have complex needs including drug and alcohol use, family breakdown, experience of trauma, ill health, and poverty. Addressing these helps cut re-offending rates and helps people to stay out of prison. UK prisons, probation and offender support programmes routinely refer to the seven pathways approach, which was included in the National Reducing Re-offending Action Plan, developed by the National Offender Management Service in 2004. Based on extensive research, the framework outlined how re-offending is reduced when support is offered around: accommodation; employment and education; drugs and alcohol; family and social support; life skills and behaviour; physical and mental health, and financial management.

The reality beneath the headline—a little more truth

When I visit prisons now, it's not just about performance. It's about recognition. I see the lads watching me the same way I once looked at the few people who'd made it out. Not famous people, not rich—just clean, balanced, breathing steady. I clock their expressions—some with arms folded tight, others with eyes fixed like they're starving. Not for food. For belief.

In one workshop, a young lad told me he'd never heard his own thoughts spoken out loud by someone else. That's the power of lived experience. That's why we need more people like me doing this work. Not because we're better qualified—but because we survived it.

I talk to the officers, too. The old guard who've seen it all, and the new recruits just trying to make it through the shift. Some come in hard-faced, all about control. Others are curious. You can tell who's going to burn out. You can also tell who might stay the course if they get the right support. The system burns everyone—staff and inmates alike.

And I'll be honest, I still carry it. The grief, the guilt, the "what ifs." They don't disappear just because you've got a mortgage now. I dream of the old days sometimes. Not because I miss them, but because they left their mark. Trauma doesn't check out. It just gets quieter—if you're lucky.

The flat I live in now? It's mine. My name is on the letterbox. I've got a kettle I don't have to hide, a mirror I can look in, and a front door I don't have to bolt from the inside. I walk my dogs by the sea. I hold my grandkids' hands on the beach. It's not a fairy tale. It's a daily decision. A routine I built piece by piece.

And every time I sit down in front of another young person, I think: you could have this too. But only if someone shows up. Only if the help comes when they ask—not six months too late.

You want to know what real hope looks like? It's when your grown daughter rings just to check in. It's when your grandson asks if you can pick him up from school. When your wife puts the kettle on before you even ask. Those are the moments that remind you this version of life is worth holding onto.

Working in residential care now, I see boys who are still figuring out whether the world wants them to survive. Some are hardened already—eyes too old for their age. Others are still holding out for someone to mean what they say. I see both versions. I was in both versions. I wish I had more to give them than a shift and a checklist. But I show up. I listen. That counts for something.

And if I could say anything to my younger self, the one standing outside school gates in glue-stained trousers, I'd say: "You're not broken, bruv. You're just waiting to be heard."

REFLECTIVE ACTIVITY

So here are some questions for you to consider: how will you respond?

Reflective Questions:

1. A 10-year-old boy stands in front of you. He hasn't eaten properly in days. Last night, he slept in a stairwell because his mum had punters over and the door was locked. He tells you he's scared of the "uncle" who babysits. He smells like piss and shame. He looks you dead in the eye and says, "What are you gonna do to help me?" What do you say?
2. Kid's hungry, mum's battered, budget's blown. Do you protect the spreadsheet–or feed the kid and fight the fallout later?
3. You meet a man just released from prison. He's got no ID, nowhere safe to go, and he's clearly traumatised. Do you see a person who needs safety and care–or a problem to manage and move on? How do you prove to someone like me that you're not just another "professional" who'll smile, nod, and disappear?

4 It's past lunchtime, and little Billy, who's been kicked out of middle school for displaying violent tendencies, saw something kind in your face when you went to his damp and dirty flat to assess his situation. He turns up at the office. Are you concerned that he found your workplace? Do you feel threatened and start thinking about professional boundaries, or see a cry for help? Did you accept a seat without showing displeasure?

We all know the answers. But the system still fails. Would you be brave enough to challenge it when it's easier to just follow protocol? Are you prepared to hold power responsibly—or will you end up causing harm with a clipboard and a smile?

Is your job to guard the budget line or stand between poverty and harm? Pick. We'll remember.

A SYSTEM UNDER PRESSURE—THE NUMBERS

Category	Statistic	Source
Prison Population	87,726 inmates in England and Wales as of June 2024	Justice Data (GOV.UK)
	Operating at 99% capacity; projected surplus of 9,500 inmates by 2028	The Guardian
Drug-Related Deaths	5,448 deaths from drug poisoning in England and Wales in 2023—the highest on record	ONS
	1,172 drug misuse deaths in Scotland in 2023, a 12% increase from 2022	National Records of Scotland
Homelessness	At least 354,000 people were homeless in England as of December 2024	Shelter
	4,667 people were sleeping rough across England in 2024—a 20% increase from the previous year	GOV.UK

Summary:

- **Prisons** are overcrowded and nearing collapse. Officers are undertrained and outnumbered.
- **Drug deaths** are at record highs, showing the scale of untreated addiction.
- **Homelessness** continues to soar, with families in unsuitable housing and rough sleeping rising fast.

Further reading, listening, or viewing

To learn more, we would recommend you read/view/listen to the following. Here's a list of UK-based media Gary thinks captures the realities of prison, poverty, and trauma:

Time (BBC Drama)—A powerful prison story set in the UK. Sean Bean's character shows how fast life can change.

Shows the emotional toll on inmates and staff alike.

Scum (1979 Film)—Set in a UK borstal. Brutal, raw, still relevant. A punch to the gut about what happens when young people are caged without care.

Top Boy (Netflix)—East London streets, housing estates, broken systems. More than gangs—it's about kids trying to survive where there's no safety net.

Blue Story (2019 Film)—Set in South London. Two friends divided by postcode war. Honest and tragic. Shows how young lives can be pushed into chaos.

The Unseen (Prison Radio)—Real UK prisoners telling their own stories. No filter, just truth. Gives people a voice who rarely get heard.

Prison: First and Last 24 Hours (Channel 4)—Follows UK prisoners at entry and release. Shows how disorienting and cold the system can be, even in those first or last moments.

Panorama: Inside HMP Belmarsh (BBC)—Documentary inside one of the UK's most infamous prisons. Pressure, violence, and staff burnout are all on show.

The Streets—"Dry Your Eyes"—Mike Skinner nails the emotional numbness and breakdown that creeps into working-class men. Not a prison track—but it hits that same spot.

George the Poet—"The System Isn't Broken"—Spoken word piece that breaks down exactly how systems keep people trapped. Intelligent and emotional. One of the best at doing it.

References

BASW (2025). Poverty, social inequality and domestic abuse: The impact on children Implications for Social Work Practice. Available at https://basw.co.uk/policy-and-practice/resources/poverty-social-inequality-and-domestic-abuse-impact-children

DWP (2025). Household below average income: for financial years ending 1995 to 2024. Available at https://www.gov.uk/government/statistics/households-below-average-income-for-financial-years-ending-1995-to-2024

End Child Poverty (2025). Local child poverty statistics 2025. Available at https://endchildpoverty.org.uk/child-poverty-2025/

Joseph Rowntree Foundation (2025). UK Poverty 2025: The essential guide to understanding poverty in the UK. Available at https://www.jrf.org.uk/uk-poverty-2025-the-essential-guide-to-understanding-poverty-in-the-uk

Websites

https://basw.co.uk/policy-and-practice/resources/poverty-social-inequality-and-domestic-abuse-impact-children

https://www.jrf.org.uk/uk-poverty-2025-the-essential-guide-to-understanding-poverty-in-the-uk

https://researchbriefings.files.parliament.uk/documents/SN07096/SN07096.pdf

https://cpag.org.uk/child-poverty/poverty-facts-and-figures

https://post.parliament.uk/children-and-young-people-and-the-criminal-justice-system/#_edn4

https://www.gov.uk/government/statistics/youth-justice-statistics-2023-to-2024/youth-justice-statistics-2023-to-2024

Prisons data—Justice Data

https://www.files.ethz.ch/isn/157081/RP12-71.pdf

12

POVERTY AND RAISING A DISABLED CHILD

Taliah Drayak and Stefan Kleipoedszus

The poem "Welcome to Holland" by Emily Perl Kingsley (1987) uses the metaphor of an unexpected journey to describe the experience of raising a disabled child. Parents may prepare for and dream of one life: the "trip to Italy," only to find themselves somewhere different: "Holland." Although it is not what they planned, it is not a terrible place; it is simply different, requiring new learning, perspectives, and appreciation. The poem acknowledges the enduring grief for the loss of a life imagined, while recognising the unexpected beauty and richness of experiences that can be found in this alternative journey.

Only, in this case, as a parent raising a disabled child in poverty, you do not have any money, not even enough to go to the toilet. You have arrived at a holiday destination where everything is ten times more expensive for you than for everyone else. And on this holiday, your child's survival is dependent on you making this work.

Introduction

Poverty is not just a statistic; it has never just been about a lack of achievement; it is a lived experience that shapes the rhythms of everyday life, the possibilities of tomorrow, and the way society views those of us who endure it. For families raising disabled children, poverty is not merely about lacking money but about constant barriers, judgements, and sacrifices that can never seem to be enough.

DOI: 10.4324/9781003638476-13

THE LINK BETWEEN DISABILITY AND POVERTY

Research indicates that families with disabled children face higher healthcare, therapy, and adaptive equipment costs, stressing their finances. Emerson and Llewellyn show that these expenses increase the risk of poverty and highlight the complex link between poverty and parental mental health issues arising from caregiving demands (Emerson and Llewellyn, 2008). Parents caring for disabled children often face employment challenges, frequently working part-time or quitting altogether, which leads to economic hardship. Risdal and Singer (2004) highlight this issue, while Emerson (2003a, 2003b) notes a higher poverty rate among such families, particularly lone mothers.

Emotional and psychological factors exacerbate these economic challenges. Parents of children with disabilities often face higher stress levels and mental health issues, which can hinder employment and financial management (Ayoola et al., 2025; Emerson, 2003a). Moreover, having a child with disabilities can lead to marital tension and family breakdowns, impacting financial stability and increasing the risk of poverty for single parents (Johnston, 2021).

Based on my experience, I would describe poverty as...

Poverty has never been just about not having enough money. It is a constant pressure that weighs down on you through every decision, every opportunity, every hope. It shapes every detail of daily life, from what food goes on the table to whether the heating goes on, and it stretches into the bigger choices too: the jobs you take, the education you pursue, and the risks you dare not try. Poverty is not only financial deprivation; it is the limitation of options.

Living in poverty feels like carrying an invisible weight that other people cannot see. From the outside, someone might say: "Well, you've got a Motability car and ALL those disability benefits." But what they don't understand is that, first, most of those hard-fought-for and direly insufficient "benefits" are incredibly fragile and unstable. The next review, the following change in government could see this thread-thin lifeline vanish. Meanwhile, the electricity bill is always just barely covered, but essential to keep my child's oxygen concentrator running. The rent is paid – not that I can afford a property with a toilet my child can access. Any unexpected cost: a broken washing machine, a school trip, a child's shoes, threatens to tip everything over. Poverty doesn't allow for breathing space. There is no cushion, no pause, no room to make mistakes.

Poverty is exhausting. It means waking up each morning already tired, calculating what you can juggle, and knowing that whatever you do, it won't be enough. It is staying up late at night worrying about bills, wondering whether the direct debit will bounce, and what letter might come through the post tomorrow. There is always too much month and too little money.

Poverty is also isolating. You decline invitations because you cannot afford the transportation, ticket, or meal out. Watching your children miss out on things their friends take for granted breaks your heart. Sometimes the isolation is not just practical but social. People withdraw when they do not understand your struggles or, worse, judge you, believing the myths that poverty is a sign of laziness or poor choices.

Which is why poverty is so shameful. When you have to decide between the cost of transportation to take one child to a hospital appointment and whether you can afford to send your other child on a school trip, it feels like constantly failing and never being enough. Poverty damages dignity as much as it damages finances.

How I think others view poverty

Poverty is terribly misunderstood by many, especially by those who have never experienced it firsthand. Poverty is depicted not by reality, but through stereotypes. Much of what society "knows" about poverty is shaped by headlines, TV, political speeches, and social media memes. These are not neutral stories; they are carefully constructed narratives that define poor people in ways that are convenient for those in power.

Poverty results from inequality, underfunded systems, and structural barriers. In society, poverty is perpetuated by blaming those in poverty (Alcañiz-Colomer et al., 2022). From this perspective, only lazy, greedy, deceitful, or undeserving people are poor. When disability is added into the mix, the stereotypes become even sharper, more cruel, and more absurd. Research indicates that parents of children with disabilities often find themselves battling societal stereotypes that view their children through a lens of deficit and incapability (Bramhe, 2019; Watanabe et al., 2021).

PREJUDICES AGAINST PARENTS WHO DEPEND ON BENEFITS

Historically, discussions about welfare have been influenced by the idea of the "undeserving poor," portraying parents on benefits as irresponsible and contributing to societal decline. Benefits are often seen not as vital support but as an unfair burden on the state, increasing hostility towards parents who rely on them.

> Public policies have often failed to support families relying on benefits. According to Daly (2023), UK income support programs can discourage work and fail to help single parents, reinforcing stereotypes that depict them as unmotivated. Beatty and Fothergill (2016) highlight that welfare reforms have disproportionately impacted families with children, reinforcing stigmas around entitlement and related behaviours.
>
> The media often reinforces prejudices by highlighting poverty and dysfunction without acknowledging the systemic issues behind them. For example, stories about families on benefits tend to be negative and rarely include the voices of those affected, many of whom are working parents trying to get by (Arthur, 2014; Beatty and Fothergill, 2016).

Let's reflect on some stereotypes here: the myths that dominate public discussion and the harm they cause families like mine.

1 **The stereotype that disability benefits are so generous that people are all "faking it" to live the high life.**
One of the most widespread and harmful stereotypes is that disabled people and their families are "on the take." So-called "benefits cheats," stories are designed to create outrage. They suggest that disability benefits are a golden ticket, making life so comfortable that people will invent illnesses or exaggerate needs to qualify. The truth could not be further from this misconception. Benefits are not generous; they are barely enough to survive on. Families raising disabled children face additional costs that far exceed what the system recognises: electricity bills for medical equipment that keep their child breathing, special diets, therapies, medical and specialised equipment, and constant transport to hospital appointments. Far from living the high life, most families are constantly in deficit, constantly juggling bills, and constantly going without.

2 **Social myths of disabled children and their "Warrior mothers": "They cost the system too much."**
This cruel stereotype depicts disabled children as a drain on resources and a burden that the system can barely afford. Headlines focus on the cost of special education, the pressure on health budgets, and the strain on social care. The media often frames mothers of disabled children as "warriors," but not always in a positive way. Instead, we are portrayed as greedy, demanding, fighting everyone around us to claim resources that other children supposedly deserve more. The narrative suggests that by advocating for our children, we are taking away from others; that we are selfish rather than protective.

3 **The myth that having a disabled child means the government hands you the keys to a "wheelchair accessible mansion."**
Needless to say, having a disabled child does not guarantee a beautiful, spacious, fully adapted home. The reality could not be more different. Families wait years, sometimes decades, living in overcrowded, unsuitable homes where wheelchairs cannot pass through doorways, where medical equipment clutters bedrooms, and where stairs become daily obstacles, an everyday reminder of necessary adaptations.
The idea of the "free mansion" is both absurd and painful. It dismisses the daily indignities families endure, carrying a growing child up the stairs, washing them in a kitchen sink because the bathroom is inaccessible, watching them sleep in pain because there is no space for proper equipment. Housing remains one of the clearest examples of how stereotypes obscure reality. Instead of recognising the desperate need for accessible, affordable homes, the myth of the "mansion" convinces the public that families like mine are already over-provided for.

4 **The idea that disabled children, like poverty itself, are the "fault" of the parents.**
Blame is a recurring theme in how society talks about both poverty and disability. Mothers are accused of drinking, smoking, or eating the wrong foods during pregnancy. This reasoning reflects the way poverty is viewed, not because of structural inequality, but as the outcome of poor personal choices. It absolves society of responsibility. If disability and poverty are individual failings, then nothing needs to change. Governments do not need to invest, communities do not need to adapt, and employers do not need to make space. The burden is placed entirely on families, who are left to carry both the care work and the shame.

5. **The myth that mothers who leave employment to care are "lazy and feckless."**
Caring for a disabled child often requires round-the-clock attention. Appointments, therapies, hospital stays, and sleepless nights are full-time jobs on top of full-time parenting. The administrative burden of caring for a disabled child is enormous. Many mothers reduce their hours or leave paid employment altogether because there simply are not enough hours in the day. Others are driven out of their employment because businesses struggle to cope with the relentless onslaught of days off for illness and hospital visits. This stereotype unfairly diminishes the value of care. It implies that unless you are earning wages, you are worthless. Parent carers of disabled children often work harder and longer than others, without breaks, holidays, or recognition.

6 **The idea that disabled children, and disabled people in general, don't contribute enough to justify what they "get."**
This belief underpins so much discrimination. It justifies underfunding services, cutting benefits, and questioning whether certain lives are "worth" the

investment. Contribution cannot be measured solely in economic terms. Disabled children contribute love, laughter, and perspective to their families and communities. They teach resilience, creativity, and the importance of inclusion. Disabled adults contribute in countless ways: through paid work where barriers are removed, through volunteering, activism, art, and relationships. Reducing human worth to financial output is dehumanising.

These stereotypes influence policy, reinforce stigma, and harm families. They create an environment where families feel judged. They silence broader conversations about inequality, because as long as poverty and disability are seen as personal failings, society avoids confronting the underlying structures that create them.

Poverty is not a personal failing, and disability is not a burden to be managed. These are matters of justice, rights, and collective responsibility.

My story (my life and experiences, the causes of poverty for me, the impact of poverty on me, and those around me)

Beginning: childhood in poverty

Growing up in poverty wasn't as stressful as it undoubtedly was for the adults making difficult decisions. Children accept things as they are, and to some extent, we don't miss what we don't know exists. Nonetheless, a childhood in poverty has a significant impact on your future opportunities and options. The stigma of being a child in poverty becomes woven into the fabric of your being as you absorb all the sideways glances and sharp comments that connect to the likelihood of your guilt for a crime and the estate upon which you reside. The hardest part wasn't going without, but knowing that society is judging you.

Middle: university, nights, and three jobs

When I left home, I was determined to escape poverty. Attending university felt like breaking a cycle. Unlike many of my peers, I didn't have a safety net. I worked mornings in a café, a lunch shift in the student union building on campus, and nights in a restaurant. While other students came to classes tired from being out socialising, I often went to lectures with little sleep, running on caffeine and sheer willpower after working a 55-hour workweek and studying.

Balancing study and multiple jobs was brutal, but it gave me a sense of pride. I was proving, at least to myself, that poverty was not laziness. I wanted to give my children, if I had any, something better. And for a while, I thought I was succeeding. Working three jobs comes at a cost. It wears down your health, your relationships, and your sense of balance. Poverty teaches you never to rest, because resting feels like a risk you can't afford.

Now: raising two complexly disabled children

Life changed in unexpected ways. Having two children with complex disabilities transformed everything. The energy I once dedicated to work was suddenly consumed by hospital appointments, surgeries, care routines, and the emotional strain of watching my children fight battles most adults could not endure.

It has been an impossible balancing act year after year. One child in one hospital undergoing brain surgery, another child in a High Dependency Unit in a hospital hundreds of miles away, my other children at home needing me too. And here I am trying to work, trying to be in three places at once, trying to hold everything together, and constantly failing in ways the outside world never sees. It is not just the exhaustion, but the judgement. No matter what I do, society still manages to paint me as lazy and overindulgent.

Raising disabled children in poverty feels like being punished for circumstances beyond your control. The barriers are endless: unsuitable housing, inaccessible transportation, long waits for equipment, and battles with bureaucracies that treat every request with suspicion. Even when I push myself beyond breaking point, it never feels like enough. There is always another letter demanding proof, another form to justify need, another sideways glance suggesting I'm not pulling my weight.

No matter the cost or exhaustion, there is love. My children are not burdens; they are beautiful, vibrant, and full of joy. They are the reason I fight so hard. They show me daily what resilience truly means. The burden is not on them; it is how society treats them, and us.

Impact of poverty on raising a disabled child

Impact on the child

For a disabled child, poverty adds an extra layer of challenge. Poverty limits access to resources, reduces opportunities, and deepens stigma. Health can be significantly affected. Families in poverty may struggle to access prompt healthcare, whether due to long waiting lists, lack of transport, or the costs associated with specialist diets, equipment, or medication not fully covered by the NHS or benefits. The expenses of running medical equipment can be significant, and challenging decisions must be made about whether to operate the washing machine or the oxygen concentrator. Disabled children in poorer households face higher risks of hospitalisation, poorer long-term outcomes, and missed preventative care (Mitra et al., 2017). For example, when a wheelchair breaks, a family with financial means can order a replacement. In poverty, a child may be left without mobility for weeks or months, even years, limiting independence and dignity. Overcrowded housing is more prone to damp and poor ventilation, having a profound effect on respiratory health and the ability to safely store medical equipment.

Education is another important area of inequality. Although inclusive schooling is theoretically a right, in practice it often requires parental advocacy, costly transport, and the purchase of materials that schools do not provide. Children in poverty are less likely to receive early intervention services, have education plans fully implemented, and are more likely to be excluded when behaviour linked to disability is misunderstood. Missed school days caused by inaccessible housing or medical crises further compound disadvantage.

Well-being is also significantly affected. Disabled children already face stigma and exclusion; poverty magnifies this. Being unable to afford school trips, adapted sports clubs, or social activities means disabled children in poverty are often doubly excluded: first by disability, then by finances. Over time, this leads to isolation, low self-esteem, and a sense of being "less than."

With limited access to education, fewer opportunities for independence, and the health impacts of deprivation, disabled children are more likely to enter adulthood already disadvantaged, perpetuating cycles of exclusion. In this sense, poverty not only impacts a child's present but also sets the stage for a lifetime of structural inequality.

Impact on siblings

Siblings of children with disabilities may take on caring responsibilities, provide emotional support, or adjust their own lives to accommodate the needs of their brother or sister. Poverty magnifies these pressures. Financial strain may mean siblings go without, as when balancing the need for a wheelchair against the desire for a trendy pair of shoes, the wheelchair is the purchase the family has to make. Siblings may have fewer chances to participate in extracurricular activities, not just due to costs but also due to the challenges of transport when their disabled sibling is in the hospital or ill. Many siblings show remarkable resilience, empathy, and compassion; however, others internalise feelings of neglect or resentment (Burke, 2010). It is not that parents love them less, but that attention, time, and money are so heavily directed towards the disabled child's needs.

School can be a spotlight for these disparities. Siblings may face bullying because of their family circumstances. Some siblings become protectors, fiercely loyal to their disabled sibling, while others withdraw socially to avoid embarrassment or pity. Studies have shown that siblings in such contexts face higher risks of anxiety and depression (Goudie et al., 2013).

Siblings often develop empathy and maturity, and many grow to possess a strong sense of justice, compassion, and responsibility. Poverty makes it harder to nurture these positives because of the stress of having to juggle access to necessary resources. For example, not only might siblings have to share a bedroom, but they may also have to accept a significantly reduced share of space. Disability tends to bring with it the need for a volume of equipment and supplies, and siblings may find themselves sharing their wardrobe not just for their clothes, but also for their disabled siblings' medical supplies.

Impact on parents

For parents, raising a disabled child in poverty is like walking a tightrope without a safety net. Every decision is high stakes, every mistake carries heavy consequences, and every day is foggy with exhaustion.

The financial pressure is immediate. Parents often face additional costs of disability, from specialist diets and therapies to hospital travel and equipment, that can amount to three times the costs of raising a non-disabled child (Contact, 2014). Benefits rarely cover this gap, and many families report ongoing debt and arrears. Employment becomes difficult or impossible. Mothers, in particular, often reduce their hours or leave work entirely to provide care, thereby reinforcing gendered inequalities in the labour market (Parish and Cloud, 2006).

Emotionally, the toll is vast. Parents face stress, sleep deprivation, and anxiety about their child's health. Studies show significantly higher rates of depression and physical ill-health among carers of disabled children (Brehaut et al., 2004). Poverty worsens this, as the inability to meet needs creates a sense of constant failure. Parents describe feeling judged as "lazy" or "feckless" even as they work harder than ever, both in paid and unpaid labour.

Socially, poverty isolates families. Bureaucratic systems often treat parents with suspicion, requiring repeated proof of disability or need. Instead of support, parents often face hostility from the very services meant to help. This creates what scholars call "bureaucratic violence," the harm inflicted when systems designed for care instead degrade dignity.

Advocacy becomes a daily practice, involving efforts to fight for education, healthcare, housing, and benefits. Mothers, in particular, are often labelled "too demanding." In reality, they are doing what love requires.

Impact on community services

Poverty significantly affects community services, which are often already underfunded. Schools, healthcare providers, and social services are facing an increasing demand but lack the necessary resources to respond. In this climate, families of disabled children are sometimes positioned as "burdens" rather than as rights-holders.

In education, this looks like exclusion; schools resisting the enrolment of disabled children because they lack staff, training, or adapted facilities. In healthcare, it often appears as long waits, inaccessible clinics, and limited respite services. In social care, it appears that eligibility thresholds are so high that only the most severe cases receive any form of help.

The story of scarcity is persuasive. Services blame families for "taking too much," while families blame services for failing to provide, when the real problem is systemic underfunding. Poverty creates competition for resources, fuelling resentment and reinforcing stereotypes.

Importantly, poverty also limits the effectiveness of otherwise good services. A therapy session offered once a week may be useless if the family cannot afford the bus fare. A wheelchair provided by the health system may be stored if the home is too cramped to accommodate its use. Without addressing poverty, even well-designed services cannot fully meet needs.

THE IMPACT OF DISABLED CHILDREN LIVING IN POVERTY ON PUBLIC SERVICES

Public services, especially child protection and welfare, are strained by austerity and rising child poverty. Bywaters et al. (2017) find that demand for children's services has increased disproportionately in high-poverty areas, resulting in disparities in access and quality across England. As poverty grows, limited resources become more stretched, further reducing support for disabled children who often require additional help (Webb et al., 2022).

Austerity cuts have reduced preventative services for families with disabled children. Webb et al. (2022) highlight that these cuts lead to inadequate prevention, which, along with poverty, heightens the risk of crises and the need for emergency intervention (Webb et al., 2020). As a result, many disabled, disadvantaged children rely on crisis-focused public services that do not meet their needs.

Practitioners aim to help vulnerable people, but austerity constraints can cause ethical dilemmas, hindering their ability to fulfil professional duties (Kerasidou and Kingori, 2019). This may reduce job satisfaction and increase turnover, exacerbating workforce pressures.

Tailored services for disabled children and their families, offering emotional, social, and educational support, and community engagement, can mitigate the adverse effects of poverty (Rakap et al., 2022). Building strong support networks enhances therapeutic and educational outcomes, boosting quality of life and reducing reliance on emergency services.

Impact on family and friends

Extended family and friends can be both a lifeline and a source of strain. In some cases, grandparents step in to provide childcare, emotional support, or financial assistance. However, for many, relatives withdraw, overwhelmed by the demands of disability and poverty.

Friendships often suffer. Socialising costs money and energy that families of disabled children in poverty do not have. Friends may not understand why so many invitations are declined. When your child is in a wheelchair and has poor temperature regulation, a playpark might be free to visit. However, the woodchips won't allow the wheels to roll across, and the cost to the whole family of a fortnight in hospital with another chest infection is too high a price to pay. Yet, without the resources to afford the cinema or the indoor play place, it can make going out and meeting with others challenging.

When family and friends do show up, the impact is transformative. A meal cooked, a lift given, a sympathetic ear; these gestures remind families they are not alone and carry us through the hardest times.

Overall impact

The impact of poverty on raising a disabled child is significant, and it is further amplified if you live rurally, are a single parent, or have more than one disabled child. It has a lifelong impact on the child, alters sibling relationships, puts parents in extreme circumstances, pressures community services, and reshapes bonds with family and friends. Poverty magnifies the difficulties of disability, not because disability itself is inherently difficult, but because of the way society is structured and how support is delivered.

Families like ours do not want or need pity. We need dignity and fair access to the resources that enable full participation. Poverty is not an inevitable part of disability; it is the result of choices made at political and societal levels. And it is within our collective power to change.

What needs to change – my message to others

Disability can affect anyone through birth, accident, illness, or old age. Poverty, too, is closer than many imagine; one job loss, one illness, one crisis away. If we pause and consider that both disability and poverty are real possibilities for every person, this perspective changes how we vote, how we speak, and how we support one another.

Having a disabled child is not a tragedy, any more than arriving in Holland, instead of Italy. It is an honour and a joy, a privilege to see the world through their eyes, to love them and be loved in return. The tragedy is the way society layers stigma and poverty on top of disability, turning love into struggle.

Poverty and disability are not personal failings. They result from policies, systems, and attitudes that cause families like mine to struggle, and then blame us for it. If there is one message I want to share, it is that change is possible, but it requires courage, compassion, and a willingness to see poverty and disability differently.

Benefits systems need to be fairer, simpler, and rooted in dignity rather than suspicion. Assessments should begin from a place of trust, not hostility. Families should not have to prove and re-prove their children's needs, and housing policies must prioritise accessible homes. We need to robustly invest in our hospitals and paediatric services. Schools need to receive proper funding and training to include children with disabilities, and respite services must be expanded so that parents are not pushed to exhaustion before help arrives.

Beyond the urgent fixes, we need a deeper cultural shift. We must dismantle the stereotypes that portray disabled children as drains or disabled adults as non-contributors. We should recognise care work for what it is: labour that sustains society and should be valued as such. Work should not be measured only by wages but by contribution, and parents who give their time and energy to care for disabled children should be supported, not penalised. We also need to change how poverty itself is understood. Instead of seeing it as an individual fault, we must recognise it as structural – the result of inequality, underfunding, and social neglect. This shift in perspective opens the door to systemic solutions: living wages, affordable housing, universal healthcare, inclusive education, and robust social security.

REFLECTIVE ACTIVITY

Take a moment to pause and reflect on the following prompts. Write down your thoughts, discuss them with a colleague, or simply sit with them. The goal is not to find the "right" answer but to challenge assumptions and deepen understanding.

1 **Think about the stereotypes.**
- Which of the common myths about poverty and disability have you heard before?
- Have you ever believed any of them? If so, why do you think that was?

2 **Reflect on your own experiences.**
- How close have you, or someone you know, come to poverty?
- How do your life circumstances (job, housing, health, and education) protect you from or expose you to poverty?

3 **Consider the role of systems.**

- In what ways are poverty and disability shaped by political and social choices rather than individual actions?
- How might things be different if society chose to value care, equity, and inclusion more highly?

4 **Imagine change.**

- What is one small change you could make – in your thinking, your language, or your actions – that could help dismantle stereotypes about poverty and disability?
- What bigger changes would you like to see in your community or country?

Reflection is the first step towards transformation. Change begins when we recognise that poverty and disability are not private shames but public responsibilities – and that every one of us has a role in shaping a fairer world.

Further reading, viewing, or listening

- *Letter to Louis* by Alison White – A UK-based memoir about the first 18 years of her son Louis, who was born prematurely and has cerebral palsy and learning difficulties.
- *Loving Fiona: A memoir about parenting, disability, and the beauty of being human* by Heather Lanier – Focuses on raising a daughter with an ultra-rare physical/developmental syndrome (Wolf-Hirschhorn).
- *Motherness: A memoir of generational autism, parenthood, and radical acceptance by* Julie M. Green – A mother discovers along the way that not only her child, but she herself is autistic.
- The Special Needs Mom Podcast by Kara Ryska – A podcast by a parent of children with special needs; she addresses everyday challenges, mental health, navigating systems, and resilience. (Apple Podcasts)
- The Skies We're Under by Rachel Wright (Born at the Right Time) – Conversations with parents of children with disabilities and those in their communities; mixing storytelling, practical tips, and emotional honesty. (Apple Podcasts)
- Welcome to Holland, poem by Emily Perl Kingsley.

Bibliography

Alcañiz-Colomer, J., Moya, M., & Valor-Segura, I. (2022). Not all Poor Are Equal: the Perpetuation of Poverty Through Blaming those Who Have Been Poor All their Lives. *Current Psychology*, 42(31), 26928–26944. https://doi.org/10.1007/s12144-022-03804-6

Arthur, R. (2014). Troubling Times for Young People and Families with Troubles – Responding to Truancy, Rioting and Families Struggling with Adversity. *Social & Legal Studies*, 24(3), 443–464. https://doi.org/10.1177/0964663914559239

Ayoola, A. A., Adeoye, O. F., & Joy, A. (2025). Maternal Mental Health and Parenting Children with Disabilities: A Systematic Review of Psychological and Social Challenges. *IJPGRR*, 2(2), 16–27. https://doi.org/10.54660/ijpgrr.2025.2.2.16-27

Baumberg, B. (2016). The stigma of claiming benefits: a quantitative study. *Journal of Social Policy*, 45(2), 181–199. doi:10.1017/S0047279415000525

Beatty, C., & Fothergill, S. (2016). The Uneven Impact of Welfare Reform. https://doi.org/10.7190/cresr.2017.5563239352

Bramhe, V. (2019). Depression and Anxiety in Mothers of Children with Autism Spectrum Disorders and Intellectual Disabilities. *Indian Journal of Mental Health*, 6(3), 272. https://doi.org/10.30877/ijmh.6.3.2019.272-279

Brehaut, J.C., Kohen, D.E., Raina, P., Walter, S.D., Russell, D.J., Swinton, M., O'Donnell, M., Rosenbaum, P. (2004). The health of primary caregivers of children with cerebral palsy: how does it compare with that of other Canadian caregivers? *Pediatrics*, 114(2), e182–91. doi: 10.1542/peds.114.2.e182

Burke, P. (2010). Brothers and Sisters of Disabled Children: The Experience of Disability by Association. *Disability & Society*, 25(1), 41–54.

Bywaters, P., Brady, G., Bunting, L., Daniel, B., Featherstone, B., Jones, C., Morris, K., Scourfield, J., Sparks, T. H., & Webb, C. (2017). Inequalities in English Child Protection Practice Under Austerity: A Universal Challenge? *Child & Family Social Work*, 23(1), 53–61. https://doi.org/10.1111/cfs.12383

Contact (2014) Counting the costs 2014 Research into the finances of more than 3,500 families with disabled children across the UK. Available at http://www.counting_the_costs_2014_uk_report.pdf

Daly, M. C. (2023). Inclusiveness and Flexibility of Income Support Policies. https://doi.org/10.31235/osf.io/pm7na

Dobson, B., & Middleton, S. (1998). *Paying to Care: The Cost of Childhood Disability*. York: Joseph Rowntree Foundation.

Dowling, M., & Dolan, L. (2001). Families with Children with Disabilities—Inequalities and the Social Model. *Disability & Society*, 16(1), 21–35.

Emerson, E. (2003a). Poverty, Disadvantage and Children with Intellectual Disabilities in the UK. *Children & Society*, 17(2), 95–109.

Emerson, E. (2003b). Mothers of Children and Adolescents With Intellectual Disability: Social and Economic Situation, Mental Health Status, and the Self-assessed Social and Psychological Impact of the Child's Difficulties. *Journal of Intellectual Disability Research*, 47(4–5), 385–399. https://doi.org/10.1046/j.1365-2788.2003.00498.x

Emerson, E., & Hatton, C. (2007). The Socio-economic Circumstances of Children at Risk of Disability in Britain. *Disability & Society*, 22(6), 563–580.

Emerson, E., & Llewellyn, G. (2008). The Mental Health of Australian Mothers and Fathers of Young Children at Risk of Disability. *Australian and New Zealand Journal of Public Health*, 32(1), 53–59. https://doi.org/10.1111/j.1753-6405.2008.00166.x

Gorman, M. (2019). Disability and Child Poverty. In Gottfried, T., & Archer, D. (Eds.), *Philosophy and Child Poverty* (pp. 187–202). Cham: Springer.

Goudie, A., Havercamp, S., Jamieson, B., Sahr, T. (2013). Assessing functional impairment in siblings living with children with disability. *Pediatrics*, 132(2):e476–e483. doi: 10.1542/peds.2013-0644

Green, S. (2007). "We're tired, not sad": Benefits and Burdens of Mothering a Child with a Disability. *Social Science & Medicine*, 64(1), 150–163.
Jacobs, S. (2025). "Some people on benefits are faking it. There, I've said it." Telegraph, some people on benefits are faking it. There, I've said it.
Johnston, E. (2021). The Child with Developmental Disabilities: The Effects on the Whole Family. What Do the Families Really Need From the 'Early Intervention' Professional System? *Human Systems Therapy Culture and Attachments*, 2(1), 20–29. https://doi.org/10.1177/26344041211062851
Kerasidou, A., & Kingori, P. (2019). Austerity Measures and the Transforming Role of A&E Professionals in a Weakening Welfare System. *PLoS One*, 14(2), e0212314. https://doi.org/10.1371/journal.pone.0212314
Kingsley, E.P. (1987). Welcome to Holland. www.emilyperlkingsley.com/welcome-to-holland
McConnell, D., & Savage, A. (2015). Stress and Resilience among Families Raising Children with Disabilities. *Journal of Child and Family Studies*, 24, 3462–3475.
McHale, S. M., & Harris, V. (1992). Sibling Relationships of Children with Disabled and Nondisabled Brothers and Sisters. *Developmental Psychology*, 28(4), 682–689.
Mitra, S., Palmer, M., Kim, H., Mont, D., Groce, N. (2017). Extra costs of living with a disability: A review and agenda for research. *Disability and Health Journal*, 10(4):475–484. doi: 10.1016/j.dhjo.2017.04.007
Naylor, A., & Prescott, P. (2004). Invisible Children? The Need for Support Groups for Siblings of Disabled Children. *British Journal of Special Education*, 31(4), 199–206.
OECD. (2011). *Doing Better for Families*. Paris: OECD Publishing.
Parish, S., & Cloud, J. (2006). Financial Well-being of Young Children with Disabilities and their Families. *Social Work*, 51(3), 223–232.
Rakap, S., Batık, M. V., Kalkan, S., Karnas, M., Sarı, H. İ., & Bayrakdar, U. (2022). The Hidden (Overlooked) Impact of Living Through a Pandemic: How Parents of Children with Disabilities Fared During COVID-19? *Frontiers in Education*, 7. https://doi.org/10.3389/feduc.2022.827230
Risdal, D., & Singer, G. (2004). Marital Adjustment in Parents of Children with Disabilities: A Historical Review and Meta-Analysis. *Research and Practice for Persons with Severe Disabilities*, 29(2), 95–103. https://doi.org/10.2511/rpsd.29.2.95
Sharpe, D., & Rossiter, L. (2002). Siblings of Children with a Chronic Illness: A Meta-analysis. *Journal of Pediatric Psychology*, 27(8), 699–710.
Shikako, K., et al. (2024). Experiences and Factors Affecting Poverty Among Families Raising a Child with a Disability: A Scoping Review. *Disability and Health Journal*.
UNESCO. (2020). *Global Education Monitoring Report: Inclusion and Education*. Paris: UNESCO.
UNICEF. (2013). *The State of the World's Children: Children with Disabilities*. New York: UNICEF.
Watanabe, M., Kibe, C., Sugawara, M., & Miyake, H. (2021). Courtesy Stigma of Parents of Children with Down Syndrome: Adaptation Process and Transcendent Stage. *Journal of Genetic Counseling*, 31(3), 746–757. https://doi.org/10.1002/jgc4.1541
Webb, C., Bennett, D., & Bywaters, P. (2022). Austerity, Poverty, and Children's Services Quality in England: Consequences for Child Welfare and Public Services. *Social Policy and Society*, 23(2), 278–299. https://doi.org/10.1017/s147474642200001x
Webb, C., Bywaters, P., Scourfield, J., McCartan, C., Bunting, L., Davidson, G., & Morris, K. (2020). Untangling Child Welfare Inequalities and the 'Inverse Intervention Law' in England. *Children and Youth Services Review*, 111, 104849. https://doi.org/10.1016/j.childyouth.2020.104849
WHO. (2011). *World Report on Disability*. Geneva: World Health Organization.

13

POVERTY AND BEING A REFUGEE

Alan Hamidi and Katharine Harrison

The United Nations High Commission for Refugees reports increasing numbers of people being forcibly displaced worldwide. Currently, 1 in every 67 people is displaced (UNHCR 12/06/2025).

"I had to flee"

My name is Alan Hamidi. I am from the Kurdish city of Kermanshah in Iran. I am a civil society and cultural rights activist who worked to defend and promote human rights, particularly Kurdish linguistic and cultural rights.

In December 2008, I was kidnapped by the agents of the Ministry of Intelligence of the Islamic Republic of Iran. For several days, I was kept in their secret torture rooms in Kermanshah and then for more than nine months in Tehran. I was detained in solitary confinement, subjected to inhumane interrogations and physical and mental torture, accused of acting against national security and espionage (common accusations for persecution and imprisonment of activists and dissidents in Iran). When I was sent for trial, the Judge in the first court dismissed the charges for lack of any evidence. The intelligence agents, using force and pressure, tried me and convicted me in another court, before transferring me to Hamedan Prison, where I was imprisoned for more than three years. Finally, after two years of detention without trial and three years of imprisonment, I was released.

Prior to my arrest and imprisonment, I had worked for the Air Force as an aircraft maintenance engineer and technical teacher, but after being released from prison, I was fired from my job.

Before my release, intelligence agents had threatened me that they would not leave me after my release and that the next time they would deal with me

DOI: 10.4324/9781003638476-14

more seriously and severely. They refused to give me a copy of the verdict; they said that with it, you will create discord and controversy against us abroad.

When I was released from prison, I tried to have a normal life and started a small business. But they threatened me twice, refusing to let me pursue any cultural activities, for example, Kurdish language teaching, poetry and literature, or education about our civil rights. They called me to go to the Intelligence Office: I knew that if I went to them, I would be arrested, with an unpredictable outcome.

I decided to leave the country for Turkey, where I registered with UNHCR (United Nations High Commission for Refugees) as an asylum seeker. Then, in a wave of arrests of Kurdish civil and cultural activists in Kermanshah, a number of my friends were detained by the security and intelligence forces. During the interrogations, they had asked my friends a lot of questions about me, my whereabouts, and the ways they could capture me. Family members informed me of their threats. The Turkish government has a long-standing enmity with the Kurds and, like Iran, violates the rights of its own Kurdish citizens. After a long period of waiting, uncertainty, and hopeful expectation, I had to flee Turkey and come to Europe, and eventually to England in September 2023.

KURDS IN THE UK

The Kurds are the world's largest ethnic group without a state of their own. Oppression of the Kurdish people in Iran is well-documented. For example, the UK government website states that

> Kurds asserting their ethnic and religious identity, engaging in or associated with civil or political activities, or promoting or perceived to be promoting separatism, may face arbitrary arrest, detention ... and in some cases the death penalty ... Kurds in Iran face systematic discrimination and barriers which affects their access to basic services such as housing, political office, employment and education ... Instruction of the Kurdish language is not taught in state schools ... Activities that may be perceived as political and as a threat to the state include students, environmentalists, musicians, attending Nowruz [new year] celebrations and other cultural activities ... Almost half of all political prisoners in Iran are Kurds and most are charged with crimes against national security. In the absence of evidence, torture, which is reported to be widespread, may be used to extract confessions.

An estimated 0.1% of the total population of England and Wales identify as Kurds (ONS 2021). Only those with evidence and details of direct persecution, or the threat of it, obtain refugee status.

"It was strange for me"

When I arrived in the UK, I had €250 as the last money that I had, and I needed to buy a phone, although I could talk with my family by the Dover camp phone by remembering our home telephone number after many years. This was happiness for me and a most important and necessary thing.

After Dover, I came to London. I had come from the hotel to the Hounslow shopping centre with two friends. We didn't have any pound sterling to pay the bus fare, but I knew enough English to show the bus driver our euros, which he accepted. My friend Hadi helped me search "Charity near me"; I hadn't heard this word before. I found a few charities on the map and went to them. But most of them were charity shops and full of second-hand clothes and other household items. It was strange for me that I saw these kinds of shops in this country. I didn´t think people in the UK bought second-hand clothes.

After a little search, I found a charity that was not a charity shop. I think it was "Afghanistan & Central Asian Association". Me and one of my friends who didn't have a phone could take two old phones with sim cards. One of them could connect to the internet, and I could install a few simple applications like WhatsApp, but its battery was damaged. Finally, I was forced to buy a better phone. I gave the old one to my friend Ahmad, whose charity phone was not smart even.

Hounslow was full of India. You thought you had come to India instead of England. The question in our mind was "Where are the British people?" Most of the staff of the hotels are from India and Pakistan, too. Where are the British guys and where do they work? As a friend said, maybe they are so rich that they don't need to work, and foreign people work for them. Many questions were on my mind.

On the third day in Hounslow, I saw my name on the list of transportation. To where? I don't know. After less than one hour, I was in another hotel in a town named Basingstoke.

"I tried continually to adapt"

There were two people in every room. I was sent to a room where an Iranian guy lived, who said, in Persian: "You cannot be here! I have a single room".

I said to him: "Hello, how are you? I wanted to take a room with one Kurdish guy but they sent me to this room. If you know a way to change it, please tell me". He finally brought his friend Shahin, and I swapped rooms with him.

A young Arabic African guy was sent to be my roommate. He was a calm guy who definitely carried a story of people's suffering. He did not know English, and I only knew a few Arabic words.

Our next challenges were applying for Section 95, an Aspen [Asylum Support Enablement] card (on which they paid us almost £9 each week), and an ARC [application registration card].

OUR ENTITLEMENTS

"Aspen" is Asylum Support Enablement, a card onto which money is paid each week. The current rate (2025) has risen to £9.95. An ARC card is an application registration card, which certifies that an asylum seeker can remain in the UK while their claim is pending. Although it contains information about their identity, it is not proof of identity.

Migrant Help (Aspen Cards) – you can find out the current entitlements from government websites or migrant support charities.

Under Sections 95 and 98 of the Immigration Act 1999, the Home Office provides housing and financial support to a person seeking asylum who is destitute.

They are not allowed to work, unless they have been waiting more than a year for a decision, and then only in a job on the Skilled Worker visa: immigration salary list (GOV.UK). Effectively, for most, this means in care work or construction.

Government legislation and policy regarding asylum in the UK are under constant review and change, making it difficult for support organisations and individuals to navigate. The information presented here is the latest at the time of writing, but you will need to access the links for the latest updates.

They gave us three meals a day and some fruit too, but the hotel's spicy food often didn't suit our tastes. We were not allowed to cook in the rooms, but some of us had small hobs and cooked sometimes. Meals came in plastic boxes, which staff reheated in microwaves. It was not healthy. I talked with the manager and was able to get special food that was not spicy.

I had some English skills, but British accents are strange and hard. The first day, I went to find the college to ask about English courses. It was possible to apply after six months.

LEARNING ENGLISH

ESOL (English for Speakers of Other Languages) courses are government-funded at the local college for those who have been in the UK for six months, but waiting lists can be long. Alan is now registered for a couple of sessions a week at the local community learning centre.

Community-Based English Language Training (GOV.UK) – there are several organisations providing this training in the UK, which is seen by the current government as a core intervention to help new and established migrants integrate into British society.

I tried continually to adapt to the new environment. A network of Christian communities, well-wishers, and charities supported the refugees. On Thursday afternoons, there was an English class in the hotel. Monday afternoon, there was another class in the United Reformed Church, and another English class in the library every Saturday morning. From our hotel to the town centre was 25 minutes walking. The most prominent volunteer was a woman named Alex, an angel in human form. Her charity was for asylum seekers, and every Saturday, there were donated clothes for us. On Tuesdays, she ran the language class, and she gave another morning to talk and help the asylum seekers in the hotel lobby.

You cannot afford to go on a short trip or go to the gym. I bought an electric razor with a part of my money. I didn't like to use second-hand clothes. One day, one of my friends sent me an app; he wanted me to install it so that he could get some free items by sharing the app. It was Temu. I downloaded it, and then I tried to share it with others in the hotel. I could take six items by sharing this app. as part of their promotion: a smart watch, a suitcase, some sports clothes, headphones, and a jacket. It made us happy.

One of my issues was finding a solicitor. One of my uncle's friends finally introduced a Kurdish solicitor, but most asylum seekers had so many issues finding one. After one year of waiting, we qualify for a limited work permit, but some want to find a job with or without a permit. Most of the "black economy" jobs are in a carwash, in construction, gardening, or mini-markets.

YOUR RIGHT TO LEGAL SUPPORT

Claiming asylum (The Law Society) – to stay in the UK as a refugee, the person must apply for asylum. As the Law Society explains, asylum law is complicated, and good legal advice is recommended to help put the person's case forward.

How to get help as an asylum seeker if you can't find legal aid (Big Issue) – although most people seeking asylum are entitled to free legal support, in practice, finding a solicitor with a legal aid contract who can take on a new case can be very difficult. It often takes many months of waiting for the solicitor to be able to act at each stage. The Big Issue found that this can further add to the trauma experienced by asylum seekers.

"Welcome to the UK"

After one and a half months in the hotel, my body started to itch. I talked with reception, and they made an appointment for me in two weeks' time. It's hard to get an appointment when you are not familiar with the system, and they must arrange an interpreter in advance. Sometimes you need to talk with (the NHS phone line): 111; they ask so many questions according to their protocol, and finally, maybe they tell you to go and buy some medicine you can't afford in a pharmacy.

One day, I went to the Emergency Department of the hospital. The receptionist asked me to wait in one room. I waited more than three hours, but there was no doctor. It was so strange. Then I told them that if the doctor doesn't come soon, I will go back to the hotel to eat my lunch. Finally, they sent an Iranian doctor. I asked him why here is so strange? He answered: "Welcome to the UK!" After examination, he said you should go to the GP, and we cannot do anything here because it is not an emergency, and we cannot give you any medicine here. I asked him, "Could you please give me a prescription to take a medicine from a pharmacy outside?". He said, "No I cannot". I was so astonished! Why can a doctor not give a prescription after examination? If I were in Iran, it would be very normal. When I have the right to use the medical service system, especially free medical care, what difference does it make whether the doctor prescribes medicine for me in a hospital or in a GP surgery?

So, I waited for a GP appointment. The first time, the doctor just gave me cream for my dry skin. After one week, the itching increased, and I had a rash and redness. I asked the staff to make me a new appointment. From searching the net and asking my friend's brother, I came to the conclusion that it was scabies. I have not experienced that before, even when I was in prison under the Iranian dictatorship. I experienced it in the UK, the centre of the developed world. Why? I don't know. The NHS system is destroyed, people say, but there are many positive points. It is a problem to meet an expert doctor. I had this illness for three months, and they gave me the wrong medicine over the phone and by photo. In the Middle East, even in Iran and Turkey, you can find better doctors. Anyone can find them; there aren't any restrictions, [gatekeepers], and obstacles.

Finding a home

After three months, the hotel in Basingstoke was closed. I was moved to a hotel in Bournemouth. After one year as an asylum seeker, I became a refugee. I received refugee status after attending two interviews with the Home Office in Portsmouth. The officer interviewed me for three hours over a screen with an interpreter. They asked many questions about my life: "Why did you leave your country?" and "What will happen if you go back to your country?"

BEING GRANTED REFUGEE STATUS

The average time to be granted refugee status in the UK is several years, typically taking between one and three years for an initial decision. In 2023, the government published a briefing looking at how asylum delays have changed over time, the possible reasons for the increase in delays, the effect of this on asylum seekers, and the Government's plans to reduce the backlog. You can read this and any updated briefings on the House of Commons Library website.

Refugee Data (UNHCR, March 2025):

85,112 asylum applications (relating to 109,343 people) were made in the UK.

109,536 people were awaiting an initial decision, one third of whom had been waiting for more than a year.

47% of initial decisions were grants of protection, meaning they have been awarded refugee status or humanitarian protection. The number of appeals lodged has increased sixfold.

Refugee Action – half of one percent of the UK's population is a refugee or a person seeking asylum. Worldwide, roughly 85% of all refugees live in developing regions, not in wealthy industrialised countries, and 73% of refugees displaced abroad live in countries neighbouring their countries of origin.

After ten days, I received their decision and a letter from Migrant Help that said: "You must leave the hotel within 28 days".

Finding a place to live is a struggle and a big issue for each refugee, especially the first time. A refugee gets a work permit with their refugee status, but nobody has work at that moment. Every estate agent asks about your job and wants to see your contract, or a work record, or requires a guarantor. A refugee doesn't have any of them. Renting a property was so hard for me.

When a refugee wants to rent, first, they must apply for Universal Credit, and at the same time, they should go to the council and register their details there. After reviewing the conditions like age and health problems (illness and disability), the council assigns a housing worker. Then this housing worker sets an appointment for the refugee (they have many others applying too). My housing officer set my appointment nearly two weeks ahead.

I started searching for a property in the very first days.

I have some English friends, and they work as volunteers at a local Church. They hold free English classes for asylum seekers two days a week. When they heard about me, one of them talked to an English teacher, and he agreed to be my guarantor. I had a good chance. It was a good advantage, but even with this, it was hard to find an appropriate property. Most people rent a shared house with several rooms; shared houses usually do not need a guarantor.

I searched for more than two weeks and visited several properties. Universal Credit gives housing benefit for renting according to age. The maximum amount that they pay is nearly £700 for a person over 36 years old, like me. It was hard to rent a studio flat on this amount. Many of the estate agents don't answer you when they know about your situation as a person who takes benefits and doesn't have a full-time work contract. It was very painful.

I chose three or four properties. Two of them were studio flats. Both were on the third floor without a lift; they didn't have any kitchen appliances such as an oven, hob, washing machine, or fridge. They were completely unfurnished.

The first one I visited was better than the others. It was furnished and on the first floor, but it had a shared bathroom. I decided to take it, but it went to another applicant. I didn't have time to wait.

Another estate agent called me to say I could visit a studio flat near the town centre. It was better than the others; on the ground floor, unfurnished, but it had basic kitchen appliances. I filled the forms out after visiting the property, and they were accepted; I paid the holding deposit and informed the council. I needed them to pay the deposit [a loan which comes out of my Universal Credit] and first rent; fortunately, the housing officer accepted it, but I had to wait three days and felt very stressed.

One day before the deadline to leave the hotel, the estate agent called me and said we received the money, and tomorrow you can collect the key at 10 a.m. I did not have a bed or a bowl, but never mind.

ASYLUM SEEKERS AND HOMELESSNESS

Speak with young refugees living in an HMO (House in Multiple Occupation), and some will describe sharing bathroom and kitchen facilities with challenging neighbours, including drug dealers, sex workers, and people who may be racist and aggressive. The testimony of those living in these situations is that, on top of trauma, language difficulties, and the stresses of navigating life in the UK, it can be hard to avoid mental health difficulties and/or criminality.

On any one night in winter 2024, an estimated up to 20 refugees could be sleeping rough in the coastal town where Alan now lives, with many others as "hidden homeless" on friends' floors. Until charities like St Mungo's provide proof of rough sleeping, and usually until someone directs them to the Town Hall, they cannot access help from the council.

In 2024, 15,200 households in England received homelessness assistance from a local authority after having to leave asylum accommodation, an increase of 39% on the year before, according to statistics from the Ministry of Housing, Communities and Local Government.

"Penalised again"

Recently, I applied for a Teaching Assistant position through an organisation that operates nationally in the UK education sector. After providing all documents and disclosures, I was informed that the company's policy prevents them from registering or employing any individual who has ever been imprisoned – regardless of the nature of the imprisonment.

I was imprisoned not for any criminal behaviour, but as a political and human rights prisoner in Iran – a non-democratic regime known internationally for human rights violations, hostage-taking, repression, and torture. My activism was in support of democratic values and human rights, values that are deeply aligned with the principles of the United Kingdom.

It is distressing to learn that a blanket policy – one that makes no distinction between criminal, political, and human rights imprisonment – now prevents me from accessing employment in the education sector. I would like to emphasise that I have no criminal record in the UK, and I am fully eligible to obtain a DBS certificate.

Refugees who fought for democracy and suffered unjust imprisonment are penalised again when seeking safety, dignity, and meaningful work in the UK.

If a blanket employment barrier is applied to all individuals with past "imprisonment", then even figures such as Nobel Peace Prize winner Narges Mohammadi, who is internationally recognised for her fight for human rights, would be judged unfit for educational roles despite their moral integrity.

"It's not just refugees"

My experience of poverty is so different from how British people talk about these things. I would describe poverty as deprivation from normal life: education, safety, peace; isolation from family and loved ones, from a minimal standard of living: food, clothing…

If you go to the jobcentre, they give you Universal Credit, which gives you this minimum. In some countries, like Iran, they don't have this, but they should. In the UK, some British people don't have a better life than me; for example, I saw some British people in a shared house… It was not good. Economic poverty is not just about refugees; it's about others too.

There are other sorts of poverty: maybe a royal person doesn't have friends and family. But economic poverty is the basis of many problems: you can't take care of your children or send them to good schools.

I don't want to be labelled as a poor person, but I want to talk about my challenges and struggles. Poverty is a common thing in the world, and in the UK, it isn't a shameful thing. Some of the people who help you don't have a better life than you. I knew a lady volunteering in English classes who doesn't own a home; she lives in a flat like me, and she was retired, and with her limited income, she had some issues, having to change her property and find a new place. When I talked with her, I learned that some people in the UK live like us, so I'm not ashamed of myself in this country.

28 DAYS TO VACATE

When refugees receive a positive decision on their asylum claim, they have 28 days to leave their Home Office accommodation, and their financial support stops. As the Refugee Council report:

> The moment someone receives a positive decision on their asylum claim should be one of celebration and relief, an end to instability and the start of a bright future where they are able to establish new lives in the UK. Instead, many newly-recognised refugees experience homelessness and/or destitution, right at this point. Faced with a cliff edge and no support to find new housing, open a bank account and secure income, among other activities needed before being evicted, many refugees are at significant risk of homelessness and/or destitution.

"What is Poverty?"

When I talk with my mother [in Iran], I say why do you complain? She has a better standard of living than some here, but in Iran, there is high inflation, over 40%, and they can't be happy. They don't have hope for the future. But here, people are stable, and they don't have those anxieties: if they are homeless, the system will help them if they want. I wasn't homeless; now I can study and follow the process to find a job. Compared with Iran, the people have different expectations. People say the system is broken and they expect better.

We live in a society, not individually. How do the wealthy make their wealth? From others. If we don't have fairness and social justice, the differences become so large. Employers can exploit employees, misuse them. The big difference between European countries and the Middle East, Africa, and parts of Asia is that they don't have a just society. They don't have a good system, democracy, human rights, responsibility, or accountability. These are the main reasons for poverty. The poverty in the UK is different: for example, maybe there is a shortage of doctors and NHS resources, and people aren't satisfied with it, and the system regresses and doesn't improve. But this poverty is different from Africa, where you don't even have clean water. Bad governments make farms turn to deserts, but in Saudi, they turn desert to farms. Iran is not a poor country, but a government can make a wealthy country poor. Venezuela is another example.

Some people do not budget well, spending more than they have on alcohol and cigarettes, and not appreciating the benefits that they have. But poverty here in the UK causes us to not have access to health and medical facilities such as specialist doctors and dentists, and to adequate education and further education. Even if we learn English, the desired social status and suitable work, as well as suitable travel, recreation, exercise, and healthy nutrition, are inaccessible. Refugees are socially and financially disadvantaged, causing much frustration and isolation. These issues make them very vulnerable to social harms.

I think every person can have some aspect of poverty in their life. I don't think I am poor, I don't think of myself as a poor person. I don't know about big cars; I am happy with my bike. If the capitalists in this world faced the people in society like me, the capitalist system would be destroyed, because most of the things they produce are not attractive to me.

Life? Have a good sense of peace and satisfaction, friends, a minimum standard of living: living in a clean place, having respect, being able to read, and living independently.

The more property you have, the more issues. But having a good economic situation isn't bad, and I will try and make it. I need it to help others get a good education and do things for people. If I were wealthy, I would do something for my nation as a Kurd, to improve education, to protect the culture…

We live in society, not alone, and we are responsible for each other. We cannot be rich without others. Happiness depends on a successful society: a level of equality and access to opportunities for all benefits everybody. The better off an individual is economically, the greater their responsibility to society will be.

Thank you to all of the people in the UK. They protect, and they help the asylum seeker. Thank you very much.

Kath's reflections on the co-authorship of this chapter

At Alan's request, I've "tidied up" his English spelling and punctuation here, but attempted to keep his voice. His official name is an Arabic/Persian name, but his chosen name, Alan, is Kurdish.

We met through a charity I was volunteering with. Realising he was passionate about justice and interested in social science, I asked him to accompany me to an event about homelessness. He was very keen to connect with the world beyond the hotel.

We connected again over a Refugee Week poetry evening, and bumped into each other on street corners and over coffee breaks during his ESOL classes (I was working elsewhere in the same building). Our friendship was consolidated when we both happened to need wardrobes from Facebook Marketplace in the same week; I had the wheels, and he brought the muscle! We've since met at the cafe run by the local foodbank, sat with other refugee friends around the firepit, and discovered strong cultural differences over our methods of washing the dishes.

Currently, the Iranian regime is hanging on to power; the nation has many ethnic minorities who would welcome a change, and Alan is anxious not to see one dictatorship replaced by another in the homeland, which he loves. While the instability and oppression continue, Alan admits that becoming integrated into UK life is a long way off. After over two years in the UK, he agrees that his head and heart are still in the Middle East, bound up with the cause in which he has invested over 20 years of his life, at enormous personal cost. "And this is a very strange country", he says with a smile.

UK poverty is something Alan admits to not really being interested in. He expects to need to work hard for everything and does not expect bureaucrats to make life simple for anyone.

There's another Alan, a musician with a great sense of humour. When he no longer needs to be preoccupied with English exams and obtaining a bolt to fix his bicycle, hopefully, there will be opportunities for Alan to flourish. I'm grateful to know him and others like him.

REFLECTIVE ACTIVITY

1. Put on your safeguarding trauma-aware thinking cap, and go and get to know the people in your community (local mini-market/corner shop, barbers, car wash, dentists...) who came to the UK as adults. Find out how their expectations matched the realities. Listen to them: what do they want you/everyone to know?
2. Can you relate to any of these from your own experience:

   - Unfairness that compelled you to speak out?
   - Getting into trouble for speaking up?
   - Losing work, status, or freedoms?
   - Physical/mental/emotional abuse?
   - Leaving home and family?
   - Loss, bereavement?
   - Physical hardship, hunger, lack of sleep?
   - Feeling unsafe in your bed? Or not having a bed?
   - Feeling let down over something you were promised?
   - Not understanding the language, and not being able to make yourself understood?
   - Having to start from scratch in a new place with new people?
   - Not knowing what the rules are?
   - Being prejudged?

- Being misjudged or underestimated?
- Not having a biro when you need one?
- Meeting hostility when you ask for help?
- Loss of agency over your life; being at the mercy of broken systems?
- Wanting to contribute but being treated as invisible?

How have they affected you? Did/do they impact your daily life and your long-term situation?

Further resources

Films

Families Like Ours – 2024 dir. Thomas Vinterberg, imagining a privileged European country needing to evacuate due to rising sea levels (currently free to watch on BBC iPlayer).

Aisha – 2022 dir. Frank Berry: a young Nigerian woman is seeking asylum in Ireland (currently free to watch on BBC iPlayer).

The Swimmers – 2022 dir. Sally El Hosaini: biographical drama about two Syrian sisters.

The Old Oak – 2023 dir. Ken Loach. Syrians arrive in the North of England.

Limbo – 2020 dir. Ben Sharrock: a group of asylum seekers on a remote Scottish island awaits the outcome of their applications.

For Sama – 2019, a self-shot account of war-torn Syria (available free on Channel 4 https://www.channel4.com/programmes/for-sama).

Name Me Lawand – 2022 dir. Edward Loveless: a deaf Kurdish boy travels from Iraq to Derby.

Books

Daughters of Smoke and Fire – Ava Homa.
The Lightless Sky – Gulwali Passerlay.
I Don't Want To Talk About Home –
The Ungrateful Refugee – Dina Nayeri.
Refugee Week – Book recommendations for 2023.
Waterstones – Refugee Awareness.

For further information and background

Charities: Refugee Council, Right To Remain, Refugee Action, Migrant Voices… and many small local groups.

Further individuals whose stories may be of interest:

Nazanin Zaghari-Ratcliffe, a British-Iranian charity worker, was unjustly imprisoned by Iran.
Lindsay and Craig Forman, a British couple, were also detained as part of Iran's politically motivated hostage-taking.

Claim asylum in the UK: Overview (GOV.UK)

Statistics are hard to pin down in a fast-moving landscape. The Migration Observatory provides a detailed analysis of the latest data.
The Refugee Council website draws together figures from the Home Office, Ministry of Justice, Tribunal, and Ministry of Housing, Communities and Local Government into a good up-to-date summary.
Refugee Data Finder (2025).
Refugee Action (Facts about refugees).

Background information on the situation for Kurds in Iran

Iran: Human rights abuses against the Kurdish minority.
The Kurds: A stateless nation striving for self-determination | FairPlanet.
See also Amnesty International, or HENGAW Organization for Human Rights, for the latest news and statistics, and footnotes for more background information.
The Kurdish Project – including, in the history and culture section, the Sykes-Picot agreement and information about the part Britain played in Kurdish history.

Further resources to watch, read, or listen to

ONS 2021 Census-based statistics UK:2021 Available at Census-based statistics UK: 2021 - Office for National Statistics.

Films

Families Like Ours – 2024 dir. Thomas Vinterberg, imagining a privileged European country needing to evacuate due to rising sea levels (currently free to watch on BBC iPlayer).
Aisha – 2022 dir. Frank Berry: a young Nigerian woman is seeking asylum in Ireland.
The Swimmers – 2022 dir. Sally El Hosaini: biographical drama about two Syrian sisters.
The Old Oak – 2023 dir. Ken Loach. Syrians arrive in the North of England.

Limbo – 2020 dir. Ben Sharrock: a group of asylum seekers on a remote Scottish island awaits the outcome of their applications.
For Sama by Waad al-Kateab 2019, a self-shot account of war-torn Syria (available free on Channel 4 https://www.channel4.com/programmes/for-sama).
Name Me Lawand – 2022 dir. Edward Loveless: a deaf Kurdish boy travels from Iraq to Derby.
Prisoner 951 – Dramatisation of the true story of Nazanin Zaghari Ratcliffe, Persian/English prisoner of the Iranian regime.
Prisoner 951 – **The Hostages Story** documentary.

Books

Daughters of Smoke and Fire – Ava Homa.
The Lightless Sky – Gulwali Passerlay.
I Don't Want To Talk About Home – by Suad Aldarra Penguin.
The Ungrateful Refugee – Dina Nayeri.

For further information and background

Charities: Refugee Council, Right To Remain, Refugee Action, Migrant Voices…& many small local groups.
For the **latest policies**, see *Claim asylum in the UK: Overview – GOV.UK*
Statistics are hard to pin down in a fast-moving landscape: https://migrationobservatory.ox.ac.uk/ provides detailed analysis of the latest data.
The Refugee Council website draws together figures from the Home Office, Ministry of Justice, Tribunal, and Ministry of Housing, Communities and Local Government into a good up-to-date summary:

https://www.refugeecouncil.org.uk/stay-informed/explainers/top-facts-from-the-latest-statistics-on-refugees-and-people-seeking-asylum/
https://www.unhcr.org/refugee-statistics
https://www.refugee-action.org.uk/about/facts-about-refugees

Background information on the situation for Kurds in Iran

Iran: Human rights abuses against the Kurdish minority.
The Kurds: A stateless nation striving for self-determination | FairPlanet.
See also Amnesty International, or https://hengaw.net/en for the latest news and statistics, and footnotes for more background information.
thekurdishproject.org – including, in the history and culture section, the Sykes-Picot agreement and information about the part Britain played in Kurdish history.

14

POVERTY AND SCHOOL

Luke James, Debbie James and Richard Williams

Debbie (Luke's mum)

When Luke was born, Social Services had long been in our lives. They had taken my eldest son into care, and I'd fought for two years to win him back. A judge ultimately ruled that their actions had been Draconian, and he returned home. But Social Services didn't go away. Because I lived in poverty and struggled with alcohol and depression, the system considered me unfit. Social Services weren't there to support us – they were there to *Police me*, joining forces with the school, while masquerading as support.

When it was time for Luke to go to secondary school, I chose not to send him to the local all-boys school. In hindsight, I think Luke may have been better off there. Most of the kids were like us, from working-class families, often struggling, living in poverty. It was closest to home, but it had a rough reputation and bad exam results. I wanted better for Luke and thought I was doing the right thing by aiming higher. I was glad when Luke gained a place at The Academy School – a middle-class school with a good Ofsted report, but little understanding of what our life looked like. He stuck out and was treated like an outsider. So was I.

Luke was labelled a "child in need". That label carried weight – it meant constant meetings, joint reviews with the school and social workers, and a long list of assumptions. They never asked what we needed. Instead, they told me what was wrong. I was accused of "neglect". My house wasn't tidy enough, my meals weren't healthy enough, and my kids weren't clean enough. The bruises on their knees, the rips in their trousers, teenage body odour – ordinary signs of boyhood – raised as concerns. Every day, parenting was twisted into a catalogue of faults and failures.

DOI: 10.4324/9781003638476-15

The school phoned me almost daily because of a hole in Luke's sock or a scrape on his knee. One time, even a chocolate bar Luke was seen eating prompted a phone call – how could I afford it? Had he stolen it? Why hadn't I provided some fruit? One day, Luke had ripped his trousers on the way to school. They called, demanding I bring a replacement pair. But that was his only pair – I couldn't just pop out and buy new ones. So, they gave him a needle and thread, made him sit in a classroom in his boxers, and had him sew them himself. Another teacher called him a "skank" because he had writing on his hand. Another one commented that a smelly cupboard "smelt like Luke". Once a food parcel was arranged for us. I was grateful until it was delivered directly to Luke's classroom in front of everyone.

I was constantly raising concerns and making complaints about how Luke was treated, but my complaints were never heard or acted on. I did eventually take Luke out of The Academy School, and he was moved to The Boys school. It was a slight improvement in attitude and environment for Luke, but his reputation had been unfairly tarnished and followed him. He was viewed as a troublemaker, spent far too much time in isolation for minor incidents, and was overlooked academically. When his exams eventually came around, the procedure was chaotic, and the results were corrupted due to COVID. His school career ultimately fizzled out during lockdown with zero ceremony or sense of accomplishment.

Luke was not fully aware of the extent to which poverty affected his education.

SCHOOL ATTAINMENT AND POVERTY

Findings have revealed an imbalance in school attainment, which is clearly and consistently stratified by socio-economic background – this disadvantage tends to gradually increase towards the end of Key Stage 4 (ages 14–16, Year 10, and Year 11), with students who are living in poverty having poorer outcomes than those who are not (Shao & Lu, 2025).

Department for Education (DfE) statistics consistently show that children's attainment is positively related to family income (e.g., DfE, 2015, 2017, 2024).

He didn't know about the sheer volume of phone calls I received or the number of meetings I attended. One thing I'm grateful for is that most of the indignity and judgement was aimed at me, personally. Conversations were private and mostly kept separate from Luke. It wasn't too difficult to shield him from the worst aspects of prejudice and discrimination. I made excuses for the rudeness of teachers and deflected their actions with humour and distraction.

Luke's sense of humour and his laid-back personality have served him well throughout his life so far. Often, I was more upset and offended by the actions of authorities than he was. He's very loyal to me and tries to shield me from difficult situations as much as I try to protect him. He doesn't like to hear me criticised. He has a deep sense of respect for me and a gratitude that I really don't deserve.

Because I lived in poverty, the authorities presumed I lacked intelligence, ability, and worth. They didn't see a family doing its best in difficult circumstances; they saw a problem to be managed. In all of that, they never saw the boy I was raising – the charismatic, kind, and resilient boy who was always far more than the sum of their assumptions and is a better man than they could have imagined.

Luke

I love my mum. I still live with her, and I have nothing but respect for her. Her own life had its share of difficulties. She has had to deal with her own addiction issues, and that has been really hard for her at times. My mother brought me and my older brother up on her own. My father did not want anything to do with me from the moment he learnt my mum was pregnant.

I am 21 years old and have lived in Bournemouth all my life. Right now, I work in security. The hours I work tend to be evenings through to the early hours of the morning. My work matters to me, and I feel proud that I can help people feel safe. It means a lot to me when people tell me how much they appreciate my work.

When I was growing up, we didn't have much at home. I had a mattress on the floor. Sometimes I had to skip dinner and make do with a packet of biscuits. The area where we lived was awful. There was lots of organised crime – drug and gang-related. There were always people coming into the house, and I think, from my memory, people often stashed stuff in the house. I was sexually assaulted by one of them – I told my mum, and she was terrified of them – she didn't want to believe it, but she did realise it was true. It was a very confusing time for me. I was about 8 years old when it happened. It wasn't till I was 15/16 before I realised what really happened, I understood the gravity of how serious it could have been. I feel lucky because I don't seem to have had any adverse effects. I also feel guilty because I know people who have had similar experiences and have been left feeling traumatised and struggle with their day-to-day lives.

My older brother was troubled, and the school he went to struggled to meet his needs, dealing with his trauma and his behaviour. When I turned up, they just assumed I was like him, and I was going to be trouble too. I went to two secondary schools – I had a "managed move" in year 8, from my first secondary school to the North school, which I joined at the beginning of year 9. The reason for the move was that I bear-hugged a Teaching Assistant and tried to force-feed him with pineapple.

Because I was labelled as the naughty kid, it seemed to me that I was never listened to when I had a genuine reason for reacting in a way that teachers saw as "naughty".

One example of this was when two female friends of mine were sitting behind me in class. We were doing ethics in a food tech classroom – they were throwing paper at me and poking me with a compass in my back. I told the teacher, and she told me to deal with it. I felt dismissed and annoyed. The compass poking continued, and one of them came around and stabbed me in the hand. I told the teacher, and I was told to stop disrupting the lesson, and that left me feeling dismissed even more and even more angry. I was sitting next to a tray of big kitchen knives. So, when one of them approached me with a pair of scissors and threatened to stab me, I picked up one of the kitchen knives and dared her. That was when the teacher got involved, and I was in trouble, including with the police.

The thing is, teachers had been telling me to talk to them if I had an issue and to try not to deal with it myself. That is exactly what I had tried to do – and had been brushed off and, yet again, forced to deal with it myself. I was asked why I didn't walk out of the classroom. I explained that if I had done so, I would have gotten into trouble. I would never have hurt her – I knew that – I just wanted her to stop stabbing me, and I found a way to stop her because nobody else was willing to try.

The result was that when the police came and talked to me about the dangers of knife crime, I couldn't take it seriously.

The school tried to help, but it was obvious to me that they were ticking boxes. I was in isolation a lot of time at my secondary school – often for multiple days in a week.

My Head of Year in Year 9 was my PE teacher and taught me Maths. He always used shouting as a last resort. He never ordered, he guided. He bantered with me and always saw me and treated me as a person. He used to take me out of isolation to be in a rugby match or to do training. He would advise me to avoid going into isolation so I could play rugby; he really encouraged me. I always felt safe around him. I could go to him if I were having difficulty, and he would help me calm down.

I enjoyed English. My English teacher always made an effort and helped me through my work. She would make the time to talk to me and to help me. Thanks to her I developed a real interest in the subject. She also helped me feel safe and feel calm.

RELATIONSHIPS WITH TEACHERS

Studies have shown that students' relationship with teachers and perception of teacher sensitivity are the strongest predictors of scholastic achievements (Banerjee, 2016)

Positive teacher expectations, support, and motivation have progressive effects on students regardless of their risk status and particularly for lower-income students (Gregory & Huang, 2013; Sorhagen, 2013).

Shao and Lu (2025) argue that positive school experiences might contribute to narrowing the deprivation-related gaps.

I enjoyed being able to challenge stuff in Ethics. It was just nice to have the opportunity to ask questions and challenge the views of different religions. Debating was encouraged and welcomed. I would put my hand up, and the teacher would use me, and when he did that, I would feel so proud. He would even ask me when I did not have my hand up. It gave me a sense of maturity. I felt I could be an adult, and I could ask questions that other classmates would feel too anxious to ask.

Science was fun. I had a flair for biology and chemistry. My teacher would plan practical lessons, and I knew he was doing this to help me and my mates to stay involved and to keep us interested – it worked. There were times when me and the teacher fell out. The difference with him was that while he did sometimes send me to isolation, he would always make himself available for a restorative meeting before he went home. I felt listened to, and I would take responsibility for my actions. I was always treated fairly by him.

COMMUNICATION

Short et al. (2018) highlight the importance of empathic, non-punitive communication as a means of resolving conflict and repairing relationships in a positive, constructive way, i.e. a restorative practice approach (RP). The authors identified RP as having a positive impact on academic attainment and on creating an emotionally and physically safe environment.

The individual teacher, social worker, or involved person can and does make a difference even when the odds seem stacked against the youngster (Williams & Pritchard, 2006)

Living in poverty has given me different life experiences than most of my friends. There is a divide: going on holiday, having nice lunches, and being able to contribute a tenner so you can go on a school trip. My Food Tech teacher would buy my ingredients so I could take part, and after the course had finished, she asked for just a pound, which I was happy to give. I don't know why she asked; maybe it was about taking responsibility. I really appreciated her help.

We could never have people round our house. I would go to a friend's house so that I could have dinner. They would have Xboxes, massive gardens, and trampolines.

When I left school, I went to a local college to study military preparation. One of the teachers was ex-military. He was so good at managing my behaviour, not me. He would tell me to run three laps to calm down, he would sit next to me and teach all of us what we needed to know, and he would talk with us. We did adventure training, built a raft, and then used it to go across the water.

Army cadets were the best. I was there from 13 to 18. It was the best time of my life. It was free, which was amazing. To get there, my detachment was a two-minute walk away from where I lived. I met the best people in my life there. I learnt I was only badly behaved when I was not interested in what I was doing. I was so passionate and wanted to do well, so I behaved well. I had so many great experiences: live firing ranges, section attacks, and getting to use radios. Drill was cool. We would go on camps, which I think were free too. And I even left as a Corporal.

Another teacher inspired me to join Wimborne Rugby Club. He was massive on positive reinforcement, and I thrived on that; "Luke you are really good", "Luke, I need you to be in training". He knew money was tight for me, and he would take me aside and offer support for me with the kit and with transport. I really felt seen. I never knew I could be good at something, and he showed me that I could be.

PROMOTING SUCCESS

Michael Rutter has been described as the father of child psychiatry. The findings of his seminal 1979 study of secondary schools apply to Luke's experience in the cadets. Rutter et al. (1979) concluded that schools that promote success demonstrate appropriate, well-conveyed high expectations, the involvement of pupils in taking responsibilities, positive rewards with feedback, clear, fair discipline, positive models of good teacher behaviour, a focus on achievement and good behaviour, and good teacher-pupil relationships in and outside the classroom.

To summarise, I guess it all ties together by learning that everyone has their own struggles and their own way of dealing with things. Trying to be as understanding as possible of people. I kind of enter situations with an open mind because it feels right for me. I have learnt to always be vigilant, but kind, not too trusting but not too worried.

If I may, I'd like to end my chapter with a guiding phrase that both me and my academic collaborator agree upon wholeheartedly:

Be curious, not judgemental

REFLECTIVE ACTIVITY

Navigating the school day

Take the time to think about how poverty might affect different aspects of the school day.

Reflect on the emotional, social, and academic challenges faced by students living in poverty.

What might school be like for someone who doesn't have enough food, clean or spare clothes, or school supplies?

Imagine the school day from getting up, getting to school, being in the classroom, and being with friends.

How might food insecurity, housing instability, lack of internet access, or having to work after school affect your day?

Thinking back to Luke's story and what helped him, if you are a teacher, social worker, caregiver, fellow student, friend? What can you do? What might help?

To understand more about poverty and education, we would recommend

To watch and to listen to via YouTube:

- Pupils speak about UK child poverty (UNICEF UK)
- Tackling the consequences of poverty (The SecEd Podcast)
- How can we help poor kids do better at school (BBC Politics)
- Unequal Britain: Child poverty and how to fix it (Donny Dorling)

And to read:

The seminal work published over four decades ago – still as relevant today:

Rutter, M., Maughan, B., Mortimore, P. & Ouston, J. (1979) *Fifteen Thousand Hours: Secondary Schools and Their Effects on Children*. Open Books.

References

Banerjee, P.A. (2016) 'A systematic review of factors linked to poor academic performance of disadvantaged students in science and maths in schools', *Cogent Education*, 3(1). doi:10.1080/2331186X.2016.1178441

Department for Education (DfE). (2015) *Measuring Disadvantaged Pupils' Attainment Gaps Over Time*. DfE.

Department for Education (DfE). (2017) *Analysing Family Circumstances and Education: A Technical Consultation Document*. DfE.

Department for Education (DfE). (2024) *Factors Influencing Secondary School Pupils' Educational Outcomes: A Literature Review Supporting the Growing Up in the 2020s Study*. DfE.

Gregory, A. & Huang, F. (2013) 'It takes a village: The effects of 10th grade college-going expectations of students, parents, and teachers four years later', *American Journal of Community Psychology*, 52, 41–55. doi:10.1007/s10464-013-9575-5

Rutter, M., Maughan, B., Mortimore, P. & Ouston, J. (1979) *Fifteen Thousand Hours: Secondary Schools and Their Effects on Children*. Open Books.

Shao, X. & Lu, B. (2025) 'An Evaluation of the attainment gaps in state schools in England: Evidence from next steps' age 25 sweep dataset', *Education Sciences*, 15(2), 179

Short, R., Case, G. & McKenzie, K. (2018) 'The long-term impact of a whole school approach of restorative practice: the views of secondary school teachers', *Pastoral Care in Education*, 36(4), 313–324. doi:10.1080/02643944.2018.1528625

Sorhagen, N. (2013) 'Early teacher expectations disproportionately affect poor children's high school performance', *Journal of Educational Psychology*, 105, 465–477

Williams, R. & Pritchard, C. (2006) *Breaking the Cycle of Educational Alienation A Multi-Professional Approach*. McGraw-Hill Educational.

15

POVERTY, TRAUMA, AND ADDICTION

Debbie James and Mel Hughes

My Name is Debbie; I am an alcoholic. I've been in recovery for around six years now. I say 'around' because recovery isn't a straight line, it's a cycle of sobriety and relapse, of falling and getting back up. What I can say with certainty is that the last time I took a drink was six years ago. I've also lived in poverty for my entire adult life. This chapter is about my lived experience of poverty, addiction to alcohol, and a broken support system. I'm not sharing it to shock or shame, and I'm not looking for pity or praise. It's simply an invitation to look beyond the case file and see the human being.

I don't know if Poverty was a result of my alcoholism, or my alcoholism was a result of Poverty, but I do know it's not that simple.

Both alcoholism and poverty go hand in hand for me. Both were the cause and the result of trauma. Both trapped me in a downward spiral and brought me to a place where I no longer recognised myself.

Neither poverty nor alcoholism are lifestyle choice. Nobody would choose to live like that. I did a lot of things I'm not proud of, and I live with the consequences.

When I was an active alcoholic, and while living in poverty, I slept around and stole money from strange men I'd slept with specifically for that purpose. I was a shop lifter; I couldn't hold down a job. I dropped out of Uni. I ended up homeless. I lost my dignity, my sanity, and my will to live.

DOI: 10.4324/9781003638476-16

LINKS BETWEEN POVERTY AND ALCOHOL USE

Research shows that the relationship between poverty and drinking is complex. Problematic drinking affects people across all income levels, and people on low incomes have been shown to drink less, on average, than those on higher incomes. Research reported by Liverpool John Moores University (Jones and Sumnall, 2016), however, shows that people of lower social and economic standing are likely to suffer greater harm from alcohol. They are more likely to die or suffer from alcohol related disease and may be less able to buffer the social and economic consequences of problem alcohol use, leading to poorer outcomes.

Early trauma and alcohol use

I can't talk about poverty and addiction without talking about trauma. Trauma has been the common theme that's influenced my choices and behaviour throughout my life. My childhood was unstable and traumatic since birth. I've lived my life ever since in a constant state of crisis, as a response to those experiences. It's not an excuse, but it's an explanation for the chaos that's nearly always surrounded me.

I don't know much about my birth. Dad told me I wasn't planned, and that Mum had wanted two children… I was the third. After I was born, she had a nervous breakdown. My parents argued frequently, mostly about money, and there was little to no affection between them. I grew up believing I was the cause of Mum's illness and my parents' loveless marriage.

When I was eight, I was sexually molested by our school bus driver. He wasn't charged due to 'lack of evidence.' It turned out I wasn't the only child he'd molested. I was the only one who spoke up.

I began drinking alcohol at the age of 9. It was served at family meals, and I stole it from my Dad's cabinet. Alcohol soon became a coping mechanism. It numbed me amid the chaos of Mum's illness and an unpredictable environment.

At the age of 10, I was diagnosed with bone cancer. Alcohol was used as a reward after chemo, and I was treated to Babychams at the local pub. These were meant as kind gestures of support from family members, which I gladly accepted, so no judgement, please.

It was around this time that Dad was made redundant from his job as a farm labourer. We lived in a tied cottage, so when he lost it, we also lost our home. We moved to a council house in a tiny village about five miles from the local town. I say 'village', but it was more of a cluster of houses, and a pub. My brother and sister soon grew up and moved out. I was left feeling alone and trapped. There was virtually no public transport. There was nothing to do and nowhere to go, unless Mum or Dad were driving into town. My Dad struggled to find steady work. He did odd temporary jobs as a self-employed Farm labourer and later as a Gardener, but it wasn't a steady income. I wasn't fully aware of how bad our financial situation was. Mum and Dad shielded me from the consequences as much as they could. I was still fed and clothed, and I received Christmas and Birthday presents. I think I was given a small amount of pocket money every weekend. It might have been enough to buy a bar of chocolate, but nothing more than that. All of this happened during my ongoing cancer treatment, which put even more of a financial burden on my parents.

Fostered and cancer-free

I was 15 when I got the all clear from cancer. It should have been a relief, a new beginning, but none of us was prepared for the toll, the events during my childhood had taken on my mind. My behaviour spiralled downwards, at school, at home, everywhere. My relationship with my parents broke down completely, and I was fostered by a teacher. She was the head of the special needs department at my school. She was well respected by the other teachers; she'd remained committed to her job during a difficult divorce and was a lone parent to her daughter. I had grown close to her since she had started to work with me on my behaviour. I had serious anger issues, and she went above and beyond her role as a teacher to keep me out of trouble. It was a private fostering arrangement. My Dad had agreed to pay a monthly amount directly to my Foster Mum for my keep. It didn't work out. Dad couldn't keep up the payments, but my Foster Mum agreed to keep me on without them. When I reached my 16th birthday, I received an amount from a savings account my Dad had opened for me when I was born. I can't remember the amount I got, probably around £300, but I gave it all to my Foster Mum to help pay for me to go on holiday to France with her and her daughter.

On the outside, I had a comfortable transition between a working-class and middle-class home. I was happy to be there. It was supposed to be a safe haven, but, behind closed doors, my Foster Mum was a narcissistic control freak, and I went through years of abuse. I kept it all inside, convinced no one would believe me.

Student life

By the age of 18, I was already drinking heavily and battling serious mental health issues. My Foster Mum dropped me off at Birmingham Polytechnic to do a Sociology course that she'd coerced me into. And then she did all she could to erase me from her life.

I arrived at the student halls with no social skills, zero self-esteem, and an almost childlike need to be loved. I stuck out like a sore thumb among my peers. I was a loner from the start and swung from feeling a deep sense of isolation to enjoying solitude and independence.

One thing that I was pleasantly surprised by, during my first year in Birmingham, was how easy it was to get bank accounts, loans, and overdrafts. I started out with a student grant. Once I'd got that, financial services were literally falling over themselves to provide perks and loopholes to what I thought were great opportunities. I was given credit cards, debit cards, and cheque books. For the first time in my life, I could afford to spend money on myself. I could choose what to spend it on and how much to spend. It was my money, and it felt like freedom. I loved it and had a great time spending it. The trouble was, I had no experience with handling money or budgeting large amounts. Without the shackles of my Foster Mum's control, I spent it badly and squandered it away on clothes, alcohol, and takeaways. My grant was gone before the end of my first year. I begged my Foster Mum for loans when I could get hold of her, but she flatly refused. I was told I was not welcome to stay with her over the summer and winter holidays, and I rarely had contact with her after that. My relationship with my parents was still almost non-existent. I was stuck in Birmingham and started to rely on overdrafts and credit cards. The government brought in Student Loans, which I squandered in a similar fashion, spending the majority of them on cigarettes and alcohol.

TRAUMA AND POVERTY

The Mental Health Foundation describes trauma and traumatic events as those that 'put you or someone close to you at risk of serious harm or death'. It can include an accident, violent attack, or natural disaster, or, as in Debbie's case, ongoing stress such as childhood and intimate partner abuse, bullying, long-term illness, living in unstable or unsafe conditions, or seeing someone else get hurt.

The Joseph Rowntree Foundation reports 'a strong association between family poverty and a child's chance of suffering child abuse or neglect. Adverse events in childhood, including abuse and neglect, are associated with a negative effect on adult economic circumstances' (Bywaters et al., 2016, p. 3).

Researchers at University College London's International Centre for Lifecourse Studies (Lacey et al., 2020) found that poverty was strongly associated with increased odds of a child reporting an adverse childhood experience. 'If people can't afford heating, lighting or have faced homelessness, there's a direct link with mental health problems and domestic and substance abuse. It's a really strong predictor of those problems, but is often overlooked', Lead author, Dr Rebecca Lacey (UCL Epidemiology and Public Health).

Homelessness

At the age of 21, I was two years into the Sociology course. I received news that my mother had died. That's when I went off the rails, and my alcoholism really kicked in. I dropped out of the course and became homeless. I began a cycle of repeated stays in homeless shelters, psychiatric wards, and rehabs. By this time, I owed thousands to the student loans company and was thousands of pounds in debt to three credit card companies. I'd lost my bank account, and my credit record was blacklisted. I was penniless.

I was homeless for approximately two years.

There was a place called Harp (Homeless Alcoholics Rehousing Project). It was like a one-stop shop. I could get something to eat, a shower, and a haircut. They offered access to legal advice, there was a doctor on site, and you had access to phones and laundry facilities. The staff there were amazing. They found me a place in a night shelter or a hostel most nights. Until they secured a longer-term placement in a hostel for homeless women.

Recovery

Eventually, I came to a treatment centre in Bournemouth and settled here. In 1997, I met John. We were both in recovery at the time and began seeing each other. John worked part-time cleaning the local shopping centre. I was still being chased for debts I'd built up in Birmingham, and the pit of late payment charges and more borrowing was already dug deep. I was living on benefits and living in a privately rented studio flat from a sympathetic landlord. I often couldn't make the rent, so the landlord would let me owe him. I bought tobacco on the black market and struggled to pay the bloke selling it. As more debts grew, my days were spent borrowing off 'Peter to pay Paul'. I tried a few different jobs, but they didn't last long. It wasn't so much a problem finding a job, it was keeping one. My mental and physical health was unpredictable and unstable for days, weeks, or months at a time. I couldn't commit long-term to anything that needed any amount of consistency.

Motherhood, relapse, and social services

I gave birth to my first child, a son, in 1998. That is when Social Services came into my life and never really left for the next 18 years. My son was put on the At-Risk Register before he was even born, because John had a criminal history. I was fairly tolerant of their involvement to start with. I was a nervous, clueless first-time mum. I knew we would need support as a family. I had a naive sense of gratitude. What I hadn't realised was that my alcoholism and psychiatric history were all laid out in my medical notes, and I was considered a risk as well. The hospital staff watched me closely from the moment my son was born.

I hardly noticed at the time. I was totally smitten. In hindsight, it is clear to see that a midwife had been assigned to watch my every move. But she was taking meticulous notes to report back to Social Services. I realised that I was not being 'supported', I was being policed.

The relationship between me and John ended when my son was 2. I relapsed when he was 3. I was not a quiet drinker. I lurched from one drink-induced crisis to another. I was a nuisance to everyone around me. Family, friends, the police, and the ambulance were all fair game. Verbally, I was always up for a fight, but I wasn't a physical danger to anyone except myself. I was a self-harmer and my own worst enemy. I don't remember how or why I relapsed, but I do remember asking his godparents on a few occasions to look after my son because I was drunk. They were people he knew well and loved spending time with. I needed time to get back on track so I could be the mother that he needed and deserved. It made sense to me at the time. Now, I can see it was the selfish and twisted logic of an alcoholic, but I did want to protect my son from my chaos, and my motives were genuine.

One day, I was picking my son up from nursery school. When I got there, I was met by a social worker, one of the godparents, and two police officers. I was informed they were taking my son because they had received reports that I'd been seen drinking in a local pub. It didn't take long to realise it was the godparents who had reported me. Helping me to take care of my son for free had become a burden, and they had their own family to think of.

My son was ripped away in front of me, and there was nothing I could do to stop it. I felt like he was being kidnapped. I tried to get to him, to tell him I loved him, and he'll be home soon. I was held back by the police. They held my arms down so I couldn't even wave goodbye. He was driven off in a police car, dazed and confused. I was left screaming and crying in the middle of the street.

Apart from the gut-wrenching loss and the feeling of betrayal, what hurt the most was the assumption that my alcoholism meant I didn't care about my son. That I was a danger to him. My alcoholism wasn't a choice; it was a response to trauma. I was trying to numb the pain that nobody saw, and that I couldn't name. No one recognised that I'd been trying to protect him from that. They only saw the alcoholic, not the mother.

My son was taken into foster care. I wasn't allowed to know where he was living, and contact was supervised. Every visit ended with my son clinging to me, begging me not to go. The social worker would peel him away from me and bundle him in the car. He'd be driven away screaming and crying for Mummy, and all I could do was stand and watch. He wasn't just ripped away from me that day at the nursery. We were ripped away from each other multiple times. Each time added to the trauma for both of us.

I was told they were putting my son up for adoption. That broke me, and my life fell apart once again. I had nothing to live for and no reason to stop drinking.

I was arrested multiple times. I attempted suicide. I lived in a state of guilt and grief that eats away at you. It was a relentless, soul-destroying void.

I was given a ray of hope when I was given the contact details of a solicitor, who took me on with legal aid.

I spent the next two years fighting to get my son back. The battle was long and brutal. I got back into recovery, jumped through every hoop, and attended every court hearing. Reports from Social Services focussed on my addiction and twisted everything I did to fit their narrative. I wasn't seen by them as someone trying to heal; I was seen as an open wound.

Finally, the judge saw through the social services' bias. He called their actions 'Draconian', ruled in my favour, and my son came home. I still thank God for that judge and the solicitor every day.

I would love to say that's the end of my story, and we lived happily ever after, but this is a life immersed in addiction, poverty, and trauma that we're talking about. Unfortunately, it doesn't get better overnight, and consequences are often lifelong.

Before my son was taken into foster care, he was a happy, outgoing little boy, and we had a close relationship. He came home to me as an emotionally damaged child. He was traumatised and suffering from separation anxiety. He had regular night terrors. He became withdrawn and anxious. He grew increasingly distant from me until he totally estranged himself in 2015, just before his 17th birthday.

Poverty and 'neglect'

I gave birth to my second son, Luke, in 2003. My recovery from alcohol use was going well, but Social Services continued to scrutinise me, often interpreting signs of poverty as proof I was 'not coping'. They put a label on it and called it 'neglect'. In their opinion, my house wasn't clean enough or tidy enough. They told me my kids smelled, and I wasn't feeding them healthily enough. They wanted me to do parenting classes, budgeting classes, and attend frequent meetings involving the school, education welfare officers, and write attendance reports. Everything was questioned. If Luke had a hole in his sock, or if my elder son had a rip in his trousers, or a bruise on his knee, it was noted. Normal stuff for young boisterous boys was scrutinised and twisted at every opportunity. I was constantly misunderstood, actions misinterpreted, and any normal parenting mistakes were immediately pounced on.

They saw everything through a blurred lens of judgement and presumption. After one of the meetings with the school, they wrote in a report that the room where we had been 'smelt of urine' after I left. They did not mention that the room was a reception classroom, and apart from me, there were four other adults in the room. They didn't consider that a child might have had an accident that had gone unnoticed. Or that one of the other adults in the room might have stank of piss. As I was someone living in poverty and with a drinking problem, they assumed it was me.

DO YOU SEE POVERTY OR NEGLECT?

The British Association of Social Workers (BASW) published an article in 2024, urging caution when equating poverty with child abuse or neglect (Gallagher 2024). The article's author, Gallagher, argues that 'we do families a disservice when we look at them as more likely to abuse or neglect their children because of poverty'.

While it is recognised that there is a correlation between poverty and neglect, one does not directly cause the other. Those working with families living in poverty, such as social workers, need to recognise that poverty and neglect are two distinct issues requiring different responses. A 2025 Community Care poll of 468 practitioners in children's services, however, showed that 68% of respondents believed that poverty was not taken into account during assessment and planning. This needs to change if the causes and impacts of poverty are to be understood and addressed.

Kelly

I think I would have admitted defeat and completely given up if it had not been for Kelly. She was the last social worker we had, and she was by far the best. I wish we had known her sooner, before my son had estranged himself, and before poverty began to destroy us. She did everything differently. She had a difficult job to begin with. I had a completely negative view of social workers when I met her, and I had absolutely no reason to believe that she would be any different. I wasted no time in telling her that. I made it plain that she was the last person I needed in our lives, and I completely resented her involvement. I certainly did not want her anywhere near my son. As it happened, Luke liked her straight away. It took me a bit longer.

Kelly never pushed herself on either of us. She never judged me. She kept me informed and included me in plans and decision making. She praised me when I achieved things, and she talked things through with me if any problems came up. She treated me like an equal and would often refer to me and Luke as a 'team'. She took time to get to know us as individuals. She spent time 1-1 with Luke and 1-1 with me, and also together.

She didn't invade our lives; she enhanced our lives, and she empowered me to become the kind of parent I'd never had the chance to be. She gave me the freedom to discover my own capability and the space to explore my own goals. She gave me and Luke the chance to grow together and support each other in our separate roles. We really did become a team, and we both had pride in that.

She couldn't solve every problem. My eldest was still estranged, we still lived in poverty, I was still depressed and sometimes struggled in recovery, but instead of trying to 'save' us, she empowered us. She went beyond what I would expect of any Social Worker. It's a shame that she was the exception and not the rule.

The present

Today I still live in poverty. My youngest son, Luke, still lives with me. He is 22 years old. He earns his own money, working as a security guard. He is happy, has a heart filled with compassion for others, and has wisdom beyond his years. He's got confidence, charisma, and a determination to overcome any obstacles, with a positive outlook that will make him a success in his life. He's in a loving relationship with a wonderful girlfriend, and he fills me with pride and joy every day. Is he a product of neglect or the result of survival? I'll let you decide.

I've not seen or heard from my estranged son for 10 years. I know that somewhere, the son I know and love is still there. I will never give up on him, and I'll never lose hope that he'll come back to us one day.

My reflections

Homelessness

Having seen how society treats people living on the streets, I believe that to tackle poverty in this country, we need to challenge current attitudes and make fundamental changes. We need to look at the real issues without getting distracted by the same discussions that are brought up every time we talk about homelessness. For example, should we give homeless people money? This is just a smokescreen and misses the point because whether you do or don't, it won't make much difference in the end. Even if you paid for them to stay in a hotel overnight, they would still be homeless in the morning.

I begged on the streets in Birmingham. I was always grateful for someone's bit of spare change. It was more than just coins. It was a token of worth. A tangible reminder that I'd been seen and heard by someone. The value of it wasn't in the amount; it was in the personal gesture from one human being to another.

As a society, I think we are all a little bit responsible for the homeless on our streets. Every single one of us could do something to help. We shouldn't forget that every single homeless person is somebody's child, brother, or sister. They all have a story that most of us don't want to hear. We could start by giving homeless people a sense of identity. That's' something that gets stripped away when you're constantly ignored or judged. If you give them a sandwich or spare change, ask their name, give them your time, and treat them like a human being. Not someone to be pitied or feared, not a problem or a liability, but someone who is worthy of respect and deserving of dignity. When we give them an identity, we give them a voice, and we might well be surprised by what they do with it. Perhaps if individually, we gave them the benefit of the doubt, we could collectively empower them to help themselves.

Social services

Social services always called their involvement 'support', but all they ever did was drive me to mental breakdown, suicide attempts, and losing the son I'd fought so hard for in the first place. I have no doubt in my mind that when they took him from the nursery, the trauma that it caused him was irreversible. It was the root cause of the breakdown in the relationship between us, and the eventual estrangement.

I am not saying I'm blameless. I'm to blame in many ways. I'm his mother, and that makes me responsible! I have taken on board all the accusations and battled the guilt. I have accepted my responsibility and done all I can to try and make amends.

I had to prove myself worthy to be a mother from the minute my eldest son was born and again from the minute Luke was born. There was always another social worker visit, another concern, another hoop to jump through. I was living under the constant threat of both my children being taken away, creating a climate of fear and anxiety that never left. Living like that changes you. It erodes your confidence and makes you question everyone around you. Trust is another luxury you can't afford.

If the authorities had spent more time getting to know me and given me a chance to work with them before they went to extremes. If they'd looked beyond the alcoholic, the chaos, and the poverty and seen the loving mother-son relationship despite everything. If they had focussed on keeping me and my son together instead of ripping us apart, I think things could have been very different. Instead, they wanted to fix something that wasn't broken, paradoxically breaking us in the process.

Tough love versus empathy

I would like to add a few personal thoughts about a phrase that I hear often in discussions about alcoholism, addiction, and mental health. That's the concept of tough love. I've been on both sides of it. I've had people walk away from me 'for my own good' and I've had people stay quietly and patiently without trying to fix me. I'm not a professional in Psychology or anything, I don't know if

Tough Love is a positive way to help someone or not. I do know in my own experience, it has been used as an excuse for some people. They can ignore a person, turn them away, and not respond to requests for help. It enables those who don't want to help a person to walk away and actually feel good about it. It gives them a smug sort of satisfaction, and if any uncomfortable feelings arise, they can say 'it was tough love'. They bleat on about how difficult it was to turn their back on a friend in need, a partner, or a family member. They get reassurance and encouragement from like-minded people, who praise them for their strength. They get all the support and comfort, while the person left behind is left in their pain, left alone to 'save themselves'.

I don't doubt that sometimes tough love comes from a genuine belief that it's the best way to deal with someone. But is it? Really? Or is it just a convenient way for people to avoid any responsibility for those in need?

People are often so 'busy', so wrapped up in their own lives, they don't even stop to notice a friend or loved one's cry for help, and if they do, they panic. They don't need the problem because it's uncomfortable, inconvenient, or hard work. It's easier to walk away and feel like a hero in doing so. When help only comes from professionals and not loved ones, it reinforces the belief that we're unworthy of care, that we're too much. That we've failed.

Empathy is different. It's about presence and actions. It's consistency and commitment. It's the difference between giving up and holding on. Not everyone can be saved, I know that, but before you walk away from someone in pain Ask yourself, have I truly given them a chance? You might be their last hope, and empathy, not tough love. might be what they need the most.

Conclusion

Throughout my life, I've often felt misunderstood, unworthy, and unlovable. It has been hard, and bad things have happened. I've made some impulsive choices and behaved in ways that I didn't fully understand. It's a harsh reality to confront the fact that the majority of my life has passed me by in a haze of chaos, destructive choices, and despair. People have said to me, 'you survived cancer, you should be grateful, you should have made better use of your life' and they're probably right. I've lived with survivor's guilt, but the harsh truth is that surviving cancer doesn't guarantee a trouble-free life. Not everyone is a hero, and we don't all have the support or resources to become the world's version of success.

Recovery isn't linear. Mine has been messy, painful, and slow, but I'm still here, and still fighting. Recently, I've begun to learn more about the nature of addiction, the impact of poverty, and the complexity of trauma. I've begun to understand my alcoholism not as a moral failing, but as a trauma response. I recognise now how poverty has limited my choices throughout my life, but not my worth. This has helped me view my life story in a more positive light. It has given me greater compassion for myself and a clearer understanding of the direction my life took.

Sharing my story and raising awareness about the struggles and challenges I've faced has become a mission that fuels my determination to keep moving forward. Through this, I've found a deeper understanding of myself and a renewed sense of purpose. I've gained an identity, and I've turned my lived experience into a teaching tool.

Living with unresolved trauma, alcoholism, and poverty has been challenging and messy, but it has all been worth it. I've realised that my life has not been without purpose; it has given me hard lessons to learn and a story to share. I now look forward to the future with hope.

REFLECTIVE ACTIVITY

Write a short story about someone struggling with poverty and addiction. Describe the barriers they come up against and their journey to recovery. It could be based on your own experience, someone you know, or a fictional one. What key aspect would you include in their story?

Reflective questions to consider:

How might poverty, trauma, and alcoholism overlap in a person's life? How can the cycle be broken?

How might poverty complicate recovery, and what role does empathy play when dealing with those obstacles?

What can you do to show empathy?

Recommended reading/viewing/listening

Films

- Barfly (1987)
- Clean and Sober (1988)
- Ironweed (1987)
- TV film My Name is Bill W. (1989)
- When a Man Loves a Woman (1994)

Songs

- Dear Alcohol—song and lyrics by Dax | Spotify
- Guilty—2008 Remaster—song and lyrics by Bonnie Raitt | Spotify

Websites

Alcohol Addiction and Homelessness (Alcohol Help)
Poverty is often overlooked in social work assessments, say practitioners (Community Care)
Trauma (Mental Health Foundation)

What to read

Brady, K. T., & Back, S. E. (2012). Childhood trauma, posttraumatic stress disorder, and alcohol dependence. *Alcohol Research*, *34*(4), 408–413. https://pmc.ncbi.nlm.nih.gov/articles/PMC3860395/

Bywaters, P. Bunting, L., Davidson, G., Hanratty, J., Mason, W., McCartan, C., & Steils, N. (2016). *The relationship between poverty, child abuse and neglect: An evidence review* Joseph Rowntree Foundation.

Gallagher, B. 2024 We must be careful when we equate poverty with child abuse or neglect. Professional Social Work. Available at: We must be careful when we equate poverty with child abuse or neglect | BASW

Jones, L, & Sumnall, H 2016 *Understanding the relationship between poverty and alcohol misuse* Centre for Public Health, Faculty of Education, Health and Community, Liverpool John Moores University. https://www.drugsandalcohol.ie/25676/1/Understanding-the-relationship-between-poverty-and-alcohol-abuse-2.pdf

Lacey, R. E., Howe, L. D., Kelly-Irving, M., Bartley, M., & Kelly, Y. (2020). The clustering of adverse childhood experiences in the Avon longitudinal study of parents and children: Are gender and poverty important? *Journal of Interpersonal Violence*, *37*(5–6), 2218–2241. https://doi.org/10.1177/0886260520935096 (Original work published 2022)

Mirsal, H., Kalyoncu, A., Pektaş, Ö., Tan, D., & Beyazyürek, M. (2004). Childhood trauma in alcoholics. *Alcohol and Alcoholism*, *39*(2), 126–129. https://doi.org/10.1093/alcalc/agh025

Moustafa, A. A., Parkes, D., Fitzgerald, L. et al. (2021). The relationship between childhood trauma, early-life stress, and alcohol and drug use, abuse, and addiction: An integrative review. *Current Psychology*, *40*, 579–584. https://doi.org/10.1007/s12144-018-9973-9

Mulia, N., Schmidt, L., Bond, J., Jacobs, L., & Korcha, R. (2008). Stress, social support and problem drinking among women in poverty. *Addiction*, *103*(8), 1283–1293. https://pmc.ncbi.nlm.nih.gov/articles/PMC2751765/

Revolving Doors Agency (2021). *The knot: An essay collection on the interconnectedness of poverty, trauma, and multiple disadvantage.* https://revolving-doors.org.uk/wp-content/uploads/2021/02/The-Knot-The-interconnectedness-of-poverty-trauma-and-multiple-disadvantage-FINAL.pdf

Schwandt, M. L., Heilig, M., Hommer, D. W., George, D. T., & Ramchandani, V. A. (2013). Childhood trauma exposure and alcohol dependence severity in adulthood: Mediation by emotional abuse severity and neuroticism. *Alcohol: Clinical & Experimental Research*, *37*(6), 984–992. https://doi.org/10.1111/acer.12053

16

POVERTY AND WHERE YOU ARE FROM

Mary Brennan and Andrew Grinnell

Neighbourhood poverty: finding hope within the disconnection

Mary will often say, 'I can't stand it when it's called a deprived area. We do not have a lot of money, but we've got lots and lots of good neighbours.' The area in question is a neighbourhood to the east of Leeds city centre. It's an area both of us have lived in. Mary moved in as a single parent with her two dual-heritage daughters. One of the things that struck her when she first arrived in the area was that there seemed to be no other people of colour living there. Yet, throughout the four decades that have followed, the ethnic make-up of the neighbourhood has significantly changed.

Andrew moved in with his family, who were part of a small team of people committed to connecting with local people in the area. The neighbourhood in many ways seemed quite empty in comparison to where he had moved from. He noticed that the roads seemed empty of cars, some of the houses were empty of people, and many of the old buildings that once had been major employers in the area stood empty. Yet, we will claim in this chapter that life in this neighbourhood should never be labelled only by its emptiness or the scarcity of its resources. Whilst we would not deny that the neighbourhood struggles against poverty, if we focus only upon these seemingly negative aspects, we will overlook other ways in which the place is rich. In fact, we argue that it is precisely because of the daily struggle that people face that deep relationships are formed through which meaningful acts of neighbourliness are practiced, which enable people to move beyond simply surviving.

We acknowledge at the start of this chapter the particularity of where we speak from. Our encounters with the neighbourhood are interpreted through our own lenses of what makes sense to us. Both of us want to highlight the best

DOI: 10.4324/9781003638476-17

in people, communities, and organisations because we have learnt that doing otherwise continues to pull the neighbourhood down. However, we do not wish to paint a romanticised version of neighbourhood life. If hope is to be found, it must be rooted in the everyday struggle where categories of good and bad seem inadequate for negotiating the complexities of the situations we have encountered.

We also recognise that we speak of one neighbourhood with its own specific histories, geographies, and communities that have shaped it in its own way. Therefore, we will try to stay away from making grand statements about how all low-income neighbourhoods function or should be engaged with. We know how frustrating it is when our own neighbourhood has been treated this way. That said, we do not think that our experiences are *extra*ordinary. There are utterly brilliant people within all low-income neighbourhoods across the UK who create an environment where the reductionist labels about them as 'no-go areas,' 'deprived,' or 'crime-ridden' are demonstrated to be inadequate.

In this chapter, we will outline why it's important to address the experience of poverty within places; describe some of the ways poverty is felt within the neighbourhood and how residents are responding to them; and make some suggestions as to how poverty might be addressed in low-income neighbourhoods in the light of these experiences. Although we will challenge unhelpful characterisations of places, our intention is to encourage you about what is already present within such places and cultivate hope about what might be for neighbourhoods struggling against poverty. As Mary is always reminding us, 'when hope is what you are left with, you can't give up on hoping.'

Neighbourhood poverty – a disconnecting experience

For several decades, the neighbourhood we have lived in has comprised a mixture of housing types – owner-occupied, privately rented, housing association, and council housing. Leeds was never a one-industry city, and so residents traditionally found work down the mines, on the railways, in the foundries, and within the textile industry. Until the 80s, many within the community were still members of the Irish families who had settled in the area the best part of a century earlier.

There was a time in the early 90s when the neighbourhood experienced very high levels of anti-social behaviour. Reflecting upon this period, Mary says, 'it was very rough. Frightening. Hard to live there.' Residents were too scared to report crime to the authorities for fear of retaliation. One of the outcomes of this was that many people sold their late Victorian through-terraced family houses and moved out of the area. Not only did this continue to break up the fabric of the established community, but many of the houses were bought by people from outside the immediate area at relatively cheap prices. Some of the larger properties were converted into houses of multiple occupancy by the new owners, many of whom would be inhabited by people with multiple and complex needs. Others were purchased by an organisation that had a government tender to house people and families who were seeking asylum.

HOUSES OF MULTIPLE OCCUPANCY (HMOS)

According to the Office for National Statistics, 'a dwelling where unrelated tenants rent their home from a private landlord is a HMO if both of the following apply: at least three unrelated individuals live there, forming more than one household; toilet, bathroom, or kitchen facilities are shared with other tenants.'[1] Accurate figures for the number of HMOs across the UK aren't available, partly due to local variations in licensing regulations. For instance, within the City of Leeds, there are 291 HMOs licensed; it is reported that there are a further 1,368 properties operating as HMOs.[2] It should be remembered that a significant number of HMOs cater to students and young professionals.

A potential outcome of this shift in housing tenure is that life in the neighbourhood became disconnected in several ways. Individuals who had no connection to the area and who had a history of vulnerability moved in to live in houses with one another. They were strangers to one another and strangers to the area. People who had stayed in the area wondered why family homes had been 'given over' to people they perceived as having challenging lifestyles. At the same time, individuals and families who had fled from their homeland to try to find sanctuary were moved into a neighbourhood that was already experiencing something of an identity crisis. As a resident, talking about the area in a film from 2005 says, 'It used to be clear who people from the neighbourhood were, it was not now… they are coming into our area, and we don't like it.' Whilst not every person in the area would have agreed with this statement, it reflects something of the struggle the neighbourhood was facing. This was further exacerbated as neither the organisations that were moving people in, nor the local authority, offered enough support either for those who were moving in or those who were staying. One of the consequences of all this was that people became disconnected from one another.

The changing population of the neighbourhood illustrates why we think it is crucial that any discussion about poverty includes consideration of how it is experienced by communities. Too often, we only refer to poverty on an individual or household level. When poverty is talked about in the media, the illustrations used predominantly focus on either specific people or families. Statistics often state the number of people who are unemployed or the number of children who are caught up in poverty. The danger of concentrating only on this is that we fail to engage with the web-like factors that trap both individuals and neighbourhoods in cycles of poverty.

The illustration of the change in housing tenure demonstrates the importance of considering collective experiences of poverty in several ways. First, it acknowledges that there is something about the 'built environment' that seems to perpetuate poverty in certain places. Maps showing where poverty exists in Leeds will look very similar from any decade for the last 100 years. The same neighbourhoods that experienced poverty in the 1950s still seem to be experiencing it today. In part, this is due to the type of housing that exists within a place. The neighbourhood's late Victorian terraces, whose front door step literally leads on to the pavement and have, at best, a small yard at the back, create an environment where it feels that everyone is living on top of one another. The natural desire for young people is to connect with one another. However, many of the communal spaces for building relationships were closing in the 1990s, and so they were either trapped in their homes or left to hang out on the streets. This vulnerable position led to unhealthy connections where they engaged in some of the anti-social behaviour that led to the challenges we have talked about in the neighbourhood. The unhealthy connection of some led to the disconnection of others.

From the housing example, a second reason why looking at low-income neighbourhoods is important. In it, we get a glimpse of how the narratives of national and international politics play out in the life of neighbourhoods. At a time when people who were seeking asylum were being moved into the neighbourhood, the British National Party spread misleading information to stoke up tensions. They preyed upon the sense of loss that many people within the neighbourhood were feeling. The loss of workplaces. The loss of a distinct identity. The loss of places where people could gather. In the ten years that Andrew lived in the neighbourhood, thirteen public houses (pubs) were closed, leaving just one within the local area. In many respects, the neighbourhood had a legitimate sense of loss or disconnection with its past, which sought to find a scapegoat to illegitimately blame. For some within the neighbourhood that has, and continues to be, people who have arrived from other nations. The political problems facing the nation were lived out in the real experience of residents within this low-income community.

The third reason the housing illustration highlights is that issues of poverty can only be partially solved if you focus only on the individual. We must widen the lens to see the connections that need to be made. The change of who lives in a particular house has implications for all the neighbours. When this is intensified by the changing residents of many houses, it creates a precarious challenge. A further example of why it is important to consider the wider context might be the many people within our neighbourhood who have, at times, been sanctioned for not attending an appointment at the job centre on time. Focussing upon the individual might provoke interventions aimed at making them take more responsibility for time management, etc. However, the problem in many cases was the poor levels of public transport in the neighbourhood. Mary tells of the many occasions she has stood waiting for the only neighbourhood bus that is timetabled every hour, only for it to 'knock,' a Leeds phrase for buses being cancelled. The bus provider's explanation for this is that if the bus gets behind on other parts of the route, it will stop in the city and turn round before it is made even later by coming through to the neighbourhood. Apart from the obvious inconvenience on a social level, if you are reliant upon public transport to get to work, to a hospital appointment, or a job centre interview, and it does not turn up, there are far-reaching consequences. Amongst other things, it leaves many local people believing that the bus would not 'knock' for a rich area and contributes to a feeling that people in the neighbourhood are second-class. Furthermore, it shows how real-life services can disconnect low-income neighbourhoods from wider society.

ACCESS TO PUBLIC TRANSPORT

According to an IPPR North report, 'cuts to bus provision have been ten times higher in the most deprived areas of England than the least deprived areas.'[3] Friends of the Earth and the University of Leeds have also shown that there is a regional dynamic to this, demonstrating that over a fifteen year period till 2023, urban bus services in London have remained at a similar level, but outside the capital have dropped by 48%.[4] New forms of public transport, like trams, are championed for increasing accessibility across a city. Yet, often the initial routes for these do not necessarily focus upon lower income neighbourhoods.[5]

These illustrations help us realise that to engage in understanding both poverty and how to effectively respond to it, we must consider the lived wisdom of low-income neighbourhoods as well as individuals or families. In doing this, we will grapple with challenges that are being faced nationally and internationally.

Neighbourhood stigma: A disconnecting narrative

Both of us have been involved with the Poverty Truth Commission in Leeds. Through it, we have realised the significant role stigma plays in how poverty is experienced. The film, 'Fighting Shame,' explores how experiencing stigma about poverty has produced shame in the lives of five women from the commission. In the film, Mary focuses on the impact of stigma on the neighbourhood. When a neighbourhood is stigmatised, it affects not only how the community feels about itself but also the behaviours they display. The result is an even greater sense of disconnection.

It is not that the stigma comes from nowhere. As we mentioned in the last section, the early 1990s were a particularly challenging time, when high levels of crime in the neighbourhood led to people feeling unsafe. Consequently, the local newspaper reported on some of these challenges, creating headlines that stigmatised the neighbourhood. The language that authorities use about the area, describing it as one of the most deprived within the city according to the Indices of Multiple Deprivation, compounds this stigma further. This labelling of the place leads to what feels like ill health in the community. It is as if the area is in some ways infected with a disease that the wider city wants to isolate from. Hearing these views can lead residents towards a sense of apathy about the area. Worse still, they may begin to believe that it is inevitable that things will always be this way. For instance, when we try to get people involved in community activities, some residents say, 'why bother. There is no point.' Furthermore, for young people, a lack of aspiration has epidemic-like proportions. 'Oh, you are from there, you won't amount to much,' is one of the worst forms of stigmatisation that young people encounter.

Conversely, the reputation of low-income neighbourhoods may also attract attention from authorities and organisations that want to help to bring positive change. Yet, if the only narrative these organisations are following is the one we have just described, we have noticed that the approach they adopt may cause further damage. In the first place, the narrative suggests that the neighbourhood and the people within it are a problem. Not only does nobody want to be labelled as a problem, but approaching the neighbourhood this way can mean that people come with grand schemes to 'fix things.' Many of these schemes have failed primarily because they haven't taken time to understand the root causes of the challenges the place was experiencing. As we will reflect later, the organisations that have engaged in the neighbourhood best are those that have listened carefully to what the problems are. Furthermore, the neighbourhood as a problem approach might assume that nothing good is happening there already. By slowing down and observing the life of the place, organisations will notice the acts of neighbourliness that are present, and the small, grassroots initiatives that hold the key to enabling change within the neighbourhood. It is to two of these examples that we will now turn to illustrate how residents are responding to the struggles a neighbourhood faces.

Connecting a neighbourhood: Wednesday meals and growing together

We had noticed that people were hungry. And by people, it was clear that it was not just a particular category of person. Yes, there were many of the men who were living in the Houses of Multiple Occupancy. But it also included people who had lived in the neighbourhood for a long time, families, and older people. We had been used to food playing a central part in how we engaged in the neighbourhood. From a monthly open house where neighbours gathered to eat together, to a cooking club that taught young people a few basic recipes and enabled them to prepare a banquet for their friends and family, we had long realised the importance of food in bringing people together. Yet this was different. It felt like some people simply could not afford to eat.

Mary was the first to notice this, as people would come around to her house asking if she had any food they could use to cook. Several people made sure that Mary's house had enough supplies for anyone who needed them, but she felt we needed to create opportunities for people who were struggling so that they might have a little more dignity. After a bit of planning and securing the use of a church hall, we began Wednesday meals. This was not to be a soup kitchen. Everyone was invited to help prepare the food. We served one another, washed up together, celebrated, cried, and laughed together. We never created publicity for Wednesday meals. Rather, we invited people in the street, knocked on their doors, and relied on people spreading the word that all were welcome. One of our strongest memories is when someone arrived who timidly opened the door. Before they had a chance to leave, someone jumped up to welcome them and exclaimed, 'come in, we are all family here.' When asked about why people came to the meals, several said that it was because the people there were the only consistent people in their lives.

At around the same time, a worker from an environmental project from another neighbourhood within the city visited the area. He listened to the ideas of local people, and they decided to establish a new activity. Together, they identified a walkway that crossed the disused railway that joined different parts of the area together. It was a place that had its fair share of anti-social behaviour. The plan was to create planters out of old railway sleepers and begin to get people from across the neighbourhood engaged in 'growing together,' the name that eventually would be adopted by the project. It worked. Before long, people from a wide variety of backgrounds, ages, and ethnicities were working together. It soon became clear that there was not enough space to do everything that they wanted to do, and so, after some negotiation, the council agreed to clear some land for Growing Together. Now, a portacabin sits on the site to provide a space to have a cuppa, act as a meeting room for the growers, is a venue for holiday activities for children, and is the new home of Wednesday meals. 'Growing Together' is a hub within the community that has even been celebrated on Radio 4's Gardeners' Question Time. However, some of the proudest moments have been when the potatoes that have been grown are used for Wednesday meals.

Both activities illustrate what we believe are important aspects of a different kind of way of understanding the impact of poverty within low-income neighbourhoods. Essentially, they are about local people offering their gifts, talents, care, and skills to one another so that they all might thrive. Several aspects are worthy of further reflection.

1 **It starts in ordinary acts of neighbourliness**. It seems to us that in every neighbourhood there are caretakers. By that, we don't mean people wearing official overalls and sweeping up. Often someone from the neighbourhood needs help filling in a form, or understanding what something means, or has experienced bad news, or simply needs some food. Caretakers are the people who are turned to in these circumstances. This neighbourhood is not unique in identifying several people who are caretakers – every place has them. Sometimes it's as simple as saying 'hello' to others you walk by in the street. We can tell of countless neighbourly acts where people have looked out for one another and sought to help each other, even when they are from groups that the media might portray as being hostile to one another. *If we want to help neighbourhoods who struggle against poverty to reconnect, we should first find the caretakers and learn from them.*
2 **Activities and projects focussing on relationships**. Earlier, we characterised part of the experience of poverty in a low-income neighbourhood as being about disconnection. Both people disconnected from one another, and the neighbourhood disconnected from the wider city. In the examples above, the focus wasn't necessarily about eating or growing in and of themselves; it was about doing these activities together. If that is the case, building relationships should permeate every aspect of the activity. It should guide how the place is set up, how people are invited to be involved, and how the activities are conducted. It should break down any sense that we are putting this activity on for you. Rather, it should enable people to come alongside one another. A great aspect of both activities is that they have enabled people from different generations to be together. Reflecting on one particular encounter, Mary remembers how, for one person, hearing the stories of older people was a vital reason why they attended. When asked why that was the case, the response was that they had grown up in care and so hadn't heard about 'the good old days.'

   Beyond these two activities, we have been involved in many other projects across the neighbourhood. Some of these have required a team of people to organise them. We might describe this as an opportunity for people to volunteer. However, we have learnt to be careful about the language we use in asking people to be involved. If they are asked to volunteer, they are likely to say no. It seems that volunteering can feel too 'official' and potentially middle class. If you say, 'can you help us with this,' the responses are often more positive. *If we want to help neighbourhoods who struggle against poverty reconnect, we should create opportunities where people can connect and get involved in doing positive things within their neighbourhood.*

3 **Local People Can't Do It on Their Own**. As we said earlier, organisations that come into the neighbourhood to do things for local people often exacerbate the stigma. Yet, it is equally problematic when local people think that they can do it on their own. Neither Wednesday Meals nor Growing Together would have happened without the help of other organisations. Whether that was simply about offering their premises as a venue or coming in to bring the skills of a project done in another area of the city to see how they might help here, support was needed. The best offers of help come from organisations that start building trust with local people by listening to them. For instance, one of the city's universities came to do some research on growing together. Local people were able to trust them because they were good listeners, got involved in doing the things that local people were doing, and brought a sense of fun. When the academics eventually shared their ideas, local people listened because they had earned the right to speak. *If organisations want to help neighbourhoods who struggle against poverty, they should start by listening, get stuck into what local people are doing, and begin to re-connect the neighbourhood back to the wider city.*

4 **Times, they are changing**. Poverty in a low-income neighbourhood is never static. Whether it's a change to the housing stock that brings new groups of people into the area, the closing of public venues, or a cost-of-living crisis, the way that poverty 'shows up' is always changing. There seems to be an ever-increasing number of people who must hold down several jobs simply to cover the costs of bringing up their children. What is primarily a personal set of circumstances impacts the kind of wider support that a neighbourhood needs to provide.

Furthermore, times are changing for the kind of support organisations can offer. We are acutely aware that financial challenges affect organisations as well as individuals. The money available to public and third-sector organisations is reducing at a time when communities and neighbourhoods need to be re-connected with wider society.

Whilst these challenges are urgent, if we want to help neighbourhoods who struggle against poverty re-connect it is important that time is given to enable communities to come to terms with how things are changing. As both activities remind us, trust is cultivated when we consistently 'show up'. Change happens when organisations join in with local people.

A hopeful neighbourhood

Urban Grimshaw and the Shed Crew is a book by Bernard Hare, who was a disaffected social worker living in our neighbourhood. The book tells the story of how he connected with a local gang, neither glorifying nor criticising their behaviour, but reflecting on how they relate to wider society. At one point, Hare describes walking with one of the gang members as they passed the abandoned Roman Catholic Church with its sign 'Keep Out, Private, Danger.' He writes 'if no one cared about the church, what message were they sending out to the kids? Had we lost faith as well as hope? And, if so, where did that leave charity?' Hare (2005)

For some, the questions Hare poses about the neighbourhood resonate with their experience. The consequences of the disconnections that dislocate neighbours from each other, the place with its past, and the area from the wider city, are felt deeply. However, we hope that something that we have shared points in a more hopeful direction. This is not a hope that hovers above reality, but one that is lived out as people rise above their struggles by connecting with one another. The neighbourhood may be described as deprived in some ways, but it is our contention that it is rich in hope. As Mary says, 'when hope is what you are left with, you can't give up on hoping.'

Notes

1 'Houses of Multiple Occupancy (HMO) Variable: Census 2021', Office for National Statistics, 6 March 2024. https://www.ons.gov.uk/census/census2021dictionary/variablesbytopic/housingvariablescensus2021/householdsofmultipleoccupancyhmo [accessed 5 November 2025].
2 'Strategic Housing Market Assessment, 2023-24,' Leeds City Council, September 2024, https://www.leeds.gov.uk/docs/leeds%20strategic%20housing%20market%20assessment%202024.pdf [accessed 5 November 2025].
3 Institute for Public Policy Research, *Change You Can Board: Delivering Better, Greener Buses*. IPPR North: Manchester, 2025.
4 'How Britain's Bus Services Have Drastically Declined', Friends of the Earth, 28 November 2023. https://policy.friendsoftheearth.uk/insight/how-britains-bus-services-have-drastically-declined (accessed 5 November 2025).
5 David Spereall, 'First Tram Routes Revealed in Country Transport Plan', BBC, 15 July 2024. https://www.bbc.co.uk/news/articles/crg70kmylrxo [accessed 5 November 2025].

To understand more about neighbourhood poverty, we recommend the following

Films

Fighting shame

Tomalin, D. (2012). Over to the East, online video recording, YouTube, 29 February.

Books

Crawford, A. (2006) 'Fixing broken promises?': Neighbourhood wardens and social capital', *Urban Studies*, 43, 957–976.
Gilchrist, A. (2009). *The Well-Connected Community: A Networking Approach to Community Development*. Bristol: Policy Press.
Hanley, L. (2007). *Estates and Intimate History*. London: Granta.
Hare, B. (2005). *Urban Grimshaw and the Shed Crew*. London: Sceptre.
Hare, B. (2011). *Urban Grimshaw and the Shed Crew* (London: Hachette UK)
McKnight, J., & Block, P.. (2010). *The Abundant Community: Awakening the Power of Families and Neighbourhoods* Chicago, IL: American Planning Association.
Patrick, R. (2017). *For Whose Benefit? The Everyday Realities of Welfare Reform.* Bristol: Policy Press.
Russell, C. & McKnight, J. (2022). *The Connected Community: Discovering the Health, Wealth, and Power of Neighbourhoods*. Oakland: Berrett-Koehler Publishers
Tallon, A. (2013). *Urban Regeneration in the UK* London: Routledge.
Tyler, I. (2021). *Stigma: The Machinery of Inequality*. London: Bloomsbury.

Articles

Green, M. (2006). 'Representing poverty and attacking representations: Perspectives on poverty from social anthropology', *The Journal of Development Studies*, 42, 1108–1129
'On the "frontline" of poverty: how public services reinforce stigma', *JRF*, 2023. https://www.ucl.ac.uk/bartlett/public-purpose/publications/2020/sep/welfare-50-why-we-need-social-revolution-and-how-make-it-happen (accessed 30 October 2025)
Taylor-Gooby, P. (2013). 'Why do people stigmatise the poor at a time of rapidly increasing inequality, and what can be done about it?' *Political Quarterly*, 84(1), 31–42. https://doi.org/10.1111/j.1467-923X.2013.02435.x
Tyler, I. & Campbell, S. (2024). 'Poverty stigma: a glue that holds poverty in place', *JRF*, 8 May. https://www.jrf.org.uk/sites/default/files/pdfs/poverty-stigma-a-glue-that-holds-poverty-in-place-6f41001b15485b3989f01492de3524f8.pdf (accessed 10 October 2025)
'Think neighbourhoods: A new approach to fixing the country's biggest policy challenges', *Independent Commission on Neighbourhoods*, 2025. https://www.neighbourhoodscommission.org.uk/wp-content/uploads/2025/03/Think-Neighbourhoods-Report-FINAL-March-2025.pdf (accessed 10 October 2025)

Websites

Asset-based community development (nurture development)
Citizen UK – bringing communities together to win change
Resolve poverty – working locally to end poverty nationally

CONCLUSION

Mel Hughes, Debbie James and Carrie-Anne Mizen

Our reflections

Carrie: *it is an honour and a privilege to be able to share other people's stories. It's good to know you are not alone, even though personally I do feel alone. It is good to know others understand these struggles. I feel like everyone just needs a big hug. There is so much courage and resilience in all the chapters. There is also so much trauma that is not of our own making – life events that are not of our own making, and that are not our fault. I was reflecting on whether there is one thing that stands out for me in the book, but there isn't. There is so much covered in the chapters, it takes time to read the whole book and take on board all of the stories and the realities. It is emotional but also heartwarming. You have to be in the right frame of mind to read some of the chapters, knowing it is going to be a tough read. I struggled with this BUT these voices need to be heard, to make a difference for the future, so the next person is not caught in the same trap. I do feel that 50% of the issues described could have been prevented had others listened better, been more receptive to the person's problems. If benefits were not as rigid. If you didn't always fall into the grey areas. My mental health is too severe for Steps to Wellbeing but not severe enough for mental health team support which has a 4-month waiting list. In the poverty truth commission, everyone is encouraged to listen with attention and speak with intention. I hope this book is read by many people in positions of power to make a difference. I hope the book has helped you to develop your understanding.*

DOI: 10.4324/9781003638476-18

Debbie: *Poverty is not just a theory; it is a real issue that needs empathy, thought, and action. By using real stories, and exploring common themes, we can see how they connect to bigger issues like fairness and inequality.*

It's aimed at students as a textbook, but I hope it's not read solely by students and not just as an academic exercise. It's a book that needs to be read by people at all levels of society, from students to professors to MPs. It should make an impact on each of them in a significant way. And most importantly, inspire change.

The things I like most about this book are the shared experiences of real people, living real lives. I think it carries a strength, and (to use the old cliché), the 'power of the people'. Each chapter is unique, personal and stands alone.

At the same time, each chapter connects to the others and becomes a unified common experience of trauma, injustice and indignity. It's in that unity that the magic happens; poverty, hardship and pain transform into a unified testimony of resilience, courage and survival. I hope it helps you think deeply, question your assumptions and find ways to make a difference.

It's been a personally powerful, emotional and valuable experience to be involved with co-editing this book and contributing a chapter. The feeling of empowerment goes above and beyond anything I've ever done before.

It's brought hope, friendship and purpose into my life. I'm proud of the achievement of all of us who have edited and contributed to this book. Even if in the end it's only read by one person. That one person has the potential to make a change. My personal call to action for anyone reading this is: aim to make one small difference every day. Be realistic but dare to think big.

Mel: *One of the poems shared in chapter three talks of how poverty is not just one thing. The stories, realities, insights, facts, and figures shared throughout this book are evidence of this. Every contribution is unique and drawn from a combination of experiences which are unique to that person's life and lived experience. What struck me most about the chapters however are the similarities, the threads that we heard repeatedly as we stepped, just for a short time, into each person's life. Whilst each contributor was asked to explore poverty through a particular lens e.g. as someone with experience of being a parent, in care, in prison, at school, we hear repeatedly of experiences of trauma, poor mental and physical health, addiction and homelessness. It is striking to see how these are both the causes and consequences of living in poverty, often creating a relentless cycle of events that compound the last. What I hope every reader takes away from this book is an understanding that poverty is something that as a society, we have caused, and we can eradicate. It is a system we have created and that we can change, rather than an individual's problem or fault. Eradicating poverty involves speaking up and coming together to co-create solutions at a policy and practice level.*

Reflecting on the measurements of poverty

Measurements of poverty cannot just be about deliberating over how much money someone needs to live on. As this book has shown, it is about dignity, support, being valued and as a society, agreeing to a standard of living for each other that goes beyond surviving and keeping your head above water, and involves creating the conditions for everyone to have a good quality of life. In the 1980s, Joanna Mack and Stewart Lansley set out what they describe as a 'consensual' approach to poverty. It starts by considering what people need (necessities) to live well. It goes beyond what people just need to survive, shifting the focus from income measures to a decent standard of living. We would encourage you to read more about the consensual approach to poverty and the subsequent minimum income standard (what the public thinks is needed for a minimal accepted stand or living in the UK) from the Joseph Rowntree Foundation website www.jrf.org.uk and to reflect on what you would add. What for you is a necessity for a good quality of life?

Our main aim for the book has been to harness lived experience expertise in the fight against poverty. It starts by being able to put yourself in the shoes of others to understand the realities of poverty, the causes and the consequences. We need to understand the root causes of poverty to be able to challenge it. Just as there is no single definition or experience of poverty, there is no single solution. As we grapple with how to eradicate poverty, we need to ensure that this is led by those with lived experience and expertise.

Your reflections

As we draw the book to a close, we invite you to reflect on what you have learnt. Take time to consider what challenged you when reading the book, what your beliefs were at the start and whether these have changed. Based on your understanding, what can you do to take action and join the fight against poverty? As an editorial team, we have devised three questions for you to consider:

1) In the introduction, we presented the two most commonly used definitions of poverty (absolute and relative). Go back and read these definitions. Has reading the realities and insights throughout the book informed your thinking about these definitions? What has changed?
2) If you could speak to one of the chapter authors, who would it be and what would you say to them? Are you able to reflect on why you were drawn to this person and this chapter? Is this something you can take forward into your everyday life and practice when speaking with others? What would you say to them?

3) You have read a number of stories about the realities of poverty for different people. What do you feel the solutions are to eradicating poverty based on this? What can you do to come together with others to make this happen?

So, what now – call to action

What can you do now? Whether in your day-to-day life, with friends, family, neighbours, people you encounter, or in your professional roles:

- Listen with attention
- Hold your judgements
- Resist the temptation to fit us into boxes
- Take time to get to know who we are and what is important to us
- Remember, we have a lot of expertise, so make time to hear it and join us in our action to end poverty
- This is our life, and we still have to go home at the end of the day, so be kind and supportive when involving us
- Aim to make one small difference every day
- Be realistic but dare to think big
- Use your power and influence to amplify the voices of others and to bring people together to explore and enact solutions to end poverty.
- Join an anti-poverty campaign
- Join or set up a poverty truth commission in your area
- Together we can change the world!

Finally, we have included some quotes from Nelson Mandela who inspires us.

> Poverty is not an accident. Like slavery and apartheid, it is man-made and can be removed by the actions of human beings.
>
> Overcoming poverty is not a gesture of charity. It is the protection of a fundamental human right to dignity and a decent life.
>
> Let's recommit to work towards our common goal: a nation where all of us are winners, all of us have shelter, food and education.

That's all we ask. What role will you play?

INDEX

Pages in **bold-*italics*** refer to boxes.

absolute poverty 4, 24–25
addiction *see* trauma
Ademuwagun, Christopher 119–131
Armstrong, Julia 106–117
Ashley's birthday bank 46
asset-based community development 28
austerity 23–24, ***156***
autism 119–131
Awaab's Law ***96***

BCP Poverty Truth Commission 1–2, 49, ***50***
Beck, D.J. ***47***
breast cancer 43–49
Brennan, Mary 198–207
British Association of Social Workers (BASW) 3, ***111–113***, ***137***, ***192***
British National Party 201

cancer: diagnosis and poverty 43–49; impact on children ***44–45***
Cancer Research UK ***44***
Caplan, P. ***47***
Care Act 2014 ***126***
care leavers 68–78
carers: definition of ***55***; financial impact 53–66
Carers UK ***55–61***
Child Poverty Action Group (CPAG) 25, ***137***
Children Act 1989 ***70***, ***73***, ***77***
Children (Leaving Care) Act 2000 ***77***
Children and Social Work Act 2017 ***70***
co-production 3–4
Corporate parenting ***70***
Crowe, Sam 19–41

debt 35, 46, 53, 58–60, ***61***
destitution 23–24, ***171***
disability: extra costs of ***89***; and poverty 80–91
domestic abuse 74, ***93***
Dorling, Danny 24
Drayak, Taliah 147–159

education: poverty and attainment 177–178
English Index of Multiple Deprivation 21
Equality Act 2010 109, ***126***
estrangement 194

food banks 47, ***57***
Fortin et al. ***48***
foster care 71–76, ***77***

Glasgow Poverty Truth Commission 32
Goodwin, Tracy 31–34
Grenfell Tower fire 107, ***108***
Grinnell, Andrew 198–207
growing together project 204–206

Hamidi, Alan 162–174
Harrison, Katharine 162–174
Harvey, Orlanda 42–50
health inequalities 20–23
homelessness 59–61, *75*, *77*, 92–103, 139–143, ***144***, ***169***
housing: access and insecurity *77*, 92–99, ***115–116***
Hughes, Mel 1–8, 133–143, ***144***, 185–196, 209–212
Human Rights Act 1998 ***126***
Huxford, Steve 80–91

income inequality 21–29
Index of Multiple Deprivation 21

James, Debbie 1–8, ***13–18***, 19, 177–183, 185–197, 209–212
James, Luke 177–178
Johnstone, Martin 31–41
Joseph Rowntree Foundation 34, ***46***, ***61***, ***80***, ***137***, ***188***, 211
judgement *see* stigma
Jupp, Kate 53–66

Kinship care 34
Kleipoedszus, Stefan 147–159
Kurds 162–174

leaving care 68–78
Lee, Gary 133–143
Lee, Sally 80–91
Lenz, Tilia 68–78
Levelling Up Strategy 27
living experience, concept of ***109***
local authority duties ***97–98***, 100, ***169***

Macmillan Cancer Support ***43–44***
Marmot Review 21
McConalogue, Tricia 31–41
McKie, Val 53–66
mental health: and poverty ***70***, 83, 119–131, ***188***
Mizen, Carrie-Anne 1–8, 42–50, 209–212
Modern Slavery Act 2015 ***73***

National Autistic Society ***120***, 131
neighbourhoods 27–29, ***112***, 198–207
NHS access and poverty ***48***

Office for National Statistics (ONS) ***200***

Parker, Kate 92–103
Personal Independence Payment (PIP) 87–89, 122, ***123***
Pickett, Kate 22–23
poverty: definitions of 4; measurement of 4–5
Poverty Truth Network 31–41

relative poverty 4
Romer, Felix 24
Russell, Cormac 22

Sam 92–103
Sarah 119–131
Shelter 92–103
Spirit Level, The (Wilkinson & Pickett) 22–23
stigma 5, 17, 22, 47, 85, ***150***, 151–157, 202–203
Sure Start 25–28

Thatcher, Margaret 23–24
Thomas, Dusty 31–41
trauma: and addiction 185–196; and care experience 69–78
Trussell Trust ***47***, ***84***, 89–90
Turner, Caitlin 68–78

universal credit 26–28, ***85***, ***87–88***, 107, 168–170
urban inequality 21–22

Watters, Dominic 106–117
Whitehead and Bird ***48***
Williams, Rachel 31–41
Williams, Richard 177–183
Woodward et al. ***48***

www.ingramcontent.com/pod-product-compliance
Ingram Content Group UK Ltd.
Pitfield, Milton Keynes, MK11 3LW, UK
UKHW020007200926
475702UK00015B/2523

9781041070238